table of contents

p. 244

p. 135

p. 161

The Great Little Kitchen Helper

At the end of the day, it's wonderful to sit down to a home-cooked meal. What's even better is if that great meal is waiting for you...no fuss, no muss on your part. You can just dish it up, relax and enjoy. Who is this magic genie that cooks all day while you're away? **THE SLOW COOKER.**

The slow cooker is so handy...just page through this collection and you'll discover just how versatile it is. You'll find entrees such as ribs, meatballs, stews, roasts, fajitas and pasta dishes. There are also recipes for hearty soups, classic sides, dips, snacks, warm beverages, puddings and fruity crisps. With **403** sensational dishes to choose from, you're sure to find several that will quickly become your go-to favorites!

You can check out **Slow Cooker Basics** for cooking tips, buying information and suggestions for converting oven or stovetop recipes to slow cooked dishes.

Slow cookers cut down on the time you need to spend in the kitchen to create a tasty, nutritious meal. Most foods can be prepped for the slow cooker in 30 minutes or less. Then you can go about the day with little if any additional kitchen work.

On the money front, slow cookers help keep your grocery budget in line. Moist low-heat cooking is ideal for less-tender, more economical cuts of meat, such as rump roasts and round steaks. They are also a "green" appliance since they use less electricity when compared to cooking the same dish in an oven. And, they give off little heat, which helps keep the kitchen cool in the summer.

Slow Cooker Basics

The slow cooker has been around for about 40 years, and the basic premise is still the same—simmering foods with low, steady heat for long time periods. While individual models vary, they usually have at least two settings, low (about 180°) and a high (about 280°). A few models have a warm setting, which is great to keep cooked food warm, particularly dips and beverages.

Newer slow cookers tend to heat up more quickly than older ones. If you have an older model and your recipe directs to cook on low, you may want to set it on the highest setting for the first hour of cooking to ensure food safety.

A range in cooking time is provided to account for variables such as thickness of meat, fullness of the slow cooker and temperature of the food to be cooked. As you become more familiar with your slow cooker, you'll be better able to judge which end of the range to use.

Buying a Slow Cooker

Slow cookers range in price from $20 to more than $200 and are available in sizes from 1-1/2 to 7 quarts. Before you purchase one, decide on a price range that fits your budget, and pick a size that is appropriate for your family (see the chart Slow Cooker Sizes, below).

Look for models with removable inserts, which make it easier to clean. Most inserts are ceramic, but some of the pricier models have aluminum inserts.

Slow Cooker Sizes

Household Size	Slow Cooker Capacity
1 to 2 people	2 to 3-1/2 quarts
3 to 4 people	3-1/2 to 4-1/2 quarts
4 to 5 people	4-1/2 to 5 quarts
6 or more people	5 to 7 quarts

Aluminum inserts allow you to brown meats directly in the insert on the stovetop. Then you can drain the meat and transfer the insert to the slow cooker. Look for inserts that are dishwasher-safe.

Slow cookers are available in the classic round shape and an oval shape. If you plan on preparing roasts in the slow cooker, you may wish to consider an oval shape. If stews and soups are your forte, then a round slow cooker is perfect for your cooking needs.

A "keep-warm" feature should be a consideration if you are planning on using the slow cooker as a chafing dish to keep items warm during a party. Some slow cookers will automatically switch to a keep-warm setting after cooking.

Think twice before you purchase a garage-sale bargain. If it is new and in its box, it probably is a bargain. If it is older and used, it might not be a smart buy. Older units can lose their cooking efficiency and might not rise to the proper temperature. To check the cooking temperature of your slow cooker, see Slow Cooker Temperature Check, below.

To find information about specific models, check online or in reputable consumer magazines for product reviews.

Slow Cooker Temperature Check

To be considered safe, a slow cooker must be able to cook slowly enough that it can be left unattended, yet it must be fast enough to keep the food at a proper temperature. Here's how to check your slow cooker:

1. Fill the slow cooker 1/2 to 2/3 full with room temperature water.
2. Cover and heat on low for 8 hours.
3. Using a thermometer, check the temperature of the water quickly since the temperature can drop quite a bit once the lid is removed.
4. The temperature should be at least 185°. If it's too hot, your meal cooked for 8 hours would likely be overdone. If the temperature is below 185°, the slow cooker is not safe to use and should be discarded.

Slow Cooker Dos and Don'ts

DO prep your ingredients the night before. It will save you time in the morning.

DO place soups and stews and other suitable recipes in the insert and refrigerate overnight. Place the insert in an unheated slow cooker.

DON'T preheat the slow cooker. Preheating could crack a ceramic insert.

DO fill the insert at least 1/2 full. If it is less than 1/2 full, the food may be burnt at the end of the cooking time.

DON'T fill the slow cooker more than 3/4 full. Foods may not cook properly and reach safe temperatures in a reasonable length of time.

DO thaw meats before adding to the slow cooker. If using purchased frozen slow cooker meals, follow manufacturer's directions for cooking.

DO spray the insert with cooking spray for easier cleanup.

DO cut large cuts of meat (over 3 pounds) in half. Cut up whole chicken before cooking.

DO brown meats and drain fat before adding to the slow cooker.

DO cut vegetables into uniform sizes. Place vegetables, such as potatoes, rutabagas, turnips, parsnips, onions and carrots, in the bottom and around the sides of the slow cooker. These firm vegetables take longer to cook than the meat.

DO taste and adjust seasonings before serving. The long, slow cooking time can weaken the flavor of some seasonings.

DON'T lift the lid. You can lose 10° to 15°, and it can take 20 to 30 minutes for the temperature to recover. Also, make sure the lid is sitting properly on the slow cooker, so heat and steam can't escape.

DO remove food from the slow cooker within 1 to 2 hours and refrigerate any leftovers.

DON'T use the slow cooker to reheat food. Use a microwave or stovetop. If your slow cooker has a warm setting, transfer the heated food to the slow cooker to keep warm.

DO allow the lid and insert to completely cool before washing.

Preparing Foods for the Slow Cooker

BEANS. Dried beans can be tricky to cook in a slow cooker. Minerals in the water and variations in voltage affect various type of beans in different ways. Dried beans should always be soaked before adding to a slow cooker. To soak beans, place them in a Dutch oven and add enough water to cover by 2 inches. Bring to a boil and boil for 2 minutes. Remove from the heat, cover and let stand for 1 to 4 hours or until beans are softened. Drain and rinse beans, discarding liquid. Sugar, salt and acidic ingredients, such as vinegar, interfere with

the beans' ability to cook and become tender. So it's best not to cook beans with these ingredients, but to add them only after the beans are fully cooked. Lentils and split peas do not need to be soaked.

DAIRY. Milk-based products tend to break down during slow cooking. Items like milk, cream, sour cream or cream cheese are best added during the last hour of cooking. Cheeses don't generally hold up during the slow cooker's extended cooking time and should be added near the end of cooking. Condensed cream soups generally hold up well in the slow cooker.

FISH & SEAFOOD. Fish and seafood cook quickly and can break down if cooked too long. They are generally added to the slow cooker toward the end of the cooking time to keep them at optimal quality.

MEAT. Meat may be browned before adding to the slow cooker. While browning is not necessary, it adds to the flavor and appearance of the meat and allows you to drain off the fat. Cut roasts over 3 pounds in half before placing in the slow cooker to ensure even cooking. Trim off excess fat from meats and poultry. Fat retains heat, and large amounts of fat could raise the temperature of the cooking liquid, causing the

meat to overcook. If you don't brown poultry before adding to the slow cooker, you may wish to remove the skin for a more appealing appearance.

OATS. Quick-cooking and old-fashioned oats are often interchangeable in recipes. However, old-fashioned oats hold up better in the slow cooker.

PASTA. If added to a slow cooker when dry, pasta tends to become very sticky. It is better to cook it according to the package directions and stir it into the slow cooker just before serving. Small pastas, such as orzo and ditalini, may be cooked in the slow cooker. To keep them from becoming mushy, add during the last hour of cooking.

COUSCOUS. Couscous is best cooked on the stovetop rather than in the slow cooker.

RICE. Converted rice is ideal for all-day cooking. If using instant rice, add it during the last 30 minutes of cooking.

VEGETABLES. Vegetables, especially potatoes and root vegetables, such as carrots, tend to cook more slowly than meat. Cut these vegetables into uniform pieces and place on the bottom and around the sides of the slow cooker. Place the meat over the vegetables. Add tender vegetables, like peas and zucchini, or ones you'd prefer to be crisp-tender, during the last 15 to 60 minutes of cooking.

Cleaning Tips

- Removable inserts make cleanup a breeze. Be sure to cool the insert before rinsing or cleaning with water to avoid cracking or warping. Do not immerse the metal base in water. Clean it with a damp sponge.

- If dishwasher-safe, place the insert in the dishwasher. Otherwise, wash in warm, soapy water. Avoid using abrasive cleansers, since they may scratch the surface.

- To remove mineral stains on a ceramic insert, fill the cooker with hot water and 1 cup white vinegar; cover. Turn the heat to high for 2 hours, then empty. When cool, wash with hot, soapy water and a cloth or sponge. Rinse well and dry with a towel.

- To remove water marks from a highly glazed ceramic insert, rub the surface with canola oil and allow to stand for 2 hours before washing with hot, soapy water.

Converting Recipes for the Slow Cooker

Almost any recipe that bakes in the oven or simmers on the stovetop can be converted for the slow cooker. Here are some guidelines:

Select recipes that simmer for at least 45 minutes. Good choices to start with are soups, stews, pot roasts, chili and one-dish meals.

Cooking Times

Conventional Time	Slow Cooker
45 minutes	LOW: 6 to 8 hours HIGH: 3 to 4 hours
50 minutes or longer	LOW: 8 to 10 hours HIGH: 4 to 5 hours

Refer to your slow cooker's guidelines or recipe booklet or this cookbook. Look for a recipe that is similar to the one you want to convert for guidance. Note the quantity and size of the meat and vegetables, heat setting, cooking time and amount of liquid.

Since there is no evaporation, you will probably need to reduce the amount of liquid the recipe calls for. If a recipe calls for 6 to 8 cups of water, start with 5 cups. All slow cooker recipes should call for some liquid. If the recipe does not call for any, add about 1/2 cup of water, broth or juice.

Use a meat thermometer to check for doneness of large cuts of meat.

Quick-cooking tapioca can be used as a thickener for stews. Add it along with other ingredients at the beginning of cooking. To thicken juices at the end of cooking, use flour or cornstarch. Mix flour or cornstarch with some water until smooth. Stir into the slow cooker. Cover and cook on high for 30 minutes or until juices are thickened. Or, strain juices and place in a saucepan. Mix flour or cornstarch with some water until smooth. Stir into juices. Bring to a boil; cook and stir for 2 minutes or until thickened.

Useful Handles for Lifting Food

Layered dishes or meat loaves, such a Slow-Cooked Taco Meat Loaf (page 46), are easier to get out of the slow cooker using foil handles. Here's how:

1. For a 3-qt. slow cooker, cut three 20- x 3-inch strips of heavy-duty foil (or 25- x 3-inch for larger slow cookers). Or cut 6-inch-wide strips from regular foil and fold in half lengthwise. Crisscross the strips so they resemble the spokes of a wheel.

2. Place strips on the bottom and up the sides of the slow cooker insert. Let strips hang over the edge of the slow cooker. Coat strips with cooking spray.

3. Place food in the center of the strips and lower until the food rest on the bottom of the slow cooker.

4. After cooking, grasp the foil strips and carefully lift food up. Remove food from foil strips and serve.

Power Outage

If you are cooking in a slow cooker and the power goes out, the USDA recommends the following:

- If you are home when the power goes out and the food is not completely cooked, immediately finish cooking the food by another method, such as a gas stove or grill.

- If you are home when the power goes out and the food is completely cooked, it can sit in the slow cooker for up to 2 hours and still be food safe. Any longer and it should be discarded.

- If you are not home when the power goes out, discard the food even if you think it is cooked. It is better to be safe than consume food that has been uncooked or sitting for a long time at unsafe temperatures.

beef

Tangy Pot Roast

(pictured at left)

PREP: 15 MIN. ■ **COOK:** 7 HOURS

Paula Beach
Milton, New York
This super-delectable roast gets its special flavor from zippy Catalina dressing. Add a salad to round out this supper.

3 medium potatoes, thinly sliced
1-1/3 cups thinly sliced fresh carrots
2/3 cup sliced onion
1 boneless beef chuck roast (3 pounds)
1 teaspoon salt
1/2 teaspoon pepper
1/2 cup Catalina salad dressing
1/4 cup dry red wine or beef broth

1 Place the potatoes, carrots and onion in a 5-qt. slow cooker. Cut roast in half; rub with salt and pepper. Place over vegetables. In a small bowl, combine salad dressing and red wine; pour over roast.

2 Cover and cook on low for 7-8 hours or until meat is tender. Skim fat from cooking juices; thicken juices if desired.

Yield: 6 servings.

Slow-Cooked Pot Roast

(pictured at right)

PREP: 10 MIN. ■ **COOK:** 6-1/2 HOURS

Vera Carroll
Medford, Massachusetts
I like to serve my fork-tender pot roast with sauteed tarragon carrots and rosemary-roasted red potatoes. This homey meal suits all tastes, and the aroma alone is satisfying.

1 large sweet onion, chopped
1 cup sliced baby portobello mushrooms
1 beef rump roast or bottom round roast (3 pounds)
1/2 teaspoon salt
1/4 teaspoon pepper
1 cup dry red wine or beef broth
1 tablespoon brown sugar
1 tablespoon Dijon mustard
1 teaspoon Worcestershire sauce
2 tablespoons cornstarch
2 tablespoons cold water

1 Place onion and mushrooms in a 5-qt. slow cooker. Rub roast with salt and pepper; cut in half and place over onion mixture. In a small bowl, combine the wine, brown sugar, mustard and Worcestershire sauce; pour over roast. Cover and cook on low for 6-7 hours or until meat is tender.

2 Mix cornstarch and water until smooth; stir into cooking juices. Cover and cook on high for 30 minutes or until the gravy is thickened.

Yield: 6 servings.

Special Slow-Cooked Beef

(pictured above)

PREP: 35 MIN. ■ COOK: 6 HOURS

Juli George
Grandville, Michigan

This hearty entree is easy to prepare for Sunday dinner. While the beef cooks, the chef has lots of time to attend to the other details. With mashed potatoes on the side, it's comfort food for the cool months.

1 boneless beef chuck roast
(3 pounds), cubed
1 tablespoon canola oil
1 tablespoon Italian seasoning
1 teaspoon salt
1 garlic clove, minced
1/2 cup sliced ripe olives,
drained

1/3 cup oil-packed
sun-dried tomatoes, drained
and chopped
1 cup beef broth
1/2 cup fresh pearl onions,
peeled
1 tablespoon cornstarch
2 tablespoons water

1 In a large skillet, brown meat in oil in batches; drain. Transfer to a 5-qt. slow cooker. Sprinkle with Italian seasoning, salt and garlic; top with olives and tomatoes. Add broth and onions. Cover and cook on low for 6-8 hours or until meat is tender.

2 With a slotted spoon, remove beef and onions to a serving platter and keep warm. Pour cooking juices into a small saucepan; skim fat. Combine cornstarch and water until smooth; gradually stir into cooking juices. Bring to a boil; cook and stir for 2 minutes or until thickened. Spoon over beef mixture.

Yield: 8 servings.

Meat Loaf from The Slow Cooker

PREP: 25 MIN. ■ COOK: 3 HOURS

Laura Burgess
Mt. Vernon, South Dakota

I really enjoy meat loaf and this one, which I've lightened up, has become one of my all-time favorite recipes.

1/2 cup tomato sauce
1/2 cup egg substitute
1/4 cup ketchup
1 teaspoon Worcestershire sauce
1 small onion, chopped
1/3 cup crushed saltines (about
10 crackers)
3/4 teaspoon minced garlic
1/2 teaspoon seasoned salt
1/8 teaspoon seasoned pepper
1-1/2 pounds lean ground beef (90% lean)
1/2 pound reduced-fat bulk pork sausage

SAUCE:

1/2 cup ketchup
3 tablespoons brown sugar
3/4 teaspoon ground mustard
1/4 teaspoon ground nutmeg

1 Cut three 25-in. x 3-in. strips of heavy-duty foil; crisscross so they resemble the spokes of a wheel. Place the strips on the bottom and up the sides of an oval 5-qt. slow cooker. Coat the strips with cooking spray.

2 In a large bowl, combine the tomato sauce, egg substitute, ketchup, Worcestershire sauce, onion, crackers and seasonings. Crumble beef and sausage over mixture and mix well (mixture will be moist). Shape into a loaf. Place meat loaf in the center of the strips.

3 In a small bowl, combine sauce ingredients. Spoon over meat loaf. Cover and cook on low 3-4 hours or until a meat thermometer reads 160°. Using foil strips as handles, remove the meat loaf to a platter.

Yield: 8 servings.

Beef 'n' Chili Beans

PREP: 15 MIN. ■ **COOK:** 6 HOURS

Anita Hudson
Savoy, Texas
I took this dish to the last church meal we had, and it was a hit! Several of the ladies requested the recipe. I have to admit it is so easy to make...just put the ingredients in the slow cooker, and dinner's ready before you know it. The tomatoes with green chilies really add some zip.

3 pounds beef stew meat, cut into 1-inch cubes

2 tablespoons brown sugar

1-1/2 teaspoons ground mustard

1 teaspoon salt

1 teaspoon paprika

1/2 teaspoon chili powder

1/4 teaspoon pepper

1 large onion, chopped

2 cans (10 ounces each) diced tomatoes and green chilies, undrained

1 can (16 ounces) ranch-style or chili beans, undrained

1 can (15-1/4 ounces) whole kernel corn, drained

1 Place the beef in a 3-qt. slow cooker. Combine the brown sugar, mustard, salt, paprika, chili powder and pepper; sprinkle over beef and toss to coat. Top with onion, tomatoes, beans and corn. Cover and cook on low for 6-8 hours or until meat is tender.

Yield: 6-8 servings.

Brown it up. *If you prefer a richer brown color to the stew meat in this dish, you can prebrown the meat before you add it to the slow cooker. In a large skillet, heat 1-2 tablespoons canola oil over medium-high heat until hot. Pat the meat dry with paper towels and brown in batches, taking care not to overcrowd the skillet.*

Tex-Mex Beef Sandwiches

(pictured above)

PREP: 25 MIN. ■ **COOK:** 8-1/4 HOURS

Brenda Theisen
Addison, Michigan
Everyone loves these hearty sandwiches when I serve them. The cocoa is the surprise ingredient that adds a depth of flavor. It's hard to identify, so I'm often asked "What's that interesting taste?"

1 boneless beef chuck roast (3 pounds)	1 large sweet red pepper, coarsely chopped
1 envelope burrito seasoning	1 large onion, chopped
2 tablespoons baking cocoa	1 cup beef broth
1 large green pepper, coarsely chopped	1/2 cup ketchup
	8 hoagie buns, split

1 Cut roast in half. Combine burrito seasoning and cocoa; rub over meat. Place peppers and onion in a 3- or 4-qt. slow cooker. Top with meat; sprinkle with any remaining burrito mixture. Combine broth and ketchup; pour over meat. Cover and cook on low for 8-10 hours or until meat is tender.

2 Remove meat; cool slightly. Skim fat from cooking juices. Shred meat with two forks and return to slow cooker; heat through. Using a slotted spoon, spoon 1/2 cup onto each bun.

Yield: 8 servings.

Poor Man's Steak

PREP: 25 MIN. + CHILLING
COOK: 4 HOURS

Susan Wright
Mineral Wells, West Virginia
These flavorful "steaks" will fit into anyone's budget. A special friend shared the recipe, and I think of her each time I make this.

---

1 cup crushed saltine crackers (about 30 crackers)

1/3 cup water

Salt and pepper to taste

2 pounds ground beef

1/4 cup all-purpose flour

2 tablespoons canola oil

2 cans (10-3/4 ounces each) condensed cream of mushroom soup, undiluted

Hot mashed potatoes or noodles

1 In a large bowl, combine cracker crumbs, water, salt and pepper. Crumble beef over mixture and mix well. Press into an ungreased 9-in. square pan. Cover and refrigerate for at least 3 hours.

2 Cut into 3-in. squares; dredge in flour. In a large skillet, cook meat squares in oil until browned on both sides. Transfer to a 3-qt. slow cooker with a slotted spatula or spoon. Add soup. Cover and cook on high for 4 hours or until meat is no longer pink. Serve with mashed potatoes or noodles.

Yield: 9 servings.

Watching calories? *You can use lean ground turkey or ground chicken breast in place of the ground beef in Poor Man's Steak. By switching to lean ground turkey, you can save up to 60 calories per 4-ounce serving.*

Flavorful Beef Stew

PREP: 25 MIN. ■ **COOK:** 6 HOURS

Jackitt
Taste of Home Online Community
This tasty and rich beef stew creates a thick sauce that goes great with bread. I find it much easier to prepare in the slow cooker than on the stovetop or in the oven.

1/2 pound medium fresh mushrooms, quartered

2 medium red potatoes, cubed

3 medium carrots, cut into 1/4-inch slices

1 medium onion, chopped

1 celery rib, thinly sliced

1/4 cup all-purpose flour

1 tablespoon paprika

3/4 teaspoon salt

1/4 teaspoon pepper

1 pound beef stew meat, cut into 1-inch cubes

1 can (14-1/2 ounces) beef broth

4-1/2 teaspoons reduced-sodium teriyaki sauce

2 garlic cloves, minced

1 bay leaf

1 In a 3-qt. slow cooker, combine the first five ingredients.

2 In a large resealable plastic bag, combine the flour, paprika, salt and pepper. Add beef, a few pieces at a time, and shake to coat. Place over vegetable mixture. In a small bowl, combine the broth, teriyaki sauce, garlic and bay leaf. Pour over beef.

3 Cover and cook on low for 6-8 hours or until meat and vegetables are tender. Discard bay leaf.

Yield: 6 servings.

Hearty Beans with Beef

(pictured above)

PREP: 10 MIN. ■ **COOK:** 3 HOURS

Jan Biehl
Leesburg, Indiana
My husband raved about this sweet bean dish after tasting it at a party, so I knew I had to get the directions. It's perfect for get-togethers because it takes mere minutes to mix and then you're done.

1 pound ground beef

1 medium onion, chopped

1 can (16 ounces) baked beans, undrained

1 can (15-1/2 ounces) butter beans, rinsed and drained

1/2 cup ketchup

1/3 cup packed brown sugar

1 tablespoon barbecue sauce

1/4 teaspoon Worcestershire sauce

1 In a large skillet, cook beef and onion over medium heat until meat is no longer pink; drain. Transfer to a 5-qt. slow cooker. Stir in the remaining ingredients. Cover and cook on high for 3-4 hours or until heated through.

Yield: 8-10 servings.

Hearty Short Ribs

PREP: 15 MIN. ■ **COOK:** 6-1/4 HOURS

Helena Ivy
St. Louis, Missouri
The whole family will love these ribs! The meat simply falls off the bone, and the gravy is perfect with either mashed potatoes or rice.

1 large onion, sliced

4 pounds bone-in beef short ribs

1/2 pound sliced fresh mushrooms

1 can (10-3/4 ounces) condensed cream of mushroom soup, undiluted

1/2 cup water

1 envelope brown gravy mix

1 teaspoon minced garlic

1/2 teaspoon dried thyme

1 tablespoon cornstarch

2 tablespoons cold water

Hot mashed potatoes

1 Place onion in a 5-qt. slow cooker; top with the ribs. Combine the mushrooms, soup, 1/2 cup water, gravy mix, garlic and thyme; pour over the ribs. Cover and cook on low for 6 to 6-1/2 hours or until the meat is tender.

2 Remove meat to serving platter; keep warm. Skim fat from cooking juices; transfer to a small saucepan. Bring to a boil. Combine cornstarch and cold water until smooth. Gradually stir into pan. Bring to a boil. Cook and stir for 2 minutes or until thickened. Serve with meat and mashed potatoes.

Yield: 6 servings.

Italian Meatball Subs

PREP: 25 MIN. ■ **COOK:** 4 HOURS

Jean Glacken
Elkton, Maryland
This is one of those recipes you always come
back to. A flavorful tomato sauce and mildly
spiced meatballs make a hearty sandwich filling,
or they can be served over pasta. I broil the
meatballs first to quickly brown them.

2 eggs, lightly beaten
1/4 cup milk
1/2 cup dry bread crumbs
2 tablespoons grated Parmesan cheese
1 teaspoon salt
1/4 teaspoon pepper
1/8 teaspoon garlic powder
1 pound ground beef
1/2 pound bulk Italian sausage

SAUCE:
1 can (15 ounces) tomato sauce
1 can (6 ounces) tomato paste
1 small onion, chopped
1/2 cup chopped green pepper
1/2 cup dry red wine or beef broth
1/3 cup water
2 garlic cloves, minced
1 teaspoon dried oregano
1 teaspoon salt
1/2 teaspoon sugar
1/2 teaspoon pepper
6 to 7 Italian rolls, split
Shredded Parmesan cheese, optional

1 In a large bowl, combine eggs and milk;
add the bread crumbs, cheese, salt,
pepper and garlic powder. Crumble beef
and sausage over mixture; mix well.
Shape into 1-in. balls. Broil 4 in. from
the heat for 4 minutes; turn and broil 3
minutes longer.

2 Transfer to a 5-qt. slow cooker. Combine
the tomato sauce and paste, onion,
green pepper, wine or broth, water and
seasonings; pour over meatballs. Cover
and cook on low for 4-5 hours.

3 Serve on rolls. Sprinkle with shredded
cheese if desired.

Yield: 6-7 servings.

Steak Burritos

(pictured above)

PREP: 15 MIN. ■ **COOK:** 8-1/4 HOURS

Valerie Jones
Portland, Maine
I spice up flank steak with convenient taco seasoning packets. Slowly
simmered all day, the beef is tender and a snap to shred. Just fill flour
tortillas and add toppings for a tasty, time-easing meal.

2 beef flank steaks (about
1 pound each)
2 envelopes taco seasoning
1 medium onion, chopped
1 can (4 ounces) chopped
green chilies
1 tablespoon white vinegar
10 flour tortillas (8 inches),
warmed
1-1/2 cups (6 ounces)
shredded Monterey Jack
cheese
1-1/2 cups chopped seeded
plum tomatoes
3/4 cup sour cream

1 Cut steaks in half; rub with taco seasoning. Place in a 3-qt.
slow cooker coated with cooking spray. Top with the onion,
chilies and vinegar. Cover and cook on low for 8-9 hours or
until the meat is tender.

2 Remove meat; cool slightly. Shred with two forks and return to
slow cooker; heat through. Spoon about 1/2 cup meat mixture
down the center of each tortilla. Top with cheese, tomato and
sour cream. Fold ends and sides over filling.

Yield: 10 servings.

Zippy Beef Fajitas

(pictured above)

PREP: 20 MIN. ■ **COOK:** 6-1/4 HOURS

Laurie Sadowski
St. Catharines, Ontario
This is a flavorful and easy way to prepare steak filling for fajitas. The yummy taste comes aromatic ingredients like garlic and gingerroot. There's even a can of cola in the recipe.

1 beef flank steak
(1-1/2 pounds)

2 teaspoons ground ginger

2 teaspoons crushed red pepper flakes

3/4 teaspoon garlic powder

1/4 teaspoon pepper

1 medium sweet red pepper, cut into strips

1 medium green pepper, cut into strips

1 can (12 ounces) cola

5 green onions, chopped

1/3 cup soy sauce

2 tablespoons minced fresh gingerroot

2 tablespoons tomato paste

1 garlic clove, minced

6 flour tortillas (8 inches), warmed

1 Cut steak in half lengthwise. In a small bowl, combine the seasonings; rub over steak. Transfer to a 3-qt. slow cooker; add red and green peppers. Combine the cola, green onions, soy sauce, gingerroot, tomato paste and garlic; pour over top. Cover and cook on low 6-7 hours or until meat is tender.

2 Remove meat; cool slightly. Shred with two forks and return to the slow cooker; heat through. Using a slotted spoon, place about 1 cupful of beef mixture off center on each tortilla. Fold sides over filling.

Yield: 6 servings.

Hearty Beef Vegetable Stew

PREP: 20 MIN. ■ **COOK:** 5 HOURS

Angela Nelson
Ruther Glen, Virginia
I received this wonderful stew from a coworker. It's awesome! It is a hit with everyone, including our two young children.

1-1/2 pounds lean boneless beef chuck roast, cut into 1-inch cubes

2 teaspoons canola oil

1-1/2 pounds red potatoes, cut into 1-inch cubes

3 medium carrots, cut into 1-inch slices

1 medium onion, chopped

1/2 cup chopped celery

1 can (28 ounces) crushed tomatoes, undrained

3 tablespoons quick-cooking tapioca

2 tablespoons dried basil

1 tablespoon sugar

1/2 teaspoon salt

1/8 teaspoon pepper

1 In a large nonstick skillet, brown meat in oil over medium heat. Meanwhile, place the potatoes, carrots, onion and celery in a 5-qt. slow cooker. Drain meat; add to slow cooker. Combine the tomatoes, tapioca, basil, sugar, salt and pepper; pour over the top.

2 Cover and cook on high for 5-6 hours or until meat and vegetables are tender.

Yield: 6 servings.

> **Experiment with herbs.** Other herbs that would be suitable for the Hearty Beef Vegetable Stew are marjoram, tarragon, thyme and savory.

Ground Beef Stew

PREP: 15 MIN. ■ **COOK:** 6 HOURS

Mary Jo Walker
Jasper, Tennessee
Since I work all day, it's great to come home knowing I have a hot, very delicious meal waiting for me. I like to serve generous helpings of this stew with corn bread muffins.

1-1/2 pounds ground beef

2 large potatoes, sliced

2 medium carrots, sliced

1 can (15 ounces) peas, drained

3 medium onions, sliced

2 celery ribs, sliced

1 can (10-3/4 ounces) condensed tomato soup, undiluted

1-1/3 cups water

1 In a large skillet, cook beef over medium heat until no longer pink; drain.

2 In a 5-qt. slow cooker, layer the vegetables in the order listed. Top with the beef. In a small bowl, combine soup and water. Pour over beef. Cover and cook on low for 6-8 hours or until vegetables are tender.

Yield: 6 servings.

Editor's Note: Bake some corn bread muffins and freeze them alongside serving-size portions of the Ground Beef Stew. Pull both packages out of the freezer when you need a quick lunch.

No-Fuss Swiss Steak

(pictured above)

PREP: 10 MIN. ■ **COOK:** 6 HOURS

Sharon Morrell
Parker, South Dakota
I received the directions for this dish from my cousin. I make it regularly because our children just love the savory steak, tangy gravy and fork-tender veggies.

3 pounds beef top round steak, cut into serving-size pieces

2 tablespoons canola oil

2 medium carrots, cut into 1/2-inch slices

2 celery ribs, cut into 1/2-inch slices

1-3/4 cups water

1 can (11 ounces) condensed tomato rice soup, undiluted

1 can (10-1/2 ounces) condensed French onion soup, undiluted

1/2 teaspoon pepper

1 bay leaf

1 In a large skillet, brown beef in oil over medium-high heat; drain. Transfer to a 5-qt. slow cooker. Add carrots and celery. Combine the remaining ingredients; pour over meat and vegetables. Cover and cook on low for 6-8 hours or until meat is tender. Discard the bay leaf before serving. Thicken cooking juices if desired.

Yield: 8-10 servings.

Texas Stew

PREP: 15 MIN. ■ **COOK:** 4 HOURS

Kim Balstad
Lewisville, Texas
I love to experiment with many different types of recipes. But as a mother, I turn to family-friendly ones more and more. Everyone enjoys this hearty stew.

- 1 can (15-1/2 ounces) hominy, drained
- 1 can (15-1/4 ounces) whole kernel corn, drained
- 1 can (15 ounces) sliced carrots, drained
- 1 can (15 ounces) sliced potatoes, drained
- 1 can (16 ounces) ranch-style or chili beans, undrained
- 1 can (14-1/2 ounces) diced tomatoes, undrained
- 1 cup water
- 1 beef bouillon cube
- 1/2 teaspoon garlic powder
- Chili powder to taste
- Dash Worcestershire sauce
- Dash hot pepper sauce
- 1-1/2 pounds ground beef
- 1 medium onion, chopped

1 In a 5-qt. slow cooker, combine the vegetables, water, bouillon, garlic powder, chili powder, Worcestershire sauce and hot pepper sauce. In a skillet, cook beef and onion over medium heat until meat is no longer pink; drain. Transfer to the slow cooker. Cover and cook on high for 4 hours or until heated through.

Yield: 10-12 servings.

Editor's Note: If your family doesn't care for hominy, you can use a 15-ounce can of green beans (drained) instead.

Pot Roast with Gravy

(pictured above)
PREP: 30 MIN. ■ **COOK:** 7-1/2 HOURS

Deborah Dailey
Vancouver, Washington
My family loves this tangy beef roast with gravy. We always hope for leftovers that I turn into a tasty sandwich spread.

- 1 beef rump roast or bottom round roast (5 pounds)
- 6 tablespoons balsamic vinegar, divided
- 1 teaspoon salt
- 1/2 teaspoon garlic powder
- 1/4 teaspoon pepper
- 2 tablespoons canola oil
- 3 garlic cloves, minced
- 4 bay leaves
- 1 large onion, thinly sliced
- 3 teaspoons beef bouillon granules
- 1/2 cup boiling water
- 1 can (10-3/4 ounces) condensed cream of mushroom soup, undiluted
- 4 to 5 tablespoons cornstarch
- 1/4 cup cold water

1 Cut roast in half; rub with 2 tablespoons vinegar. Combine the salt, garlic powder and pepper; rub over meat. In a large skillet, brown roast in oil on all sides. Transfer to a 5-qt. slow cooker.

2 Place the garlic, bay leaves and onion over roast. In a small bowl, dissolve bouillon in boiling water; stir in soup and remaining vinegar. Slowly pour over roast. Cover and cook on low for 7-8 hours or until meat is tender.

3 Remove roast; keep warm. Discard bay leaves. Whisk cornstarch and cold water until smooth; stir into cooking juices. Cover and cook on high for 30 minutes or until gravy is thickened. Slice roast; return to slow cooker and heat through.

Yield: 10 servings.

Flank Steak Roll-Up

PREP: 15 MIN. ■ **COOK:** 8 HOURS

Sheryl Johnson
Las Vegas, Nevada

As a working mom with hungry boys, I rely on my slow cooker to give me a head start on meals. I roll stuffing mix and mushrooms into flank steak before simmering it in an easy gravy.

1 can (4 ounces) mushroom stems and pieces, undrained
2 tablespoons butter, melted
1 package (6 ounces) seasoned stuffing mix
1 beef flank steak (1-3/4 pounds)
1 envelope brown gravy mix
1/4 cup chopped green onion
1/4 cup dry red wine or beef broth

1 In bowl, toss the mushrooms, butter and dry stuffing mix. Spread over steak to within 1 in. of edges. Roll up jelly-roll style, starting with a long side; tie with kitchen string. Place in a 3-qt. slow cooker.

2 Prepare gravy mix according to package directions; add onions and wine or broth. Pour over meat. Cover and cook on low for 8-10 hours. Remove meat to a serving platter and keep warm. Strain cooking juices and thicken if desired. Remove string from roll-up; slice and serve with gravy.

Yield: 6 servings.

Dressed up stuffing. You can enhance the stuffing for the flank steak with one or more of the following suggestions. Saute a 1/2 cup chopped onion and 1/4 cup chopped celery in 1 tablespoon canola oil; stir in with mushrooms. Toss in 1/2 cup thawed frozen corn and 2 tablespoons chopped fresh parsley. Or, add a chopped tart apple to the stuffing mix.

Bavarian Meatballs

(pictured above)

PREP: 15 MIN. ■ **COOK:** 3-1/2 HOURS

Peggy Rios
Mechanicsville, Virginia

Unless my husband decides to grill for me, I usually reach for my slow cooker and one of my favorite recipes such as these mouthwatering meatballs. They're a guaranteed crowd-pleaser when I serve them as a yummy sandwich filling spooned over crusty rolls and topped with cheese.

1 package (32 ounces) frozen fully cooked Italian meatballs
1/2 cup chopped onion
1/4 cup packed brown sugar
1 envelope onion soup mix
1 can (12 ounces) beer or nonalcoholic beer
12 hoagie buns, split
3 cups (12 ounces) shredded Swiss cheese

1 In a 3-qt. slow cooker, combine the meatballs, onion, brown sugar, soup mix and beer. Cover and cook on low for 3-1/2 to 4-1/2 hours or until heated through.

2 Place six meatballs on each bun bottom. Sprinkle each sandwich with 1/4 cup cheese. Place on baking sheets. Broil 4-6 in. from the heat for 2-3 minutes or until cheese is melted. Replace bun tops.

Yield: 12 servings.

Beef Roast Dinner

(pictured above)

PREP: 20 MIN. ■ **COOK:** 8-1/4 HOURS

Sandra Dudley
Bemidji, Minnesota
Because this healthy dish is slow cooked, you can use less-expensive roasts with results as mouthwatering as the more costly cuts. Change up the veggies for variety, nutrition or to suit your tastes!

1 pound red potatoes (about 4 medium), cubed

1/4 pound small fresh mushrooms

1-1/2 cups fresh baby carrots

1 medium green pepper, chopped

1 medium parsnip, chopped

1 small red onion, chopped

1 beef rump roast or bottom round roast (3 pounds)

1 can (14-1/2 ounces) beef broth

3/4 teaspoon salt

3/4 teaspoon dried oregano

1/4 teaspoon pepper

3 tablespoons cornstarch

1/4 cup cold water

1 Place vegetables in a 5-qt. slow cooker. Cut roast in half; place in slow cooker. Combine the broth, salt, oregano and pepper; pour over meat. Cover and cook on low for 8 hours or until meat is tender.

2 Remove meat and vegetables to a serving platter; keep warm. Skim fat from cooking juices; transfer to a small saucepan. Bring liquid to a boil. Combine cornstarch and cold water until smooth. Gradually stir into the pan. Bring to a boil; cook and stir for 2 minutes or until sauce is thickened. Serve with meat and vegetables.

Yield: 10 servings.

German-Style Short Ribs

PREP: 15 MIN. ■ **COOK:** 8 HOURS

Bregitte Rugman
Shanty Bay, Ontario
Our whole family is thrilled when I make these fall-off-the-bone tender ribs. We like them served over rice or egg noodles.

3/4 cup dry red wine or beef broth

1/2 cup mango chutney

3 tablespoons quick-cooking tapioca

1/4 cup water

3 tablespoons brown sugar

3 tablespoons cider vinegar

1 tablespoon Worcestershire sauce

1/2 teaspoon salt

1/2 teaspoon ground mustard

1/2 teaspoon chili powder

1/2 teaspoon pepper

4 pounds bone-in beef short ribs

2 medium onions, sliced

Hot cooked egg noodles

1 In a 5-qt. slow cooker, combine the wine, chutney, tapioca, water, sugar, vinegar, Worcestershire sauce and seasonings. Add ribs and turn to coat. Top with onions. Cover and cook on low for 8-10 hours or until meat is tender.

2 Remove the ribs from the slow cooker. Skim fat from cooking juices; serve juices with ribs and noodles.

Yield: 8 servings.

Slow-Cooked Enchilada Dinner

PREP: 25 MIN. ■ **COOK:** 2 HOURS

Judy Ragsdale
Queen City, Texas
This layered Southwestern meal just can't be beat. It gets its spicy flavor from green chilies, chili powder and cumin. Using a purchased slow cooker liner makes it easier to lift and remove the meal so it can be cut into individual wedges.

---

1 pound lean ground beef (90% lean)

1 small onion, chopped

1 can (15 ounces) ranch-style beans, undrained

1 can (10 ounces) diced tomatoes with mild green chilies, undrained

1/4 cup chopped green pepper

1 teaspoon chili powder

1/2 teaspoon salt

1/2 teaspoon ground cumin

1/4 teaspoon pepper

1 cup (4 ounces) shredded Monterey Jack cheese

1 cup (4 ounces) shredded cheddar cheese

6 flour tortillas (6 inches)

1 In a large skillet, cook beef and onion over medium heat until meat is no longer pink; drain. Stir in the beans, tomatoes, green pepper, chili powder, salt, cumin and pepper. In a small bowl, combine the cheeses; set aside.

2 In a 5-qt. slow cooker coated with cooking spray or lined with a slow cooker liner, place two tortillas side by side, overlapping if necessary. Layer with a third of the beef mixture and cheese. Repeat layers twice. Cover and cook on low for 2 to 2-1/2 hours or until heated through.

Yield: 6 servings.

Chipotle Beef Sandwiches

PREP: 25 MIN. ■ **COOK:** 7-1/4 HOURS

Jessica Ring
Madison, Wisconsin
A jar of chipotle salsa makes it easy to spice up beef sirloin for my flavorful sandwiches. Keep this no-stress recipe in mind the next time you have to feed a hungry crowd.

> 1 large sweet onion, halved and thinly sliced
> 1 beef sirloin tip roast (3 pounds)
> 1 jar (16 ounces) chipotle salsa
> 1/2 cup beer or nonalcoholic beer
> 1 envelope beefy onion soup mix
> 10 kaiser rolls, split

1 Place onion in a 5-qt. slow cooker. Cut roast in half; place over onion. Combine the salsa, beer and soup mix. Pour over top. Cover and cook on low for 7-8 hours or until meat is tender.

2 Remove roast; cool slightly. Shred with two forks and return to the slow cooker; heat through. Using a slotted spoon, spoon shredded meat onto each roll.

Yield: 10 servings.

> **Wrap it.** Instead of using a kaiser roll, place this savory beef filling on a corn or flour tortilla. Add some shredded radishes and chopped avocado for an extra-special treat.

Hungarian Stew

PREP: 30 MIN. ■ **COOK:** 8-1/4 HOURS

Susan Kain
Woodbine, Maryland
As the owner of a fitness center, I rely on a slow cooker many days to create a wonderful meal for my family. This hearty stew is chock-full of herbs and spices reminiscent of the old days.

4 medium potatoes, cut into 1-inch cubes

2 medium onions, chopped

1 pound beef stew meat, cut into 1-inch cubes

2 tablespoons canola oil

1-1/2 cups hot water

3 teaspoons paprika

1 teaspoon salt

1 teaspoon caraway seeds

1 teaspoon tomato paste

1 garlic clove, minced

2 medium green peppers, cut into 1-inch pieces

2 medium tomatoes, peeled, seeded and chopped

3 tablespoons all-purpose flour

3 tablespoons cold water

1/2 cup sour cream

1 Place potatoes and onions in a 3-qt. slow cooker. In a large skillet, brown meat in oil on all sides. Place over potato mixture.

2 Pour off the excess fat from skillet. Add the hot water to the drippings, stirring to loosen browned bits from pan. Stir in the paprika, salt, caraway seeds, tomato paste and garlic. Pour tomato paste mixture into the slow cooker. Cover and cook on low for 7 hours.

3 Add green peppers and tomatoes; cover and cook 1 hour longer or until meat and vegetables are tender. With a slotted spoon, transfer meat and vegetables to a large serving bowl; cover and keep warm.

4 Pour cooking juices into a small saucepan. Combine flour and cold water until smooth; gradually whisk into the pan. Bring to a boil; cook and stir for 2 minutes or until thickened. Remove from the heat; whisk in sour cream. Stir into meat mixture.

Yield: 6 servings.

Green Chili Beef Burritos

(pictured above)

PREP: 30 MIN. ■ **COOK:** 9 HOURS

Jenny Flake
Newport Beach, California
This recipe gets raves every time I make it. The shredded beef has a fantastic taste that you can't get anywhere else.

1 boneless beef chuck roast (3 pounds)

1 can (14-1/2 ounces) beef broth

2 cups green enchilada sauce

1 can (4 ounces) chopped green chilies

1/2 cup Mexican-style hot tomato sauce

1/2 teaspoon salt

1/2 teaspoon garlic powder

1/2 teaspoon pepper

12 flour tortillas (12 inches)

Optional toppings: shredded lettuce, chopped tomatoes, shredded cheddar cheese and sour cream

1 Cut roast in half and place in a 3- or 4-qt. slow cooker. Add broth. Cover and cook on low for 8-9 hours or until meat is tender.

2 Remove meat; cool slightly. Skim fat from cooking juices; reserve 1/2 cup cooking juices. Shred meat with two forks and return to slow cooker. Add reserved liquid.

3 Stir in the enchilada sauce, green chilies, tomato sauce, salt, garlic powder and pepper. Cover and cook on low for 1 hour or until heated through.

4 Spoon beef mixture down the center of tortillas; add toppings of your choice. Roll up.

Yield: 12 servings.

Editor's Note: This recipe was tested with El Pato brand Mexican-style hot tomato sauce. If you cannot find Mexican-style hot tomato sauce, substitute 1/2 cup tomato sauce, 1 teaspoon hot pepper sauce and 1/8 teaspoon each onion powder and chili powder.

Mushroom Pepper Steak

PREP: 15 MIN. ■ **COOK:** 6-1/4 HOURS

Katie Goble
Valparaiso, Indiana
This budget-friendly recipe takes a round steak and gently simmers it until it's so tender. It's topped with colorful pepper gravy.

    2 pounds beef top round steak

    2 cups each sliced green, sweet red and yellow peppers (1/2-inch strips)

    1 can (7 ounces) mushroom stems and pieces, drained

    2 medium onions, quartered and sliced

    1/2 cup water

    1 teaspoon salt

    1/2 teaspoon pepper

    1 can (15 ounces) tomato sauce

    1/4 cup cornstarch

    1/4 cup cold water

    Hot mashed potatoes

1 Cut steak into serving-size pieces. Place in a 5-qt. slow cooker. Add the peppers, mushrooms, onions, water, salt and pepper. Pour tomato sauce over the top. Cover and cook on low for 6 to 6-1/2 hours or until meat is tender.

2 Using a slotted spoon, remove beef and vegetables; keep warm. In a small bowl, combine cornstarch and cold water until smooth. Gradually stir into cooking juices; cover and cook on high for 15 minutes or until thickened. Serve with beef, vegetables and mashed potatoes.

Yield: 8 servings.

Italian Stuffed Peppers

(pictured above)

PREP: 25 MIN. ■ **COOK:** 4 HOURS

Taste of Home Test Kitchen
Cooking these stuffed peppers in a slow cooker is not only convenient, but the long cooking process develops the delicious flavor of the filling.

    6 large sweet red or green peppers

    1 pound lean ground beef (90% lean)

    2 cups cubed part-skim mozzarella cheese (1/4-inch cubes)

    1 cup uncooked converted rice

    1 small onion, chopped

    2 garlic cloves, minced

    1 teaspoon minced fresh parsley

    1 teaspoon salt

    1/2 teaspoon pepper

    1 cup beef broth

    1 can (28 ounces) crushed tomatoes

    1/2 cup grated Parmesan cheese

    Additional minced fresh parsley

1 Cut tops off peppers and remove seeds; set aside. In a large bowl, combine the beef, mozzarella cheese, rice, onion, garlic, parsley, salt and pepper; spoon into peppers. Transfer to an oval 5- or 6-qt. slow cooker. Pour the broth over the peppers; top with tomatoes.

2 Cover and cook on low for 4-5 hours or until a meat thermometer reaches 160° and peppers are tender. Sprinkle with Parmesan cheese and additional parsley.

Yield: 6 servings.

Loaded Vegetable Beef Stew

PREP: 40 MIN. ■ **COOK:** 8-1/2 HOURS

Kari Caven
Post Falls, Idaho
I first had this dish during a trip to Argentina a few years ago. It inspired me to re-create it at home. It turned out so well. I wrote "Yum!" on the recipe card.

___

8 bacon strips, diced

3 pounds beef stew meat, cut into 1-inch cubes

6 medium carrots, cut into 1-inch pieces

6 medium tomatoes, peeled and cut into wedges

4 medium potatoes, peeled and cubed

3 cups cubed peeled butternut squash

2 medium green peppers, chopped

2 teaspoons dried thyme

2 garlic cloves, minced

2 cans (14-1/2 ounces each) beef broth

6 cups chopped cabbage

1/2 teaspoon pepper

1 In a large skillet, cook bacon over medium heat until crisp. Using a slotted spoon, remove to paper towels to drain. In the drippings, brown beef in batches. Refrigerate the bacon until serving.

2 In a 5-qt. slow cooker, combine the carrots, tomatoes, potatoes, squash, green peppers, thyme and garlic. Top with beef. Pour broth over the top. Cover and cook on low for 8 hours.

3 Stir in cabbage and pepper. Cover and cook on high for 30 minutes or until cabbage is tender. Sprinkle each serving with bacon.

Yield: 12 servings (1-1/3 cups each).

___

Soak up the goodness. *The wonderful stew above is just packed with vegetables, which flavor the savory broth. To help get every last drop of the fabulous broth, serve the stew over cooked rice, couscous or noodles.*

Meal-In-One Casserole

PREP: 15 MIN. ■ **COOK:** 4 HOURS

Dorothy Pritchett
Wills Point, Texas
Salsa gives zip to this hearty meal. This dish makes more than my husband and I can eat, so I freeze half of it. We think it tastes even better the second time.

> 1 pound ground beef
>
> 1 medium onion, chopped
>
> 1 medium green pepper, chopped
>
> 1 can (15-1/4 ounces) whole kernel corn, drained
>
> 1 can (4 ounces) mushroom stems and pieces, drained
>
> 1 teaspoon salt
>
> 1/4 teaspoon pepper
>
> 1-1/3 cups salsa
>
> 5 cups cooked medium egg noodles
>
> 1 can (28 ounces) diced tomatoes, undrained
>
> 1 cup water
>
> 1 cup (4 ounces) shredded cheddar cheese or blend of cheddar, Monterey Jack and American cheese

1 In a large skillet, cook beef and onion over medium heat until meat is no longer pink; drain.

2 Transfer to a 5-qt. slow cooker. Top with the green pepper, corn and mushrooms. Sprinkle with salt and pepper. Pour salsa over mushrooms. Top with noodles. Pour tomatoes and water over all. Sprinkle with cheese. Cover and cook on low for 4 hours or until heated through.

Yield: 4-6 servings.

Picante Beef Roast

(pictured above)

PREP: 10 MIN. ■ **COOK:** 8-1/4 HOURS

Margaret Thiel
Devittown, Pennsylvania
Before putting the roast into the slow cooker, trim the fat from it to avoid greasy gravy. The south-of-the-border flavor is sure to please your family.

> 1 beef rump roast or bottom round roast (3 pounds), trimmed and halved
>
> 1 jar (16 ounces) picante sauce
>
> 1 can (15 ounces) tomato sauce
>
> 1 envelope taco seasoning
>
> 3 tablespoons cornstarch
>
> 1/4 cup water

1 Cut roast in half; place in a 5-qt. slow cooker. In a large bowl, combine the picante sauce, tomato sauce and taco seasoning; pour over roast. Cover and cook on low for 8-9 hours or until meat is tender.

2 Remove meat to a serving platter; keep warm. Skim fat from cooking juices; transfer 3 cups to a small saucepan. Bring liquid to a boil. Combine cornstarch and water until smooth. Gradually stir into pan. Bring to a boil; cook and stir for 2 minutes or until thickened. Slice roast; serve with gravy.

Yield: 8 servings.

Seasoned Short Ribs

PREP: 15 MIN. ■ **COOK:** 6-1/4 HOURS

Taste of Home Test Kitchen
These juicy, barbecue-style short ribs are sure to be a hit with your family. Line your broiler pan with foil for easy cleanup.

- 1-1/2 cups tomato juice
- 1/2 cup maple syrup
- 1/4 cup chopped onion
- 3 tablespoons cider vinegar
- 1 tablespoon Worcestershire sauce
- 1 tablespoon Dijon mustard
- 2 teaspoons minced garlic
- 1/4 teaspoon ground cinnamon
- 1/4 teaspoon ground cloves
- 4 pounds bone-in beef short ribs
- 1 teaspoon pepper
- 1 tablespoon cornstarch
- 2 tablespoons cold water

1 In a small bowl, combine the tomato juice, syrup, onion, vinegar, Worcestershire sauce, mustard, garlic, cinnamon and cloves; set aside.

2 Cut ribs into serving-size pieces; place on a broiler pan. Sprinkle with pepper.

3 Broil 4-6 in. from the heat for 3-5 minutes on each side or until browned; drain on paper towels.

4 Place ribs in a 5-qt. slow cooker; top with tomato juice mixture. Cover and cook on low for 6-7 hours or until meat is tender.

5 Pour 1 cup cooking juices into a small saucepan; skim off fat and bring to a boil. In a small bowl, combine cornstarch and cold water until smooth. Stir into cooking juices. Return to a boil; cook and stir for 2 minutes or until thickened. Serve the sauce over the ribs.

Yield: 4 servings.

Pot Roast with Mushroom Gravy

(pictured above)

PREP: 20 MIN. ■ **COOK:** 8 HOURS

Tyler Sherman
Madison, Wisconsin
You just can't beat the comforting goodness of a pot roast...especially one that simmers extra slowly in its own juices during the day. Hearty vegetables like potatoes, carrots, mushrooms, celery and onion make it a great meal-in-one.

- 1 pound small red potatoes, halved
- 2 cups fresh baby carrots
- 1 package (8 ounces) sliced fresh mushrooms
- 1 medium onion, cut into six wedges
- 2 celery ribs, cut into 1-inch pieces
- 1 boneless beef chuck roast (3 pounds)
- 1 can (14-1/2 ounces) reduced-sodium beef broth
- 1 can (10-1/2 ounces) mushroom gravy
- 1 package (1-1/2 ounces) beef stew seasoning mix

1 Place the potatoes, carrots, mushrooms, onion and celery in a 5-qt. slow cooker. Cut the roast in half; place over vegetables. In a small bowl, combine the broth, gravy and seasoning mix; pour over the roast. Cover and cook on low for 8-9 hours or until meat is tender.

Yield: 8 servings.

Slow-Cooked Caribbean Pot Roast

(pictured above)

PREP: 30 MIN. ■ **COOK:** 6 HOURS

Jenn Tidwell
Fair Oaks, California
I put this dish together throughout the fall and winter seasons, but considering how simple it is to prepare, it's great in any season.

2 medium sweet potatoes, cubed

2 large carrots, sliced

1/4 cup chopped celery

1 boneless beef chuck roast (2-1/2 pounds)

1 tablespoon canola oil

1 large onion, chopped

2 garlic cloves, minced

1 tablespoon all-purpose flour

1 tablespoon sugar

1 tablespoon brown sugar

1 teaspoon ground cumin

3/4 teaspoon salt

3/4 teaspoon ground coriander

3/4 teaspoon chili powder

1/2 teaspoon dried oregano

1/8 teaspoon ground cinnamon

3/4 teaspoon grated orange peel

3/4 teaspoon baking cocoa

1 can (15 ounces) tomato sauce

1 Place potatoes, carrots and celery in a 5-qt. slow cooker. In a large skillet, brown meat in oil on all sides. Transfer meat to slow cooker.

2 In the same skillet, saute onion in drippings until tender. Add garlic; cook 1 minute longer. Combine the flour, sugar, brown sugar, seasonings, orange peel and cocoa. Stir in tomato sauce; add to skillet and heat through. Pour over beef. Cover and cook on low for 6-8 hours or until beef and vegetables are tender.

Yield: 10 servings.

Round Steak Italiano

PREP: 15 MIN. ■ **COOK:** 7-1/4 HOURS

Deanne Stephens
McMinnville, Oregon
My mom used to make this wonderful dish, and it's always been one that I love. I especially like how the thick gravy drapes over both the meat and the potatoes.

2 pounds beef top round steak

1 can (8 ounces) tomato sauce

2 tablespoons onion soup mix

2 tablespoons canola oil

2 tablespoons red wine vinegar

1 teaspoon ground oregano

1/2 teaspoon garlic powder

1/4 teaspoon pepper

8 medium potatoes (7 to 8 ounces each)

1 tablespoon cornstarch

1 tablespoon cold water

1 Cut steak into serving-size pieces; place in a 5-qt. slow cooker. In a large bowl, combine the tomato sauce, soup mix, oil, vinegar, oregano, garlic powder and pepper; pour over meat. Scrub and pierce potatoes; place over meat. Cover and cook on low for 7 to 7-1/2 hours or until meat and potatoes are tender.

2 Remove meat and potatoes; keep warm. Pour cooking juices into a small saucepan; skim fat. Combine cornstarch and water until smooth; gradually stir into juices. Bring to a boil; cook and stir for 2 minutes or until thickened. Serve with meat and potatoes.

Yield: 8 servings.

Add a touch of wine. *For a more authentic Italian flavor, substitute a full-bodied red wine, such as Cabernet Sauvignon or Chianti, or lighter-bodied wine, like Merlot, for the red wine vinegar. Use about 1/4 cup. And remember, use a wine that is suitable for drinking, and serve a glass with the meal.*

Corned Beef Supper

PREP: 25 MIN. ■ **COOK:** 4 HOURS

Dawn Fagerstrom
Warren, Minnesota

What better way to celebrate St. Patrick's Day than with this classic one-pot meal. I often prepare it for the holiday, but it's good any time of the year.

1 small onion, sliced

4 small carrots, cut into chunks

2 medium potatoes, cut into chunks

1 corned beef brisket with spice packet (1 pound)

1/3 cup unsweetened apple juice

2 whole cloves

1 tablespoon brown sugar

1/2 teaspoon grated orange peel

1/2 teaspoon prepared mustard

2 cabbage wedges

1 Place onion in a 3-qt. slow cooker. Top with the carrots, potatoes and brisket. Combine the apple juice, cloves, brown sugar, orange peel, mustard and contents of spice packet; pour over brisket. Cover and cook on high for 3-1/2 to 4 hours.

2 Add the cabbage wedges; cover and cook 30 minutes longer or until the meat and vegetables are tender. Strain and discard the cloves; serve pan juices with corned beef and vegetables.

Yield: 2 servings.

Traditional Beef Stew

(pictured above)

PREP: 15 MIN. ■ **COOK:** 8 HOURS

Rosana Pape
Hamilton, Indiana

The aroma of this classic beef stew is irresistible, making it impossible not to dig in the moment you walk in the door.

1 pound beef stew meat, cut into 1-inch cubes

1 pound fresh baby carrots

2 medium potatoes, cut into chunks

2 medium onions, cut into wedges

1 cup drained diced tomatoes

1 cup beef broth

1 celery rib, cut into 1/2-inch pieces

2 tablespoons quick-cooking tapioca

1 teaspoon Worcestershire sauce

1/4 teaspoon salt

1/4 teaspoon pepper

1 In a 3-qt. slow cooker, combine all the ingredients. Cover and cook on low for 8-10 hours or until the meat and vegetables are tender.

Yield: 4 servings.

All-Day Brisket with Potatoes

PREP: 30 MIN. ■ **COOK:** 8 HOURS

Lana Gryga
Glen Flora, Wisconsin
I think the slow cooker was invented with brisket in mind. This sweet and savory version is perfection itself, because it melts in your mouth. It's very important to buy "first-cut" or "flat-cut" brisket, which has far less fat than other cuts.

2 medium potatoes, peeled and cut into 1/4-inch slices
2 celery ribs, sliced
1 fresh beef brisket (3 pounds)
1 tablespoon canola oil
1 large onion, sliced
2 garlic cloves, minced
1 can (12 ounces) beer
1/2 teaspoon beef bouillon granules
3/4 cup stewed tomatoes
1/3 cup tomato paste
1/4 cup red wine vinegar
3 tablespoons brown sugar
3 tablespoons Dijon mustard
3 tablespoons soy sauce
2 tablespoons molasses
1/2 teaspoon paprika
1/4 teaspoon salt
1/8 teaspoon pepper
1 bay leaf

1 Place potatoes and celery in a 5-qt. slow cooker. Cut brisket in half. In a large skillet, brown beef in oil on all sides; transfer to slow cooker. In the same pan, saute onion until tender. Add garlic; cook 1 minute longer. Add to slow cooker.

2 Stir in beer and bouillon granules to skillet, stirring to loosen browned bits from pan; pour over meat. In a large bowl, combine the remaining ingredients; add to slow cooker.

3 Cover and cook on low for 8-10 hours or until meat and vegetables are tender. Discard bay leaf. To serve, thinly slice across the grain.

Yield: 8 servings.

Editor's Note: This is a fresh beef brisket, not corned beef.

Artichoke Beef Stew

PREP: 25 MIN. ■ COOK: 7-1/2 HOURS

Janell Schmidt
Athelstane, Wisconsin
The recipe for this special stew was given to me by a dear friend before she moved to another state. She served it with dumplings, but my husband prefers noodles.

> 1/3 cup all-purpose flour
>
> 1 teaspoon salt
>
> 1/2 teaspoon pepper
>
> 2-1/2 pounds beef stew meat, cut into 1-inch cubes
>
> 3 tablespoons canola oil
>
> 1 can (10-1/2 ounces) condensed beef consomme, undiluted
>
> 2 medium onions, halved and sliced
>
> 1 cup red wine or beef broth
>
> 1 garlic clove, minced
>
> 1/2 teaspoon dill weed
>
> 2 jars (6-1/2 ounces each) marinated artichoke hearts, drained and chopped
>
> 20 small fresh mushrooms, halved
>
> Hot cooked noodles

1 In a large resealable plastic bag, combine the flour, salt and pepper. Add beef and toss to coat. In a skillet, brown beef in oil.

2 Using a slotted spoon, transfer beef to a 3-qt. slow cooker. Gradually add the consomme to the skillet. Bring to a boil; stir to loosen browned bits from pan. Stir in the onions, wine, garlic and dill. Pour over beef.

3 Cover and cook on low for 7-8 hours or until the meat is tender. Stir in the artichokes and mushrooms; cook 30 minutes longer or until heated through. Serve with noodles.

Yield: 6-8 servings.

Glazed Corned Beef Dinner

(pictured above)

PREP: 20 MIN. ■ COOK: 8-1/4 HOURS

Shannon Strate
Salt Lake City, Utah
This recipe is so tasty that it's the only way my family will eat corned beef. The glaze is the kicker!

> 8 medium red potatoes, quartered
>
> 2 medium carrots, sliced
>
> 1 medium onion, sliced
>
> 1 corned beef brisket with spice packet (3 pounds)
>
> 1-1/2 cups water
>
> 4 orange peel strips (3 inches)
>
> 3 tablespoons orange juice concentrate
>
> 3 tablespoons honey
>
> 1 tablespoon Dijon mustard

1 Place the potatoes, carrots and onion in a 5-qt. slow cooker. Cut brisket in half; place over vegetables. Add the water, orange peel and contents of spice packet.

2 Cover and cook on low for 8-9 hours or until meat and vegetables are tender.

3 Using a slotted spoon, transfer corned beef and vegetables to a 13-in. x 9-in. baking dish. Discard orange peel. Combine the orange juice concentrate, honey and mustard; pour over meat. Bake, uncovered, at 375° for 15-20 minutes, basting occasionally.

Yield: 8 servings.

Confetti Casserole

PREP: 20 MIN. ■ COOK: 8 HOURS

Joy Vincent
Newport, North Carolina
To create this comforting casserole, I adapted a recipe from the cookbook that came with my first slow cooker. I love to serve it with fresh bread from my bread maker.

    1 pound ground beef
    1 medium onion, finely chopped
    1 teaspoon garlic powder
    4 medium potatoes, peeled and quartered
    3 medium carrots, cut into 1-inch chunks
    1 package (9 ounces) frozen cut
      green beans
    1 package (10 ounces) frozen corn
    1 can (14-1/2 ounces) Italian diced
      tomatoes, undrained

1 In a large skillet, cook the beef, onion and garlic powder over medium heat until meat is no longer pink; drain.

2 In a 3-qt. slow cooker, layer with potatoes, carrots, beans and corn. Top with beef mixture. Pour tomatoes over the top. Cover and cook on low for 8-10 hours or until the potatoes are tender.

Yield: 8 servings.

Add some vegetables. This ground beef casserole is so versatile. For a Tex-Mex inspired dish, substitute Mexican diced tomatoes for the Italian version and add a chopped jalapeno to the vegetables. Or, switch out the vegetables and try frozen peas, broccoli or cauliflower.

Roast Beef and Gravy

(pictured above)

PREP: 15 MIN. ■ COOK: 8 HOURS

Abby Metzger
Larchwood, Iowa
This is by far the simplest way to make roast beef and gravy. On busy days, I can put this main dish in the slow cooker and get on with my day. My family likes it with mashed potatoes and fruit salad.

    1 boneless beef chuck roast
      (3 pounds)
    2 cans (10-3/4 ounces
      each) condensed cream of
      mushroom soup, undiluted
    1/3 cup sherry or beef broth
    1 envelope onion soup mix

1 Cut roast in half; place in a 3-qt. slow cooker. In a large bowl, combine the remaining ingredients; pour over roast. Cover and cook on low for 8-9 hours or until meat is tender.

Yield: 8-10 servings.

Double-Onion Beef Brisket

PREP: 25 MIN. ■ **COOK:** 6 HOURS

Elaine Sweet
Dallas, Texas
It's the gentle, long cooking that makes my brisket so tender. It gets a wonderfully sweet-tangy flavor from chili sauce, cider vinegar and brown sugar.

1 fresh beef brisket (4 pounds)

1-1/2 teaspoons kosher salt

1-1/2 teaspoons coarsely ground pepper

2 tablespoons olive oil

3 medium onions, halved and sliced, divided

3 celery ribs, chopped

1 cup chili sauce

1/4 cup packed brown sugar

1/4 cup cider vinegar

1 envelope onion soup mix

1 Cut the brisket in half; sprinkle all sides with salt and pepper. In a large skillet, brown brisket in oil; remove and set aside. In the same skillet, cook and stir onions on low heat for 8-10 minutes or until onions are caramelized.

2 Place half of the onions in a 5-qt. slow cooker; top with celery and brisket. Combine the chili sauce, brown sugar, vinegar and soup mix. Pour over brisket; top with remaining onions.

3 Cover and cook on low for 6-7 hours or until meat is tender. Let stand for 5 minutes before slicing. Skim fat from cooking juices and serve with meat.

Yield: 10 servings.

Editor's Note: This is a fresh beef brisket, not corned beef.

Italian Pot Roast

PREP: 20 MIN. ■ **COOK:** 5 HOURS

Debbie Daly
Buckingham, Illinois
I make this regularly, as it's a favorite of my husband's. You'll love how this moist pot roast seems to melt in your mouth.

1 boneless beef chuck roast (3 to 4 pounds)

1 can (28 ounces) diced tomatoes, drained

3/4 cup chopped onion

3/4 cup Burgundy wine or beef broth

1-1/2 teaspoons salt

1 teaspoon dried basil

1/2 teaspoon dried oregano

1/2 teaspoon minced garlic

1/4 teaspoon pepper

1/4 cup cornstarch

1/2 cup cold water

1 Cut roast in half. Place in a 5-qt. slow cooker. Add tomatoes, onion, wine, salt, basil, oregano, garlic and pepper. Cover and cook on low for 5 to 5-1/2 hours.

2 Remove meat to a serving platter; keep warm. Skim fat from cooking juices; transfer to a small saucepan. Combine cornstarch and water until smooth. Gradually stir into pan. Bring to a boil; cook and stir for 2 minutes or until thickened. Serve with meat.

Yield: 8 servings.

Perk up the flavor. To add a little more zip to this pot roast, substitute 2 cans (14-1/2 ounces each) diced tomatoes with green peppers and onions or diced tomatoes with mild green chilies for the 28-ounce can of diced tomatoes.

Burgundy Beef

PREP: 20 MIN. ■ **COOK:** 8 HOURS

Lora Snyder
Columbus, Massachusetts
On chilly days, it's a pleasure coming home
to this savory pot roast that's ready to enjoy.
The tender beef, vegetables and tasty gravy are
delicious over a bed of noodles.

1/2 pound sliced fresh mushrooms

1/2 pound fresh baby carrots

1 medium green pepper, julienned

1 boneless beef chuck roast (2-1/2 pounds)

1 can (10-3/4 ounces) condensed golden
mushroom soup, undiluted

1/4 cup Burgundy wine or beef broth

1 tablespoon Worcestershire sauce

1 envelope onion soup mix

1/4 teaspoon pepper

2 to 3 tablespoons cornstarch

2 tablespoons cold water

Hot cooked wide egg noodles

1 In a 5-qt. slow cooker, combine the
mushrooms, carrots and green pepper;
place roast on top. In a large bowl,
combine the soup, wine, Worcestershire
sauce, soup mix and pepper; pour over
roast. Cover and cook on low for 8-9
hours or until meat is tender.

2 Transfer roast and vegetables to a serving
platter; keep warm. Strain cooking juices
and skim fat; place in a large saucepan.
Combine cornstarch and cold water
until smooth; gradually stir into cooking
juices. Bring to a boil; cook and stir for
2 minutes or until thickened. Serve with
the beef, vegetables and noodles.

Yield: 6-8 servings.

Sloppy Joe Supper

(pictured above)

PREP: 15 MIN. ■ **COOK:** 4 HOURS

Karla Wiederholt
Cuba City, Wisconsin
Here's an easy way to serve up the flavor of sloppy joes in a one-dish
dinner. It's great to have a family-pleasing meal just waiting for you at
the end of the day.

1 package (32 ounces) frozen
shredded hash bown potatoes,
thawed

1 can (10-3/4 ounces)
condensed cheddar cheese
soup, undiluted

1/4 cup egg substitute

1 teaspoon salt

1/2 teaspoon pepper

2 pounds ground beef

2 tablespoons finely chopped
onion

1 can (15-1/2 ounces) sloppy
joe sauce

1 In a large bowl, combine the potatoes, soup, egg substitute, salt
and pepper. Spread into a lightly greased 5-qt. slow cooker.

2 In a large skillet, cook beef and onion over medium heat until
meat is no longer pink; drain. Stir in sloppy joe sauce. Spoon
over potato mixture. Cover and cook on low for 4 to 4-1/2 hours
or until heated through.

Yield: 8 servings.

Texas Beef Barbecue

PREP: 15 MIN. ■ **COOK:** 8 HOURS

Jennifer Bauer
Lansing, Michigan
A boneless beef roast stews for hours in a slightly sweet sauce before it's shredded and tucked into rolls to make hearty sandwiches.

> 1 beef sirloin tip roast (4 pounds)
> 1 can (5-1/2 ounces) spicy hot V8 juice
> 1/2 cup water
> 1/4 cup white vinegar
> 1/4 cup ketchup
> 2 tablespoons Worcestershire sauce
> 1/2 cup packed brown sugar
> 1 teaspoon salt
> 1 teaspoon ground mustard
> 1 teaspoon paprika
> 1/4 teaspoon chili powder
> 1/8 teaspoon pepper
> 16 kaiser rolls, split

1 Cut roast in half; place in a 5-qt. slow cooker. Combine the V8 juice, water, vinegar, ketchup, Worcestershire sauce, brown sugar and seasonings; pour over roast. Cover and cook on low for 8-10 hours or until meat is tender.

2 Remove meat; cool slightly. Shred with two forks and return to slow cooker; heat through. Spoon 1/2 cup meat mixture onto each roll.

Yield: 16 servings.

Freeze the extra. Texas Beef Barbecue makes a Texas-size amount of sandwich filling. Freeze any leftovers for future meals. Place single-serving portions in a plastic freezer bag or small freezer container. Label and freeze for up to 3 months.

Hungarian Goulash

(pictured above)

PREP: 15 MIN. ■ **COOK:** 8-1/4 HOURS

Jackie Kohn
Duluth, Minnesota
The rich, creamy sauce in this family dish is certain to satisfy goulash lovers. This one's terrific for potluck suppers, too.

> 2 pounds beef top round steak, cut into 1-inch cubes
> 1 cup chopped onion
> 2 tablespoons all-purpose flour
> 1-1/2 teaspoons paprika
> 1 teaspoon garlic salt
> 1/2 teaspoon pepper
> 1 can (14-1/2 ounces) diced tomatoes, undrained
> 1 bay leaf
> 1 cup (8 ounces) sour cream
> Hot cooked noodles
> Minced fresh parsley, optional

1 Place beef and onion in a 3-qt. slow cooker. Combine the flour, paprika, garlic salt and pepper; sprinkle over beef and stir to coat. Stir in tomatoes. Add bay leaf. Cover and cook on low for 8-10 hours or until meat is tender.

2 Discard bay leaf. Just before serving, stir in sour cream; heat through. Serve with noodles. Sprinkle with parsley if desired.

Yield: 6-8 servings.

Slow Cooker Sauerbraten

PREP: 20 MIN. ■ **COOK:** 6-1/4 HOURS

Norma English
Baden, Pennsylvania

My family is of German-Lutheran descent, and although we enjoy this traditional beef roast, I never liked the amount of time and fuss it takes to make it. This version is so good and oh-so-easy. It's great served with dumplings, spaetzle, veggies or a salad.

1 boneless beef chuck roast or rump roast
(3 to 4 pounds)
4 cups water
1 bottle (14 ounces) ketchup
1 large onion, chopped
3/4 cup packed brown sugar
3/4 cup cider vinegar
1 tablespoon mixed pickling spices
3 bay leaves
30 gingersnap cookies, crushed

GRAVY:

2 tablespoons cornstarch
1/4 cup cold water

1 Cut roast in half. Place in a 5-qt. slow cooker; add water. In a large bowl, combine the ketchup, onion, brown sugar and vinegar; pour over roast.

2 Place pickling spices and bay leaves on a double thickness of cheesecloth; bring up corners of cloth and tie with string to form a bag. Add spice bag and cookie crumbs to slow cooker. Cover and cook on low for 6-8 hours or until meat is tender.

3 Remove roast and keep warm. Discard spice bag. Strain cooking juices; transfer 4 cups to a large saucepan. Combine cornstarch and water until smooth; stir into cooking juices. Bring to a boil; cook and stir for 2 minutes or until thickened. Slice roast; serve with gravy.

Yield: 10 servings.

Mushroom 'n' Steak Stroganoff

(pictured above)

PREP: 15 MIN. ■ **COOK:** 6-1/4 HOURS

Marilyn Shehane
Colorado Springs, Colorado
I rely on this recipe when we have family visiting. After a day of sightseeing, I can relax with the rest of the group, since dinner is ready to serve without any effort on my part.

2 tablespoons all-purpose flour
1/2 teaspoon garlic powder
1/2 teaspoon pepper
1/4 teaspoon paprika
1-3/4 pounds beef top round steak, cut into 1-1/2-inch strips
1 can (10-3/4 ounces) condensed cream of mushroom soup, undiluted
1/2 cup water
1/4 cup onion mushroom soup mix
2 jars (4-1/2 ounces each) sliced mushrooms, drained
1/2 cup sour cream
1 tablespoon minced fresh parsley
Hot cooked egg noodles, optional

1 In a large resealable plastic bag, combine the flour, garlic powder, pepper and paprika. Add beef strips and shake to coat. Transfer to a 3-qt. slow cooker. In a small bowl, combine the soup, water and soup mix; pour over beef. Cover and cook on low for 6-7 hours or until meat is tender.

2 Stir in the mushrooms, sour cream and parsley. Cover and cook 15 minutes longer or until sauce is thickened. Serve with noodles if desired.

Yield: 6 servings.

Vegetable Beef Stew

PREP: 10 MIN. ■ **COOK:** 5-1/2 HOURS

Ruth Rodriguez
Fort Myers Beach, Florida
Here is a variation of an interesting beef stew that I came across. With sweet flavor from apricots and squash, we think it has wonderful South American or Cuban flair. The addition of corn makes it even more satisfying.

3/4 pound beef stew meat, cut into 1/2-inch cubes
2 teaspoons canola oil
1 can (14-1/2 ounces) beef broth
1 can (14-1/2 ounces) stewed tomatoes, cut up
1-1/2 cups cubed peeled butternut squash
1 cup frozen corn, thawed
6 dried apricot or peach halves, quartered
1/2 cup chopped carrot
1 teaspoon dried oregano
1/4 teaspoon salt
1/4 teaspoon pepper
2 tablespoons cornstarch
1/4 cup water
2 tablespoons minced fresh parsley

1 In a nonstick skillet, cook beef over medium heat in oil until no longer pink; drain. Transfer to a 3-qt. slow cooker. Add the broth, tomatoes, squash, corn, apricots, carrot, oregano, salt and pepper. Cover and cook on high for 5-6 hours or until vegetables and meat are tender.

2 Combine cornstarch and water until smooth; gradually stir into stew. Cover and cook on high for 30 minutes or until gravy is thickened. Stir in parsley.

Yield: 4 servings.

Meatball Stew

PREP: 15 MIN. ■ **COOK:** 9 HOURS

Iris Schultz
Miamisburg, Ohio
I came up with this hearty meal-in-one as another way to use frozen meatballs. It's so easy to prepare and tastes great...a perfect recipe for a weeknight supper.

> 3 medium potatoes, peeled and cut into 1/2-inch cubes
>
> 1 pound fresh baby carrots, quartered
>
> 1 large onion, chopped
>
> 3 celery ribs, sliced
>
> 1 package (12 ounces) frozen fully cooked homestyle meatballs
>
> 1 can (10-3/4 ounces) condensed tomato soup, undiluted
>
> 1 can (10-1/2 ounces) beef gravy
>
> 1 cup water
>
> 1 envelope onion soup mix
>
> 2 teaspoons beef bouillon granules

1 Place the potatoes, carrots, onion, celery and meatballs in a 5-qt. slow cooker. In a small bowl, combine the remaining ingredients. Pour over meatball mixture. Cover and cook on low for 9-10 hours or until the vegetables are crisp-tender.

Yield: 6 servings.

New life to celery. Give limp celery a second chance to season entrees, soups and stews. Cut end from limp stalk. Place in a glass of cold water in the refrigerator for several hours or overnight. You'll be surprised how crunchy it will be.

Southwestern Beef Tortillas

(pictured above)
PREP: 25 MIN. ■ **COOK:** 8-3/4 HOURS

Marie Rizzio
Interlochen, Michigan
Beef chuck roast makes for a savory filling in these satisfying tortillas. Slow cooked to perfection, it's treated to an easy jalapeno-flavored sauce.

> 1 boneless beef chuck roast (2 pounds)
>
> 1/2 cup water
>
> 4 large tomatoes, peeled and chopped
>
> 1 large green pepper, thinly sliced
>
> 1 medium onion, chopped
>
> 1 garlic clove, minced
>
> 1 bay leaf
>
> 2 tablespoons canola oil
>
> 3/4 cup ketchup
>
> 1/2 cup pickled jalapeno slices
>
> 1 tablespoon juice from pickled jalapeno slices
>
> 1 tablespoon cider vinegar
>
> 1 teaspoon salt
>
> 1/8 teaspoon garlic salt
>
> 8 flour tortillas (8 inches), warmed

1 Place roast and water in a 3-qt. slow cooker. Cover and cook on low for 8-9 hours or until meat is tender.

2 Remove meat; cool slightly. Skim fat from cooking juices; set aside 1/2 cup. Shred meat with two forks.

3 In a large skillet, cook the tomatoes, green pepper, onion, garlic and bay leaf in oil for 18-22 minutes or until the liquid is reduced to 2 tablespoons.

4 Stir in the ketchup, jalapeno slices and juice, vinegar, salt, garlic salt and reserved cooking juices. Bring to a boil. Stir in shredded beef; heat through. Discard bay leaf. Serve on tortillas.

Yield: 8 servings.

Sweet 'n' Tender Cabbage Rolls

(pictured above)

PREP: 40 MIN. ■ COOK: 7 HOURS

Sonja Benz
Carmel, Indiana

One of my favorite go-to dishes, this has been a dinnertime staple for years. I always make two batches because they go so fast. You can assemble it the night before and cook it the next day.

1 large head cabbage	1 teaspoon dried basil
2 eggs, lightly beaten	1/2 teaspoon pepper
1/2 cup 2% milk	2 pounds lean ground beef
2 cups cooked long grain rice	(90% lean)
2 jars (4-1/2 ounces each) sliced mushrooms, well drained	**SAUCE:**
	2 cans (8 ounces each) tomato sauce
1 small onion, chopped	1/2 cup packed brown sugar
2 teaspoons salt	2 tablespoons lemon juice
1 teaspoon dried parsley flakes	2 teaspoons Worcestershire sauce
1 teaspoon dried oregano	

1 Cook cabbage in boiling water just until leaves fall off head. Set aside 14 large leaves for rolls. (Refrigerate remaining cabbage for another use.) Cut out the thick vein from the bottom of each reserved leaf, making a V-shaped cut.

2 In a large bowl, combine the eggs, milk, rice, mushrooms, onion and seasonings. Crumble beef over mixture and mix well. Place about 1/2 cup on each cabbage leaf; overlap cut ends and fold in sides, beginning from the cut end. Roll up completely to enclose filling.

3 Place seven rolls, seam side down, in a 5-qt. slow cooker. Combine sauce ingredients; pour half over cabbage rolls. Top with remaining rolls and sauce. Cover and cook on low for 7-8 hours or until a meat thermometer reads 160°.

Yield: 7 servings.

Bavarian Pot Roast

PREP: 10 MIN. ■ COOK: 7 HOURS

Patricia Gasmund
Rockford, Illinois

I grew up eating pot roast but disliked it until I got this delightful recipe and changed a few ingredients to suit my taste. My child especially loves the seasoned apple gravy.

1 beef top round roast
(2 pounds)

1 cup unsweetened apple juice

1/2 cup tomato sauce

1 small onion, chopped

1 tablespoon white vinegar

1-1/2 teaspoons minced fresh gingerroot

1 teaspoon salt

1 teaspoon ground cinnamon

2 tablespoons cornstarch

1/4 cup water

1 In a large skillet coated with cooking spray, brown roast on all sides; drain. Transfer to a 3-qt. slow cooker.

2 In a small bowl, combine the juice, tomato sauce, onion, vinegar, ginger, salt and cinnamon; pour over roast. Cover and cook on low for 6 hours.

3 In a small bowl, combine cornstarch and water until smooth; stir into cooking juices until well combined. Cover and cook 1 hour longer or until the meat is tender and gravy begins to thicken.

Yield: 6 servings.

Mexican Beef Stew

PREP: 15 MIN. ■ **COOK:** 6-1/4 HOURS

Pat Dazis
Charlotte, North Carolina
Instead of chuck roast, you can also use eye of round for this recipe. To complete the meal, serve it with noodles, rice or flour tortillas.

4 medium potatoes, peeled and cubed

1 can (16 ounces) fat-free refried beans

2 cups frozen corn

1 large red onion, chopped

1 can (4 ounces) chopped green chilies

2 tablespoons chopped pickled jalapeno slices

1 can (14-1/2 ounces) reduced-sodium beef broth

1 can (10 ounces) enchilada sauce

1 tablespoon lime juice

1 teaspoon ground cumin

Dash crushed red pepper flakes

1 boneless beef chuck roast (3 to 4 pounds)

Sour cream

1 In a 5-qt. slow cooker, combine the vegetables, chilies, jalapeno, broth, enchilada sauce, lime juice, cumin and pepper flakes. Cut roast in half; transfer to slow cooker. Cover and cook on low for 6-8 hours or until meat and vegetables are tender.

2 Remove the meat; cool slightly. Cut the meat into bite-sized pieces and return to slow cooker; heat through. Serve with the sour cream.

Yield: 8 servings.

Some like it hot. For a touch more zip in Mexican Beef Stew, use a medium or hot enchilada sauce and add some chopped chipotle peppers in adobo sauce.

Texas-Style Beef Brisket

(pictured above)

PREP: 25 MIN. + MARINATING ■ **COOK:** 6-1/2 HOURS

Vivian Warner
Elkhart, Kansas
A friend tried this recipe and liked it, so I thought I would try it, too. When my husband told me how much he liked it, I knew I'd be making it often.

3 tablespoons Worcestershire sauce

1 tablespoon chili powder

2 bay leaves

2 garlic cloves, minced

1 teaspoon celery salt

1 teaspoon pepper

1 teaspoon Liquid Smoke, optional

1 fresh beef brisket (6 pounds)

1/2 cup beef broth

BARBECUE SAUCE:

1 medium onion, chopped

2 tablespoons canola oil

2 garlic cloves, minced

1 cup ketchup

1/2 cup molasses

1/4 cup cider vinegar

2 teaspoons chili powder

1/2 teaspoon ground mustard

1 In a large resealable plastic bag, combine the Worcestershire sauce, chili powder, bay leaves, garlic, celery salt, pepper and Liquid Smoke if desired. Cut brisket in half; add to bag. Seal bag and turn to coat. Refrigerate overnight. Transfer beef to a 5- or 6-qt. slow cooker; add broth. Cover and cook on low for 6-8 hours or until tender.

2 For sauce, in a small saucepan, saute onion in oil until tender. Add garlic; cook 1 minute longer. Stir in the remaining ingredients; heat through.

3 Remove brisket from the slow cooker; discard bay leaves. Place 1 cup cooking juices in a measuring cup; skim fat. Add to the barbecue sauce. Discard remaining juices. Return brisket to the slow cooker; top with sauce mixture. Cover and cook on high for 30 minutes to allow flavors to blend. Thinly slice across the grain; serve with sauce.

Yield: 12 servings.

Editor's Note: This is a fresh beef brisket, not corned beef.

Polynesian Roast Beef

PREP: 15 MIN. ■ **COOK:** 8 HOURS

Annette Mosbarger
Peyton, Colorado
This easy and delicious dish came from my sister and has been a family favorite for years. Pineapple and peppers add great color and taste.

> 1 beef top round roast (3-1/4 pounds)
>
> 2 tablespoons browning sauce, optional
>
> 1/4 cup all-purpose flour
>
> 1 teaspoon salt
>
> 1/4 teaspoon pepper
>
> 1 medium onion, sliced
>
> 1 can (8 ounces) unsweetened sliced pineapple
>
> 1/4 cup packed brown sugar
>
> 2 tablespoons cornstarch
>
> 1/4 teaspoon ground ginger
>
> 1/2 cup beef broth
>
> 1/4 cup soy sauce
>
> 1/2 teaspoon minced garlic
>
> 1 medium green pepper, sliced

1 Cut roast in half; brush with the browning sauce if desired. Combine flour, salt and pepper; rub over meat. Place onion in a 3-qt. slow cooker; top with roast.

2 Drain pineapple, reserving juice; refrigerate the pineapple. In a small bowl, combine the brown sugar, cornstarch and ginger; whisk in the broth, soy sauce, garlic and reserved pineapple juice until smooth. Pour over meat. Cover and cook on low for 7-8 hours.

3 Add pineapple and green pepper. Cook 1 hour longer or until meat and green pepper are tender.

Yield: 10-11 servings.

Asian-Style Round Steak

PREP: 20 MIN. ■ **COOK:** 7 HOURS

Marilyn Wolfe
Des Moines, Iowa
A friend gave me this recipe two decades ago.
I added a little more meat, the celery and
mushrooms to suit my family's appetites.

2 pounds beef top round steak, cut into
3-inch strips
2 tablespoons canola oil
1 cup chopped onion
3 celery ribs, chopped
1/4 cup soy sauce
1 teaspoon sugar
1/2 teaspoon salt
1/2 teaspoon minced garlic
1/4 teaspoon ground ginger
1/4 teaspoon pepper
2 medium green peppers, julienned
1 can (15 ounces) tomato sauce
1 can (14 ounces) bean sprouts, rinsed and
drained
1 can (8 ounces) sliced water chestnuts,
drained
1 jar (4-1/2 ounces) sliced mushrooms,
drained
1 tablespoon cornstarch
1/2 cup cold water
Hot cooked rice

1 In a large skillet, brown meat in oil on
all sides. Transfer meat and drippings to
a 5-qt. slow cooker. Combine the onion,
celery, soy sauce, sugar, salt, garlic,
ginger and pepper; pour over meat. Cover
and cook on low for 5-1/2 to 6 hours or
until meat is tender.

2 Add the green peppers, tomato sauce,
bean sprouts, water chestnuts and
mushrooms; cover and cook on low 1
hour longer.

3 In a small bowl, combine cornstarch and
water until smooth; stir into beef mixture.
Cover and cook on high for 30 minutes or
until gravy is thickened. Serve with rice.

Yield: 8 servings.

Brisket 'n' Bean Burritos

(pictured above)
PREP: 20 MIN. ■ **COOK:** 4-1/2 HOURS

Ruth Weatherford
Huntington Beach, California
Smoky bacon and tender beef make these easy burritos a real winner. And
if you like brisket, this is a fresh, different way to prepare it.

1 fresh beef brisket (2 pounds)
1 cup chopped onion
3 bacon strips, diced
1 can (8 ounces) tomato sauce
3/4 teaspoon pepper
1/4 teaspoon salt
1 can (16 ounces) refried
beans
1/2 cup salsa
1 can (4 ounces) chopped
green chilies
1-1/2 cups (6 ounces)
shredded Monterey Jack
cheese
10 flour tortillas (10 inches),
warmed

1 Place the brisket in a 5-qt. slow cooker; top with onion and
bacon. Combine the tomato sauce, pepper and salt; pour over
the meat. Cover and cook on low for 4-1/2 to 5 hours or until
the meat is tender.

2 In a microwave-safe bowl, combine the refried beans, salsa and
chilies. Cover and microwave on high for 2-3 minutes or until
heated through.

3 Remove meat; cool slightly. Shred with two forks. Layer the
bean mixture, meat and cheese off-center on each tortilla.
Fold sides and ends over filling and roll up.

Yield: 10 servings.

Editor's Note: This is a fresh beef brisket, not corned beef.

Slow Cooker Sloppy Joes

(pictured above)

PREP: 15 MIN. ■ **COOK:** 4 HOURS

Joeanne Steras
Garrett, Pennsylvania
Slow cook your way to a crowd-pleasing entree! Ground beef is transformed into a classic sandwich filling with just a few pantry staples.

2 pounds ground beef	2 envelopes sloppy joe mix
1 cup chopped green pepper	2 tablespoons brown sugar
2/3 cup chopped onion	1 teaspoon prepared mustard
2 cups ketchup	12 hamburger buns, split

1 In a large skillet, cook the beef, pepper and onion over medium heat until meat is no longer pink; drain. Stir in the ketchup, sloppy joe mix, brown sugar and mustard. Transfer to a 3-qt. slow cooker. Cover and cook on low for 4 hours or until flavors are blended. Spoon 1/2 cup onto each bun.

Yield: 12 servings.

Extra onion. *If you chopped an onion and have more than the 2/3 cup called for in the Slow Cooker Sloppy Joes, you can just add it to the recipe if it is a little extra. Otherwise, store the extra onion in an airtight container, such as a glass jar with a lid, for up to 5 days. The aroma from the chopped onion will fill your refrigerator if the container is not airtight.*

Steak Strips With Dumplings

PREP: 25 MIN. ■ **COOK:** 5 HOURS

John Smalldridge
Princeton, Idaho
This is old-fashioned, comfort food at its best. The cook gets to play while dinner is simmering!

3/4 pound beef top round steak, cut into 1/2-inch strips

1/4 teaspoon pepper

2 teaspoons canola oil

2/3 cup condensed cream of chicken soup, undiluted

1/2 cup beef broth

4 large fresh mushrooms, sliced

1/4 cup each chopped onion, green pepper and celery

DUMPLINGS:

1/2 cup all-purpose flour

3/4 teaspoon baking powder

1/4 teaspoon salt

2 tablespoons beaten egg

3 tablespoons 2% milk

1/2 teaspoon dried parsley flakes

1 Sprinkle steak with pepper. In a small skillet, brown steak in oil over medium-high heat. Transfer to a 1-1/2-qt. slow cooker. Combine the soup, broth and vegetables; pour over steak. Cover and cook on low for 4-5 hours.

2 For dumplings, in a small bowl, combine the flour, baking powder and salt. Stir in egg and milk just until blended. Drop by tablespoonfuls onto meat mixture. Sprinkle with parsley. Cover and cook on high for 1 hour or until a toothpick inserted in a dumpling comes out clean (do not lift the cover while cooking).

Yield: 2 servings.

Slow Cooker Lasagna

PREP: 45 MIN. ■ **COOK:** 4-1/4 HOURS + STANDING

Rebecca Goodwin
Bowling Green, Kentucky
This traditional favorite is super easy to make. The finished dish even cuts well for nice individual servings. You may need to break the lasagna noodles so they fit into the slow cooker crock.

1 pound ground beef

1 medium green pepper, chopped

1 medium onion, chopped

1 jar (26 ounces) herb and garlic pasta sauce

4 cups (16 ounces) shredded part-skim mozzarella cheese

1 carton (15 ounces) ricotta cheese

1 tablespoon Italian seasoning

1/2 teaspoon garlic powder

1/2 teaspoon salt

1/4 teaspoon pepper

4 no-cook lasagna noodles

2 tablespoons shredded Parmesan cheese

1 In a large skillet, cook the beef, green pepper and onion over medium heat until meat is no longer pink; drain. Stir in pasta sauce; heat through. In a large bowl, combine the mozzarella and ricotta cheeses, Italian seasoning, garlic powder, salt and pepper.

2 Spread 1 cup meat sauce in an oval 3-qt. slow cooker. Break one lasagna noodle into three pieces. Layer 1-1/3 noodles, 2/3 cup meat sauce and 1 cup cheese mixture in slow cooker. Repeat layers twice. Top with remaining sauce. Cover and cook on low for 4-5 hours or until noodles are tender.

3 Sprinkle with Parmesan cheese. Cover and cook for 15 minutes. Let stand for 10 minutes before cutting.

Yield: 6 servings.

Slow-Cooked Taco Meat Loaf

PREP: 20 MIN.
COOK: 3 HOURS + STANDING

Lacey Kirsch
Thornton, Colorado
This meat loaf is a hit with my family. My three sons eat two pieces each, which is incredible, considering that they can be very picky eaters. The Southwest-style meat loaf is topped with a sweet and tangy sauce.

> 2 cups crushed tortilla chips
> 1 cup (4 ounces) shredded cheddar cheese
> 1 cup salsa
> 1/2 cup egg substitute
> 1/4 cup sliced ripe olives
> 1 envelope taco seasoning
> 2 pounds lean ground beef (90% lean)
> 1/2 cup ketchup
> 1/4 cup packed brown sugar
> 2 tablespoons Louisiana-style hot sauce

1 Cut three 20-in. x 3-in. strips of heavy-duty aluminum foil; crisscross so they resemble spokes of a wheel. Place the strips on the bottom and up the sides of a 3-qt. slow cooker. Coat the strips with cooking spray.

2 In a large bowl, combine the chips, cheese, salsa, egg substitute, olives and taco seasoning. Crumble beef over mixture; mix well. Shape into a round loaf. Place meat loaf in the center of the strips. Cover and cook on low for 3-4 hours or until a meat thermometer reads 160° and juices run clear.

3 Combine the ketchup, brown sugar and hot sauce; pour over meat loaf during the last hour of cooking. Let stand for 10 minutes. Using foil strips as handles, remove the meat loaf to a platter.

Yield: 8 servings.

Southwestern Beef Stew

(pictured above)
PREP: 30 MIN. ■ COOK: 8-1/4 HOURS

Regina Stock
Topeka, Kansas
This zippy stew seasoned with picante sauce makes a warm and satisfying dinner on cold winter evenings.

> 2 pounds beef stew meat, cut into 1-inch cubes
> 1 jar (16 ounces) picante sauce
> 2 medium potatoes, peeled and cut into 1/2-inch cubes
> 4 medium carrots, cut into 1/2-inch slices
> 1 large onion, chopped
> 1 teaspoon chili powder
> 1/4 teaspoon salt
> 1/4 teaspoon ground cumin
> 1 tablespoon cornstarch
> 1/4 cup cold water

1 In a large nonstick skillet coated with cooking spray, brown beef on all sides; drain. Transfer to a 3-qt. slow cooker. Stir in the picante sauce, potatoes, carrots, onion, chili powder, salt and cumin. Cover and cook on low for 8-9 hours or until meat and vegetables are tender.

2 In a small bowl, combine cornstarch and water until smooth; stir into stew. Cover and cook on high for 15 minutes or until gravy is thickened.

Yield: 7 servings.

Coffee-Flavored Beef Roast

PREP: 35 MIN. ■ **COOK:** 6-1/4 HOURS

Jean Collier
Hanford, California
Coming home to a complete meal is a delightful way to end the day. Who would think that something so easy to make would taste so delicious?

6 medium red potatoes, cut into wedges

6 medium carrots, cut into 1-inch lengths

2 beef sirloin tip roasts (2 to 3 pounds each)

1 teaspoon salt, divided

1/2 teaspoon pepper, divided

2 teaspoons canola oil

1 medium onion, halved and sliced

2 cups whole fresh mushrooms, quartered

2 garlic cloves, minced

1-1/2 cups brewed coffee

1 teaspoon chili powder

3 tablespoons cornstarch

1/4 cup cold water

1 Place potatoes and carrots in a 5-qt. slow cooker. Sprinkle beef with half of the salt and pepper. In a large skillet, brown beef in oil on all sides. Transfer to slow cooker.

2 In same skillet, saute onion and mushrooms in drippings for 2 minutes. Add garlic; cook 1 minute longer. Stir in coffee, chili powder and remaining salt and pepper. Pour over meat. Cover and cook on low for 6-8 hours or until meat is tender.

3 Remove meat and vegetables to a serving platter; keep warm. Skim fat from cooking juices; transfer to a small saucepan. Bring liquid to a boil. Combine cornstarch and water until smooth; gradually stir into the pan. Bring to a boil; cook and stir for 2 minutes or until thickened. Serve with meat and vegetables.

Yield: 8 servings (2 cups gravy).

Slow Cooker Fajitas

PREP: 25 MIN. ■ **COOK:** 8 HOURS

Katie Urso
Seneca, Illinois
I love fajitas like they serve in Mexican restaurants, but when I prepared them at home the meat was always chewy. Then I tried this recipe in my slow cooker, and my husband and I savored every last bite. Fresh cilantro gives these fajitas the extra punch that makes them taste truly authentic.

1 each medium green, sweet red and yellow pepper, cut into 1/2-inch strips

1 sweet onion, cut into 1/2-inch strips

2 pounds beef top sirloin steaks, cut into thin strips

3/4 cup water

2 tablespoons red wine vinegar

1 tablespoon lime juice

1 teaspoon ground cumin

1 teaspoon chili powder

1/2 teaspoon salt

1/2 teaspoon garlic powder

1/2 teaspoon pepper

1/2 teaspoon cayenne pepper

8 flour tortillas (8 inches), warmed

1/2 cup salsa

1/2 cup shredded reduced-fat cheddar cheese

8 teaspoons minced fresh cilantro

1 Place peppers and onion in a 5-qt. slow cooker. Top with beef. Combine the water, vinegar, lime juice and seasonings; pour over meat. Cover and cook on low for 8-9 hours or until tender.

2 Using a slotted spoon, place about 3/4 cup meat mixture down the center of each tortilla. Top with 1 tablespoon salsa, 1 tablespoon cheese and 1 teaspoon cilantro; roll up.

Yield: 8 servings.

Garlic Beef Stroganoff

PREP: 20 MIN. ■ **COOK:** 7 HOURS

Erika Anderson
Wausau, Wisconsin
Because I work full time, I rely on my slow cooker to cook up weeknight dinners. This Stroganoff is perfect because I can get it ready in the morning before the kids get up.

2 teaspoons beef bouillon granules

1 cup boiling water

1 can (10-3/4 ounces) condensed cream of mushroom soup, undiluted

2 jars (4-1/2 ounces each) sliced mushrooms, drained

1 large onion, chopped

3 garlic cloves, minced

1 tablespoon Worcestershire sauce

1-1/2 to 2 pounds boneless round steak, trimmed and cut into thin strips

2 tablespoons canola oil

1 package (8 ounces) cream cheese, cubed

Hot cooked noodles

1 In a 3-qt. slow cooker, dissolve bouillon in water. Add the soup, mushrooms, onion, garlic and Worcestershire sauce. In a skillet, brown beef in oil.

2 Transfer to the slow cooker. Cover and cook on low for 7-8 hours or until the meat is tender. Stir in cream cheese until smooth. Serve with noodles.

Yield: 6-8 servings.

Add some variety. *The flavor of the Stroganoff can be easily changed for variety. Use cream of asparagus, broccoli, celery or chicken soup for the mushroom soup. You can also use chicken bouillon granules for the beef granules and marinade for chicken for the Worcestershire sauce.*

Spicy Goulash

(pictured above)

PREP: 25 MIN. ■ **COOK:** 5-1/2 HOURS

Melissa Polk
West Lafayette, Indiana
Ground cumin, chili powder and a can of Mexican diced tomatoes jazz up my hearty goulash recipe. It's so simple that even the elbow macaroni is prepared in the slow cooker.

1 pound lean ground beef (90% lean)

4 cans (14-1/2 ounces each) Mexican diced tomatoes, undrained

2 cans (16 ounces each) kidney beans, rinsed and drained

2 cups water

1 medium onion, chopped

1 medium green pepper, chopped

1/4 cup red wine vinegar

2 tablespoons chili powder

1 tablespoon Worcestershire sauce

2 teaspoons beef bouillon granules

1 teaspoon dried basil

1 teaspoon dried parsley flakes

1 teaspoon ground cumin

1/4 teaspoon pepper

2 cups uncooked elbow macaroni

1 In a large skillet, cook beef over medium heat until no longer pink; drain. Transfer to a 5-qt. slow cooker. Stir in the tomatoes, beans, water, onion, green pepper, vinegar, chili powder, Worcestershire sauce, bouillon and seasonings. Cover and cook on low for 5-5 hours or until heated through.

2 Stir in macaroni; cover and cook 30 minutes longer or until macaroni is tender.

Yield: 12 servings.

Hearty French Dip Sandwiches

PREP: 30 MIN. ■ **COOK:** 6 HOURS

Dorothy Connelley
Belle Fourche, South Dakota
My husband, who is nicknamed "The Beef Man" because we sell USDA beef in our retail store, says this is one of his favorite sandwiches. Served with a green salad, this makes a wonderful evening meal. It would also work great for sandwiches at a football game party.

1 large onion, sliced

1 boneless beef rump roast (3 pounds)

2 cans (10-1/2 ounces each) condensed French onion soup

1 loaf (1 pound) French bread, halved lengthwise

1/4 cup butter, softened

1 tablespoon grated Parmesan cheese

1/2 teaspoon garlic salt

8 slices part-skim mozzarella cheese

1 Place onion in a 5-qt. slow cooker. Cut roast in half; place over onion. Pour soup over beef. Cover and cook on low for 6-8 hours or until meat is tender.

2 Remove meat to a cutting board. Let stand for 10 minutes. Thinly slice meat across the grain and return to the slow cooker. Heat through.

3 Place bread on an ungreased baking sheet. Combine the butter, Parmesan cheese and garlic salt; spread over bread. Bake at 400° for 10-12 minutes or until lightly browned.

4 Layer bottom of the bread with mozzarella cheese, beef and onion. Replace bread top; cut into eight portions. Serve with cooking juices.

Yield: 8 servings.

Cajun-Style Pot Roast

(pictured above)

PREP: 15 MIN. ■ **COOK:** 6 HOURS

Ginger Menzies
Oak Creek, Colorado
This zippy roast is one of my go-to recipes when cooking for dinner guests. It gives me time to visit, and everyone always enjoys it...even my friend who's a chef.

1 boneless beef chuck roast (2 to 3 pounds)

2 tablespoons Cajun seasoning

1 tablespoon olive oil

2 cans (10 ounces each) diced tomatoes and green chilies

1 medium sweet red pepper, chopped

1-1/2 cups chopped celery

3/4 cup chopped onion

1/4 cup quick-cooking tapioca

1-1/2 teaspoons minced garlic

1 teaspoon salt

Hot cooked rice

1 Cut roast in half; sprinkle with Cajun seasoning. In a large skillet, brown roast in oil on all sides; drain.

2 Transfer to a 5-qt. slow cooker. Combine the tomatoes, red pepper, celery, onion, tapioca, garlic and salt; pour over roast. Cover and cook on low for 6-8 hours or until meat is tender. Slice and serve with rice.

Yield: 6 servings.

Slow-Cooked Short Ribs

PREP: 25 MIN. ■ **COOK:** 9 HOURS

Pam Halfhill
Wapakoneta, Ohio
Smothered in a finger-licking barbecue sauce, these meaty beef ribs are a winner everywhere I take them.

- 2/3 cup all-purpose flour
- 2 teaspoons salt
- 1/2 teaspoon pepper
- 4 to 4-1/2 pounds boneless beef short ribs
- 1/4 to 1/3 cup butter
- 1 large onion, chopped
- 1-1/2 cups beef broth
- 3/4 cup red wine vinegar
- 3/4 cup packed brown sugar
- 1/2 cup chili sauce
- 1/3 cup ketchup
- 1/3 cup Worcestershire sauce
- 5 garlic cloves, minced
- 1-1/2 teaspoons chili powder

1 In a large resealable plastic bag, combine the flour, salt and pepper. Add ribs in batches and shake to coat. In a large skillet, brown ribs in butter.

2 Transfer to a 6-qt. slow cooker. In the same skillet, combine the remaining ingredients. Cook and stir until mixture comes to a boil; pour over ribs. Cover and cook on low for 9-10 hours or until meat is tender.

Yield: 12 servings.

Party-Pleasing Beef Dish

(pictured above)

PREP: 15 MIN. ■ **COOK:** 4-1/5 HOURS

Glee Witzke
Crete, Nebraska
Mild and saucy, this mixture is served over tortilla chips and topped with popular taco ingredients. My guests can't get enough of it!

- 1 pound ground beef
- 1 medium onion, chopped
- 3/4 cup water
- 1 can (8 ounces) tomato sauce
- 1 can (6 ounces) tomato paste
- 2 teaspoons sugar
- 1 garlic clove, minced
- 1 teaspoon chili powder
- 1 teaspoon ground cumin
- 1 teaspoon dried oregano
- 1 cup cooked rice
- Tortilla chips
- Shredded cheddar cheese, chopped green onions, sliced ripe olives, sour cream, chopped tomatoes and taco sauce

1 In a large skillet, cook beef and onion over medium heat until meat is no longer pink; drain. Transfer to a 3-qt. slow cooker. Add the water, tomato sauce, tomato paste, sugar and seasonings; mix well. Cover and cook on low for 4 hours or until heated through.

2 Add rice; cover and cook 10 minutes longer. Serve over tortilla chips with toppings of your choice.

Yield: 6-8 servings.

Italian Roast with Alfredo Potatoes

PREP: 15 MIN. ■ **COOK:** 7-1/4 HOURS

Taste of Home Test Kitchen
This hearty meal is a great way to start the week. And since it cooks while you're away, you will have very little to do to put a satisfying supper on the table.

- 1 boneless beef chuck roast (4 pounds), trimmed
- 1 envelope brown gravy mix
- 1 envelope Italian salad dressing mix
- 1/2 cup water
- 1 medium sweet red pepper, cut into 1-inch pieces
- 1 cup chopped green pepper
- 2/3 cup chopped onion
- 8 medium red potatoes, quartered
- 2 tablespoons cornstarch
- 1/4 cup cold water
- 3/4 cup refrigerated Alfredo sauce
- 2 tablespoons butter
- 1/4 teaspoon pepper
- 1 tablespoon minced chives

1 Cut roast in half; place in a 5-qt. slow cooker. In a small bowl, combine the gravy mix, dressing mix and water; pour over roast. Top with peppers and onion. Cover and cook on low for 7-8 hours or until meat is tender.

2 Place potatoes in a large saucepan; cover with water. Bring to a boil. Reduce heat; cover and simmer for 15-20 minutes or until tender.

3 Meanwhile, slice the beef and keep warm. Skim fat from cooking juices if necessary; pour into a large saucepan. Combine the cornstarch and cold water until smooth; stir into cooking juices. Bring to a boil; cook and stir for 2 minutes or until thickened.

4 Drain potatoes; mash with Alfredo sauce, butter and pepper. Sprinkle with chives. Serve with sliced beef and gravy.

Yield: 6 servings.

Brisket with Cranberry Gravy

(pictured above)
PREP: 15 MIN. ■ **COOK:** 5-3/4 HOURS

Noelle LaBrecque
Round Rock, Texas
With just a few minutes of hands-on work, this tender beef brisket simmers into a delectable entree. The meat and gravy are fantastic for sandwiches and leftovers the next day.

- 1 medium onion, sliced
- 1 fresh beef brisket (3 pounds), halved
- 1 can (14 ounces) jellied cranberry sauce
- 1/2 cup thawed cranberry juice concentrate
- 2 tablespoons cornstarch
- 1/4 cup water

1 Place onion in a 5-qt. slow cooker; top with brisket. Combine the cranberry sauce and juice concentrate; pour over beef. Cover and cook on low for 5-1/2 to 6 hours or until the meat is tender.

2 Remove brisket and keep warm. Strain cooking juices, discarding onion; skim fat.

3 In a small saucepan, combine cornstarch and water until smooth; stir in the cooking juices. Bring to a boil over medium heat, stirring constantly. Cook and stir for 2 minutes or until thickened. Thinly slice brisket across the grain; serve with gravy.

Yield: 12 servings.

Editor's Note: This is a fresh beef brisket, not corned beef.

Pizza Casserole

PREP: 25 MIN. ■ **COOK:** 1 HOUR

Julie Sterchi
Harrisburg, Illinois
A friend from church gave me the recipe for this pleasing slow cooker casserole. It's always one of the first dishes emptied at potlucks, and it can easily be adapted to personal tastes.

- 3 pounds ground beef
- 1/2 cup chopped onion
- 1 jar (28 ounces) spaghetti sauce
- 2 jars (4-1/2 ounces each) sliced mushrooms, drained
- 1 teaspoon salt
- 1/2 teaspoon garlic powder
- 1/2 teaspoon dried oregano
- Dash pepper
- 1 package (16 ounces) wide egg noodles, cooked and drained
- 2 packages (3-1/2 ounces each) sliced pepperoni
- 2 cups (8 ounces) shredded cheddar cheese
- 2 cups (8 ounces) shredded part-skim mozzarella cheese

1 In a Dutch oven, brown beef and onion over medium heat until meat is no longer pink; drain. Add the spaghetti sauce, mushrooms, salt, garlic powder, oregano and pepper; heat through.

2 Spoon 4 cups beef mixture into a 5-qt. slow cooker. Top with half of the noodles, pepperoni and cheeses. Repeat the layers. Cover and cook on high for 1 hour or until cheese is melted.

Yield: 12 servings.

Italian Beef on Rolls

(pictured above)

PREP: 15 MIN. ■ **COOK:** 8-1/4 HOURS

Jamie Hilker
Harrison, Arkansas
Moist and delicious describes this no-fuss sandwich. It makes enough for eight, which means for me there will be leftovers. Freeze the leftovers, in individual portions for a quick supper on another night.

- 1 beef sirloin tip roast (2 pounds)
- 1 can (14-1/2 ounces) diced tomatoes, undrained
- 1 medium green pepper, chopped
- 1/2 cup water
- 1 tablespoon sesame seeds
- 1-1/2 teaspoons garlic powder
- 1 teaspoon fennel seed, crushed
- 1/2 teaspoon salt
- 1/2 teaspoon pepper
- 8 hard rolls, split

1 Place the roast in a 3-qt. slow cooker. In a small bowl, combine the tomatoes, green pepper, water, sesame seeds and seasonings; pour over roast. Cover and cook on low for 8-9 hours or until meat is very tender.

2 Remove meat; cool slightly. Skim fat from cooking juices. Shred beef with two forks and return to the slow cooker; heat through. Serve on rolls.

Yield: 8 servings.

Slow-Cooked Coffee Beef Roast

PREP: 15 MIN. ■ **COOK:** 8-1/4 HOURS

Charles Trahan
San Dimas, California
Day-old coffee is the key to this flavorful beef roast that simmers until it's fall-apart tender. Try it once, and I'm sure you'll cook it again.

1 beef sirloin tip roast (2-1/2 pounds), cut in half

2 teaspoons canola oil

1-1/2 cups sliced fresh mushrooms

1/3 cup sliced green onions

2 garlic cloves, minced

1-1/2 cups brewed coffee

1 teaspoon Liquid Smoke, optional

1/2 teaspoon salt

1/2 teaspoon chili powder

1/4 teaspoon pepper

1/4 cup cornstarch

1/3 cup cold water

1 In a large nonstick skillet, brown roast on all sides in oil over medium-high heat. Place in a 5-qt. slow cooker.

2 In the same skillet, saute mushrooms, onions and garlic until tender; stir in the coffee, Liquid Smoke if desired, salt, chili powder and pepper. Pour over roast. Cover and cook on low for 8-10 hours or until meat is tender.

3 Remove roast and keep warm. Pour cooking juices into a 2-cup measuring cup; skim fat. In a small saucepan, combine cornstarch and water until smooth. Gradually stir in 2 cups cooking juices. Bring to a boil; cook and stir for 2 minutes or until thickened. Serve with sliced beef.

Yield: 6 servings.

Tender Beef Brisket

(pictured above)

PREP: 15 MIN. ■ **COOK:** 8 HOURS

Jenni Arnold
Woodbury, Tennessee
Brisket can be difficult to cook, but this recipe always turns out great. I live in the country and have a 60-mile commute to work each day, so I use the slow cooker often. It's a wonderful way to get a good meal on the table for my family after a long day.

1 fresh beef brisket (4 pounds)	**2 tablespoons balsamic vinegar**
1 can (15 ounces) tomato sauce	**2 tablespoons Worcestershire sauce**
1 can (12 ounces) beer or nonalcoholic beer	**2 teaspoons prepared mustard**
1 cup chopped green pepper	**1 teaspoon salt**
2/3 cup chopped onion	**1 teaspoon garlic powder**
2 tablespoons brown sugar	**1/2 teaspoon pepper**

1 Cut brisket into thirds; place in a 5-qt. slow cooker. In a large bowl, combine the remaining ingredients; pour over beef. Cover and cook on low for 8-9 hours or until meat is tender.

2 Thinly slice meat across the grain. If desired, thicken pan juices.

Yield: 10 servings.

Editor's Note: This is a fresh beef brisket, not corned beef.

Beef and Lamb Stew

PREP: 50 MIN. + MARINATING ■ **COOK:** 8-1/2 HOURS

Dennis Kuyper
Creston, Iowa
I asked for this recipe after a recent trip to South Africa with my church. This stew includes lots of fresh garden vegetables and meat. I've made it for my friends on several occasions, and they thought it was great and enjoyed the interesting combination of flavors. It's traditionally served with brown rice or pumpkin fritters.

1/2 cup dry red wine or beef broth
1/2 cup olive oil
4 garlic cloves, minced, divided
1-1/2 teaspoons salt, divided
1-1/2 teaspoons dried thyme, divided
1-1/4 teaspoons dried marjoram, divided
3/4 teaspoon dried rosemary, crushed, divided
3/4 teaspoon pepper, divided
1 pound beef stew meat, cut into 1- inch cubes
1 pound lamb stew meat, cut into 1-inch cubes
10 small red potatoes, halved
1/2 pound medium fresh mushrooms, halved
2 medium onions, thinly sliced
2 cups fresh cauliflowerets
1 can (16 ounces) kidney beans, rinsed and drained
1-1/2 cups fresh green beans, trimmed and cut in half
3 medium carrots, cut into 1/2-inch slices
1 celery rib, thinly sliced
1 cup beef broth
2 tablespoons minced fresh parsley
2 teaspoons sugar
3 tablespoons cornstarch
1/4 cup cold water
6 cups cooked brown rice

1 In a large resealable plastic bag, combine the wine, oil, 2 minced garlic cloves, 1/2 teaspoon salt, 1 teaspoon thyme, 3/4 teaspoon marjoram, 1/2 teaspoon rosemary and 1/4 teaspoon pepper; add beef and lamb. Seal bag and turn to coat; refrigerate for 8 hours.

2 In a 5- or 6-qt. slow cooker, layer the potatoes, mushrooms, onions, cauliflower, kidney beans, green beans, carrots and celery. Drain and discard the marinade from the meat. Place meat over vegetables. Combine the broth, parsley, sugar and remaining garlic, salt, thyme, marjoram, rosemary and pepper; pour over meat.

3 Cover and cook on low for 8-10 hours or until meat and vegetables are tender. Combine cornstarch and water until smooth; stir into stew. Cover and cook for 30 minutes longer or until thickened. Serve with rice.

Yield: 12 servings (3 quarts).

Barbecued Beef Short Ribs

PREP: 25 MIN. ■ **COOK:** 5 HOURS

Erin Glas
White Hall, Maryland
These tender ribs with a tangy sauce are a cinch to make.
They're great for picnics and parties.

4 pounds bone-in beef short ribs, trimmed

2 tablespoons canola oil

1 large sweet onion, halved and sliced

1 bottle (12 ounces) chili sauce

3/4 cup plum preserves or preserves of your choice

2 tablespoons brown sugar

2 tablespoons red wine vinegar

2 tablespoons Worcestershire sauce

2 tablespoons Dijon mustard

1/4 teaspoon ground cloves

1 In a large skillet, brown ribs in oil in batches. Place onion in a 5-qt. slow cooker; add ribs. Cover and cook on low for 4-1/2 to 5 hours or until the meat is tender.

2 In a small saucepan, combine the remaining ingredients. Cook and stir over medium heat for 4-6 minutes or until heated through.

3 Remove ribs from slow cooker. Skim fat from cooking juices. Return ribs to slow cooker; pour sauce over ribs. Cover and cook on high for 25-30 minutes or until sauce is thickened.

Yield: 8 servings.

Slow-Cooked Steak Fajitas

PREP: 10 MIN. ■ **COOK:** 8-1/2 HOURS

Twila Burkholder
Middleburg, Pennsylvania
We enjoy the flavors of Mexican food, so I was glad when I spotted the recipe for this spicy entree. I simmer the beef all-day...and it always comes out nice and moist.

- 1 beef flank steak (1-1/2 pounds)
- 1 can (14-1/2 ounces) diced tomatoes with garlic and onion, undrained
- 1 jalapeno pepper, seeded and chopped
- 2 garlic cloves, minced
- 1 teaspoon ground coriander
- 1 teaspoon ground cumin
- 1 teaspoon chili powder
- 1/2 teaspoon salt
- 1 medium onion, sliced
- 1 medium green pepper, julienned
- 1 medium sweet red pepper, julienned
- 1 tablespoon minced fresh cilantro
- 2 teaspoons cornstarch
- 1 tablespoon water
- 12 flour tortillas (6 inches), warmed
- 3/4 cup fat-free sour cream
- 3/4 cup salsa

1 Thinly slice steak across the grain into strips; place in a 5-qt. slow cooker. Add the tomatoes, jalapeno, garlic, coriander, cumin, chili powder and salt. Cover and cook on low for 7 hours.

2 Add the onion, peppers and cilantro. Cover and cook 1-2 hours longer or until meat is tender.

3 Combine cornstarch and water until smooth; gradually stir into the slow cooker. Cover and cook on high for 30 minutes or until slightly thickened.

4 Using a slotted spoon, spoon about 1/2 cup meat mixture down the center of each tortilla. Fold bottom of tortilla over filling and roll up. Serve with sour cream and salsa.

Yield: 12 servings.

Editor's Note: When cutting hot peppers, disposable gloves are recommended. Avoid touching your face.

Sweet-Sour Beef

(pictured above)
PREP: 15 MIN. ■ **COOK:** 7 HOURS

Beth Husband
Billings, Montana
Pasta fans will savor this sweet and sour specialty over noodles. Chock-full of delectable beef, sliced carrots, green pepper and onion, this saucy stew is also a hit over rice.

- 2 pounds beef top round steak or boneless beef chuck roast, cut into 1-inch cubes
- 2 tablespoons canola oil
- 2 cans (8 ounces each) tomato sauce
- 2 cups sliced carrots
- 2 cups pearl onions or 2 small onions, cut into wedges
- 1 large green pepper, cut into 1-inch pieces
- 1/2 cup molasses
- 1/3 cup cider vinegar
- 1/4 cup sugar
- 2 teaspoons chili powder
- 2 teaspoons paprika
- 1 teaspoon salt
- Hot cooked pasta, optional

1 In a large skillet, brown steak in oil; transfer to a 5-qt. slow cooker. Add the tomato sauce, vegetables, molasses, vinegar, sugar and seasonings; stir well. Cover and cook on low for 7-8 hours or until meat is tender. Thicken if desired. Serve with pasta if desired.

Yield: 10-12 servings.

Butternut Beef Stew

PREP: 30 MIN. ■ **COOK:** 7 HOURS

Erin Lembke
Monroe, Washington
I tweaked this recipe I found in a magazine to suit my taste for sweet and spicy. I found that pureeing the tomatoes added a thicker consistency without using flour.

1-1/4 pounds beef stew meat, cut
into 1-inch cubes
1 tablespoon canola oil
1-1/2 cups cubed peeled butternut squash
1 cup chopped cabbage
1/2 cup coarsely chopped sweet red pepper
1 celery rib with leaves, chopped
1 can (10 ounces) diced tomatoes and
green chilies
1/4 cup packed brown sugar
1 can (14-1/2 ounces) beef broth
1 tablespoon adobo sauce
1 teaspoon dried oregano
1/4 teaspoon salt
1/8 teaspoon pepper

1 In a large skillet, brown meat in oil on all sides; drain. Transfer to a 3-qt. slow cooker. Stir in the squash, cabbage, red pepper and celery.

2 In a blender, combine tomatoes and brown sugar. Cover and process until blended. Pour over vegetables. Combine the broth, adobo sauce, oregano, salt and pepper; add to slow cooker.

3 Cover and cook on low for 7-8 hours or until meat and vegetables are tender. If desired, thicken pan juices.

Yield: 4 servings.

Smothered Round Steak

(pictured above)
PREP: 20 MIN. ■ **COOK:** 7 HOURS

Kathy Garret
Camden, West Virginia
Try less expensive round steak and gravy served over egg noodles for a hearty meal. Meaty and chock-full of veggies, this creation will take the worry out of what's-for-supper any weeknight.

1/3 cup all-purpose flour
1 teaspoon salt
1/4 teaspoon pepper
1-1/2 pounds beef top round
steak, cut into 1-1/2-inch
strips
1 large onion, sliced
1 large green pepper, sliced

1 can (14-1/2 ounces) diced
tomatoes, undrained
1 jar (4 ounces) sliced
mushrooms, drained
3 tablespoons soy sauce
2 tablespoons molasses
Hot cooked egg noodles,
optional

1 In a large resealable plastic bag, combine the flour, salt and pepper. Add beef and shake to coat. Transfer to a 3-qt. slow cooker. Add the onion, green pepper, tomatoes, mushrooms, soy sauce and molasses. Cover and cook on low for 7-8 hours or until meat is tender. Serve with noodles if desired.

Yield: 4 servings.

Swiss Steak Supper

PREP: 20 MIN. ■ **COOK:** 5-1/2 HOURS

Kathleen Romaniuk
Chomedey, Quebec
This is a satisfying, wholesome meal that anyone would be
happy to see on the dinner table.

1-1/2 pounds beef top round steak

1/2 teaspoon seasoned salt

1/4 teaspoon coarsely ground pepper

1 tablespoon canola oil

3 medium potatoes

1-1/2 cups fresh baby carrots

1 medium onion, sliced

1 can (14-1/2 ounces) Italian diced tomatoes

1 jar (12 ounces) home-style beef gravy

1 tablespoon minced fresh parsley

1 Cut steak into six serving-size pieces; flatten to
1/4-in. thickness. Rub with seasoned salt and
pepper. In a large skillet, brown beef in oil on
both sides; drain.

2 Cut each potato into eight wedges. In a 5-qt. slow
cooker, layer the potatoes, carrots, beef and onion.
Combine tomatoes and gravy; pour over the top.
Cover and cook on low for 5-1/2 to 6 hours or
until the meat and vegetables are tender. Sprinkle
with the parsley.

Yield: 6 servings.

> *Herbs for extra flavor.* If you like, add some dried
> basil, oregano or thyme to the diced tomatoes and
> gravy mixture. Try about 1/2 to 1 teaspoon total of
> one herb or a combination of herbs.

pork

Saucy Pork Chops

(pictured at left)

PREP: 15 MIN. ■ **COOK:** 4-1/4 HOURS

Jennifer Ruberg
Two Harbors, Minnesota
I don't always have time to fix the home-cooked meals my family desires, so I've come to rely on my slow cooker. I prepare these tangy chops at least once every week because we all love them, and they are so simple to make.

4 bone-in pork loin chops (8 ounces each)

1 teaspoon garlic powder

1/2 teaspoon salt

1/4 teaspoon pepper

2 tablespoons canola oil

2 cups ketchup

1/2 cup packed brown sugar

1 teaspoon Liquid Smoke, optional

1 Sprinkle pork chops with garlic powder, salt and pepper. In a large skillet, brown chops in oil on both sides; drain.

2 In a small bowl, combine the ketchup, brown sugar and Liquid Smoke if desired. Pour half of the sauce into a 3-qt. slow cooker. Top with pork chops and remaining sauce. Cover and cook on low for 4-1/4 to 5-1/4 hours or until meat is tender.

Yield: 4 servings.

Sweet Sausage 'n' Beans

(pictured at right)

PREP: 10 MIN. ■ **COOK:** 4 HOURS

Doris Heath
Franklin, North Carolina
This is a super-easy version of a traditional French dish called cassoulet. It is sweet, saucy and chock-full of beans, smoked sausage and vegetables.

1/2 cup thinly sliced carrots

1/2 cup chopped onion

2 cups frozen lima beans, thawed

2 cups frozen cut green beans, thawed

1 pound smoked sausage, cut into 1/4-inch slices

1 can (16 ounces) baked beans

1/2 cup ketchup

1/3 cup packed brown sugar

1 tablespoon cider vinegar

1 teaspoon prepared mustard

1 In a 3-qt. slow cooker, layer the carrots, onion, lima beans, green beans, sausage and baked beans. In a small bowl, combine the ketchup, brown sugar, vinegar and mustard; pour over beans. Cover and cook on high for 4 hours or until vegetables are tender. Stir before serving.

Yield: 4-6 servings.

Pork Chops & Acorn Squash

PREP: 15 MIN. ■ COOK: 4 HOURS

Mary Johnson
Coloma, Wisconsin
My husband and I can never get enough fresh buttery squash from our garden. When the squash is paired with pork chops, the results are a delicious, comforting meal.

6 boneless pork loin chops (4 ounces each)

2 medium acorn squash, peeled and cubed

1/2 cup packed brown sugar

2 tablespoons butter, melted

1 tablespoon orange juice

3/4 teaspoon salt

1/2 teaspoon grated orange peel

3/4 teaspoon browning sauce, optional

1 Place the pork chops in a 5-qt. slow cooker; add squash. Combine the brown sugar, butter, orange juice, salt, orange peel and browning sauce if desired; pour over the squash. Cover and cook on low for 4 hours or until meat and squash are tender.

Yield: 6 servings.

Chopping acorn squash. Acorn squash is quite firm and can be hard to cut up. Begin by cutting the stem end from the squash so it will sit flat on the surface. Stand the squash up and use a large sharp knife to cut squash in half. Scoop out the seeds with a spoon and discard. Place the halves cut side down on the cutting board and cut into 1-inch slices. With a paring knife, remove the rind, then cut the flesh into cubes.

Hawaiian Pork Roast

(pictured above)

PREP: 30 MIN. ■ COOK: 4 HOURS + STANDING

Ruth Chiarenza
La Vale, Maryland
This is one of my favorite slow-cooker recipes. It's wonderful with rice or potatoes and any vegetable. It also reheats well for lunch the next day.

1 boneless whole pork loin roast (3 pounds)

1/2 teaspoon salt

1/4 teaspoon pepper

3 tablespoons canola oil

2 cups unsweetened pineapple juice

1 can (8 ounces) unsweetened crushed pineapple, undrained

1/2 cup packed brown sugar

1/2 cup sliced celery

1/2 cup cider vinegar

1/2 cup soy sauce

1/4 cup cornstarch

1/3 cup cold water

1 Cut pork roast in half. Sprinkle with salt and pepper. In a large skillet, brown roast in oil on all sides; drain. Transfer to a 5-qt. slow cooker. In a large bowl, combine the pineapple juice, pineapple, brown sugar, celery, vinegar and soy sauce. Pour over the roast. Cover and cook on low for 4 to 6 hours or until a meat thermometer reads 160°.

2 Remove roast and keep warm. Let stand for 10 minutes before slicing. Meanwhile, strain cooking juices; transfer to a large saucepan. Combine cornstarch and water until smooth; stir into cooking juices. Bring to a boil; cook and stir for 2 minutes or until thickened. Serve with pork.

Yield: 8 servings.

Lazy Man's Ribs

PREP: 20 MIN. ■ **COOK:** 5-1/2 HOURS

Allan Stackhouse Jr.
Jennings, Louisiana
I have to admit these ribs are finger-lickin' good and fall-off-the-bone fantastic. I've made them for a lot of my buddies...including my preacher...and some have even suggested that I try bottling my sauce and selling it to the public.

2-1/2 pounds pork baby back ribs, cut into eight pieces

2 teaspoons Cajun seasoning

1 medium onion, sliced

1 cup ketchup

1/2 cup packed brown sugar

1/3 cup orange juice

1/3 cup cider vinegar

1/4 cup molasses

2 tablespoons Worcestershire sauce

1 tablespoon barbecue sauce

1 teaspoon stone-ground mustard

1 teaspoon paprika

1/2 teaspoon garlic powder

1/2 teaspoon Liquid Smoke, optional

Dash salt

5 teaspoons cornstarch

1 tablespoon water

1 Rub ribs with Cajun seasoning. Layer ribs and onion in a 5-qt. slow cooker. In a small bowl, combine the ketchup, brown sugar, orange juice, vinegar, molasses, Worcestershire sauce, barbecue sauce, mustard, paprika, garlic powder, Liquid Smoke if desired and salt. Pour over ribs. Cover and cook on low for 5-1/2 to 6-1/2 hours or until meat is tender.

2 Remove ribs and keep warm. Strain cooking juices and skim fat; transfer to a small saucepan. Combine cornstarch and water until smooth; stir into juices. Bring to a boil; cook and stir for 2 minutes or until thickened. Serve with ribs.

Yield: 4 servings.

San Francisco Chops

PREP: 20 MIN. ■ **COOK:** 7-1/2 HOURS

Tara Bonesteel,
Dayton, New Jersey
Both friends and family love these fast-to-fix chops. Simmering all day in a tangy sauce makes them practically melt in your mouth.

4 bone-in pork loin chops (1 inch thick and 8 ounces each)
1 to 2 tablespoons canola oil
1 garlic clove, minced
1/4 cup soy sauce
1/4 cup red wine or chicken broth
2 tablespoons brown sugar
1/4 teaspoon crushed red pepper flakes
1 tablespoon cornstarch
1 tablespoon cold water
Hot cooked rice

1 In a large skillet, brown pork chops on both sides in oil; transfer to a 3-qt. slow cooker. Add garlic to drippings; cook and stir for 1 minute. Stir in the soy sauce, wine, brown sugar and pepper flakes; cook and stir until sugar is dissolved. Pour over chops. Cover and cook on low for 7-8 hours or until meat is tender.

2 Remove chops. Combine cornstarch and cold water until smooth; gradually stir into slow cooker. Return chops to slow cooker. Cover and cook for at least 30 minutes or until slightly thickened. Serve with rice.

Yield: 4 servings.

Slow-Cooked Shredded Pork

(pictured above)
PREP: 20 MIN. ■ **COOK:** 6-1/4 HOURS

Shirleymae Haefner
O'Fallon, Missouri
The tasty pork filling for these sandwiches requires very little work. The mild, sweet sauce is appealing and nicely coats the meat.

1 boneless whole pork loin roast (2 to 3 pounds)
1 large onion, thinly sliced
1 cup beer or nonalcoholic beer
1 cup chili sauce
2 tablespoons brown sugar
1 tablespoon prepared horseradish
8 sandwich rolls, split

1 Place the roast in a 3-qt. slow cooker. Top with onion. Combine the beer, chili sauce, brown sugar and horseradish; pour over pork and onion. Cover and cook on low for 6 to 7 hours or until meat is very tender.

2 Remove meat; cool slightly. Shred with two forks and return to slow cooker; heat through. Use a slotted spoon to serve on rolls.

Yield: 8 servings.

Pork 'n' Pepper Tortillas

PREP: 15 MIN. ■ **COOK:** 8-1/2 HOURS

Rita Hahnbaum
Muscatine, Iowa
This pork roast is gently cooked with onions, garlic and spices, which allows the flavors to infuse the meat. It is then shredded, placed in wraps and topped with colorful peppers.

1 boneless pork shoulder roast (2-1/2 to 3 pounds)

1 cup boiling water

2 teaspoons beef bouillon granules

3 garlic cloves, minced

1 tablespoon dried basil

1 tablespoon dried oregano

1 teaspoon ground cumin

1 teaspoon pepper

1 teaspoon dried tarragon

1 teaspoon white pepper

2 medium onions, sliced

1 each large green, sweet red and yellow pepper, sliced

1 tablespoon butter

12 flour tortillas (8 inches), warmed

Shredded lettuce, chopped ripe olives, sliced jalapeno peppers and sour cream, optional

1 Cut roast in half. Place roast in a 5-qt. slow cooker. Combine the water, bouillon, garlic and seasonings; pour over roast. Top with onions. Cover and cook on high for 1 hour. Reduce heat to low. Cook for 7-8 hours or until pork is very tender.

2 Remove meat; cool slightly. Shred with two forks and return to slow cooker; heat through. Meanwhile, in a skillet, saute peppers in butter until tender.

3 Using a slotted spoon, place about 1/2 cup pork and onion mixture down the center of each tortilla; top with peppers. Add the lettuce, olives, jalapenos and sour cream if desired. Fold sides of tortilla over filling; serve immediately.

Yield: 12 servings.

Apricot Pork Roast

(pictured above)
PREP: 15 MIN. ■ **COOK:** 6-1/4 HOURS

Patricia Defosse
Wilmington, Delaware
Serve this delightful roast with rice or mashed potatoes and veggies. We like leftovers with gravy on buns the next night.

1 boneless whole pork loin roast (2 to 3 pounds)

1 jar (12 ounces) apricot preserves

1 cup vegetable broth

2 tablespoons cornstarch

1/4 cup cold water

1 Place roast in a 3-qt. slow cooker. In a small bowl, combine preserves and broth; pour over roast. Cover and cook on low for 6-7 hours or until a meat thermometer reads 160°.

2 Remove meat to a serving platter; keep warm. Skim fat from cooking juices; transfer to a small saucepan. Bring liquid to a boil. Combine cornstarch and water until smooth. Gradually stir into pan. Bring to a boil; cook and stir for 2 minutes or until thickened. Serve with pork.

Yield: 6 servings.

Herbed Pork Roast

PREP: 25 MIN. ■ **COOK:** 8 HOURS

Shelia Letchworth
Versailles, Missouri
The herb rub and sliced onion add loads of flavor to this pork roast. I like to serve it with a side of parsleyed potatoes and a green salad for a well-rounded dinner.

1 boneless whole pork loin roast (4 pounds)

1 cup water

1/4 cup butter, softened

2 tablespoons rubbed sage

2 tablespoons dried parsley flakes

2 teaspoons pepper

1 teaspoon minced garlic

1 teaspoon dried oregano

1/2 teaspoon salt

1 small onion, thinly sliced

1 teaspoon browning sauce, optional

1 Cut roast in half. Place pork and water in a 4-qt. slow cooker. Spread butter over meat. Combine the sage, parsley, pepper, garlic, oregano and salt; sprinkle over meat. Top with onion. Cover and cook on low for 8-10 hours or until a meat thermometer reads 160°. If desired, thicken cooking juices. Stir in browning sauce if desired.

Yield: 12 servings.

Peachy Pork Steaks

PREP: 10 MIN. ■ **COOK:** 5-1/4 HOURS

Sandra McKenzie
Braham, Minnesota
My mom has been making this pork dish for years. She always found it a surefire way to get picky children to eat meat. No one can refuse these succulent steaks!

4 pork steaks (1/2 inch thick and 7 ounces each), trimmed

2 tablespoons canola oil

3/4 teaspoon dried basil

1/4 teaspoon salt

Dash pepper

1 can (15-1/4 ounces) peach slices in heavy syrup, undrained

2 tablespoons white vinegar

1 tablespoon beef bouillon granules

2 tablespoons cornstarch

1/4 cup cold water

Hot cooked rice

1 In a large skillet, brown pork in oil; sprinkle with the basil, salt and pepper. Drain peaches, reserving juice. Place peaches in a 5-qt. slow cooker; top with the pork.

2 In a small bowl, combine the juice, vinegar and bouillon; pour over pork. Cover and cook on high for 1 hour. Reduce heat to low and cook 4 hours longer or until meat is tender. Remove pork and peaches to a serving platter; keep warm.

3 Skim and discard fat from cooking juices; pour into a small saucepan. Combine cornstarch and cold water until smooth; stir into cooking juices. Bring to a boil; boil and stir for 2 minutes or until thickened. Serve the pork, peaches and sauce with rice.

Yield: 4 servings.

Pork Burritos

(pictured above)

PREP: 20 MIN. ■ **COOK:** 8 HOURS

Sharon Belmont
Lincoln, Nebraska
I have been making this recipe for years, changing it here and there until I devised this delicious version, which is how I prepare it. Your company will enjoy it as much as your family.

1 boneless pork sirloin roast (3 pounds)

1/4 cup reduced-sodium chicken broth

1 envelope reduced-sodium taco seasoning

1 tablespoon dried parsley flakes

2 garlic cloves, minced

1/2 teaspoon pepper

1/4 teaspoon salt

1 can (16 ounces) refried beans

1 can (4 ounces) chopped green chilies

14 flour tortillas (8 inches), warmed

Optional toppings: shredded lettuce, chopped tomatoes, chopped green pepper, guacamole, reduced-fat sour cream and shredded reduced-fat cheddar cheese

1 Cut roast in half; place in a 4- or 5-qt. slow cooker. In a small bowl, combine the broth, taco seasoning, parsley, garlic, pepper and salt. Pour over roast. Cover and cook on low for 8-10 hours or until meat is very tender.

2 Remove pork; cool slightly. Shred with two forks; set aside. Skim fat from the cooking liquid; stir in beans and chilies. Return pork to the slow cooker; heat through. Spoon 1/2 cup pork mixture down the center of each tortilla; add toppings of your choice. Fold sides and ends over filling and roll up.

Yield: 14 servings.

Sesame Pork Roast

PREP: 15 MIN. ■ **COOK:** 9-1/4 HOURS

Sue Brown
San Miguel, California

I marinate a boneless pork roast in a tangy sauce overnight before slowly cooking it the next day. The result is a tasty roast that's fall-apart tender.

> 1 boneless pork shoulder roast (4 pounds), trimmed
> 2 cups water
> 1/2 cup soy sauce
> 1/4 cup sesame seeds, toasted
> 1/4 cup molasses
> 1/4 cup cider or white wine vinegar
> 4 green onions, sliced
> 2 teaspoons garlic powder
> 1/4 teaspoon cayenne pepper
> 3 tablespoons cornstarch
> 1/4 cup cold water

1 Cut roast in half; place in a large resealable plastic bag. In a small bowl, combine the water, soy sauce, sesame seeds, molasses, vinegar, onions, garlic powder and cayenne. Pour half over the roast. Seal bag and turn to coat; refrigerate overnight. Cover and refrigerate remaining marinade.

2 Drain and discard marinade from pork. Place roast in a 5-qt. slow cooker; add the reserved marinade. Cover and cook on high for 1 hour. Reduce temperature to low; cook 8-9 hours longer or until meat is tender.

3 Remove meat to a serving platter; keep warm. Skim fat from cooking juices; transfer to a small saucepan. Bring liquid to a boil. Combine cornstarch and water until smooth. Gradually stir into the pan. Bring to a boil; cook and stir for 2 minutes or until thickened. Serve with the meat.

Yield: 8 servings.

Pork Chops & Potatoes in Mushroom Sauce

(pictured above)

PREP: 25 MIN. ■ **COOK:** 3-1/2 HOURS

Linda Foreman
Locust Grove, Oklahoma

This recipe is really a keeper! Everyone loves the flavor of the saucy potatoes, and they always go back for seconds.

> 1 can (10-3/4 ounces) condensed cream of mushroom soup, undiluted
> 1/4 cup chicken broth
> 1/4 cup country-style Dijon mustard
> 1 garlic clove, minced
> 1/2 teaspoon dried thyme
>
> 1/4 teaspoon salt
> 1/4 teaspoon pepper
> 6 medium red potatoes, sliced
> 1 medium onion, halved and thinly sliced
> 6 boneless pork loin chops (5 ounces each)

1 In a 5-qt. slow cooker, combine the soup, broth, mustard, garlic and seasonings. Stir in potatoes and onion. Top with pork chops. Cover and cook on low for 3-1/2 to 4-1/2 hours or until meat is tender.

Yield: 6 servings.

Peachy Spareribs

PREP: 10 MIN. ■ **COOK:** 5-3/4 HOURS

Jeanne Brino
Woodbury, Minnesota
Canned peaches make a delightful addition to the sauce I use to coat my spareribs. These sweet-tangy ribs make a sensational meal any time of the year.

- **4 pounds pork spareribs**
- **1 can (15-1/4 ounces) sliced peaches, undrained**
- **1/2 cup packed brown sugar**
- **1/4 cup ketchup**
- **1/4 cup white vinegar**
- **2 tablespoons soy sauce**
- **1 garlic clove, minced**
- **1 teaspoon salt**
- **1 teaspoon pepper**
- **2 tablespoons cornstarch**
- **2 tablespoons cold water**
- **Hot cooked rice**

1 Cut ribs into serving-size pieces. In a large skillet, brown ribs on all sides; drain. Transfer to a 5-qt. slow cooker.

2 Combine the peaches, brown sugar, ketchup, vinegar, soy sauce, garlic, salt and pepper; pour over ribs. Cover and cook on low for 5-1/2 to 6 hours or until meat is tender.

3 Remove pork and peaches to a serving platter; keep warm. Skim fat from cooking juices; transfer to a small saucepan. Bring liquid to a boil. Combine cornstarch and water until smooth. Gradually stir into the pan. Bring to a boil; cook and stir for 2 minutes or until thickened. Serve with pork and rice.

Yield: 8 servings.

Pork Sandwiches with Root Beer Barbecue Sauce

(pictured above)

PREP: 30 MIN. ■ **COOK:** 9-1/2 HOURS

Karen Currie
Kirkwood, Missouri
I love the subtle kick and hint of sweetness in this dish. These sandwiches go great with coleslaw and pickles. They're real crowd-pleasers.

- **1 boneless pork sirloin roast (2 pounds)**
- **1 medium onion, sliced**
- **2 tablespoons dried minced garlic**
- **3 cups root beer, divided**
- **1 bottle (12 ounces) chili sauce**
- **1/8 teaspoon hot pepper sauce**
- **8 kaiser rolls, split**

1 Place roast in a 3-qt. slow cooker. Add the onion, garlic and 1 cup root beer. Cover and cook on low for 9-10 hours or until meat is tender.

2 In a small saucepan, combine the chili sauce, hot pepper sauce and remaining root beer. Bring to a boil. Reduce heat; simmer, uncovered, for 20-25 minutes or until thickened.

3 Remove meat; cool slightly. Discard cooking juices. Shred pork with two forks and return to slow cooker. Stir in barbecue sauce. Cover and cook on low for 30 minutes or until heated through. Serve on rolls.

Yield: 8 servings.

Fruity Pork Roast

PREP: 25 MIN.
COOK: 8 HOURS + STANDING

Mary Jeppesen-Davis
St. Cloud, Minnesota

I like using the slow cooker for our meals because it frees the oven, and it usually doesn't matter if you serve dinner later than planned.

1/2 medium lemon, sliced
1/2 cup dried cranberries
1/3 cup golden raisins
1/3 cup unsweetened apple juice
3 tablespoons sherry or additional unsweetened apple juice
1 teaspoon minced garlic
1/2 teaspoon ground mustard
1 boneless whole pork loin roast (about 3 pounds)
1/2 teaspoon salt
1/4 teaspoon pepper
1/8 to 1/4 teaspoon ground ginger
1 medium apple, peeled and sliced
1/2 cup packed fresh parsley sprigs

1 In a small bowl, combine the lemon, cranberries, raisins, juice, sherry, garlic and mustard; set aside. Cut roast in half. Sprinkle with salt, pepper and ginger. Transfer to a 3-qt. slow cooker.

2 Pour fruit mixture over roast. Place apple and parsley around roast. Cover and cook on low for 8-9 hours or until a meat thermometer reads 160°. Transfer meat to a serving platter. Let stand for 10 minutes before slicing.

Yield: 8 servings.

Cranberry Pork Tenderloin

(pictured above)
PREP: 10 MIN. ■ **COOK:** 5-1/4 HOURS

Betty Helton
Melbourne, Florida

I rely on a can of cranberry sauce to create the sweet sauce for this tender pork entree. The orange juice and ground cloves nicely season the sauce as it simmers.

1 pork tenderloin (1 pound)
1 can (14 ounces) whole-berry cranberry sauce
1/2 cup orange juice
1/4 cup sugar
1 tablespoon brown sugar
1 teaspoon ground mustard
1/4 to 1/2 teaspoon ground cloves
2 tablespoons cornstarch
3 tablespoons cold water

1 Place the tenderloin in a 3-qt. slow cooker. In a small bowl, combine the cranberry sauce, orange juice, sugars, mustard and cloves; pour over pork. Cover and cook on low for 5-6 hours or until a meat thermometer reads 160°.

2 Remove pork and keep warm. In a small bowl, combine cornstarch and cold water until smooth; gradually stir into cranberry mixture. Cover and cook on high for 15 minutes longer or until thickened. Serve with pork.

Yield: 4 servings.

Pork and Sauerkraut With Potatoes

PREP: 15 MIN. ■ **COOK:** 5 HOURS

Valerie Hay
Longmont, Colorado
This is a wintertime favorite in our home. The down-home flavors of pork and sauerkraut are complemented by potatoes and apples. The aroma is irresistible as it cooks.

2 cans (14 ounces each) sauerkraut, undrained

1 cup thinly sliced onion

2 medium tart apples, peeled and sliced

1/2 cup dark corn syrup

2 bay leaves

1 teaspoon caraway seeds

1/2 teaspoon pepper

3 large potatoes, peeled and cut into 2-inch chunks

6 bone-in pork loin chops (3/4 inch thick and 7 ounces each)

1 In a large bowl, combine the sauerkraut, onion, apples, corn syrup, bay leaves, caraway and pepper. Spoon half into a 5-qt. slow cooker; top with potatoes.

2 Broil pork chops 6 in. from the heat for 3-4 minutes on each side or until browned; place over potatoes. Spoon remaining sauerkraut mixture over pork.

3 Cover and cook on high for 1 hour. Reduce heat to low; cook 4-5 hours longer or until a meat is tender. Discard bay leaves.

Yield: 6 servings.

Picking a tart apple. Not sure what type of apple to use for Pork and Sauerkraut with Potatoes? A Granny Smith is a great tart apple that will hold up well during the long cooking process. Another good choice is an Empire apple. If you're not a fan of tart apples, then try the popular all-purpose Golden Delicious apple.

Hearty Pork Stew
(pictured above)

PREP: 10 MIN. ■ **COOK:** 8-1/2 HOURS

Rebecca Overy
Evanston, Wyoming
Chunks of pork are combined with colorful tomatoes and green peppers to create this spicy stew. I garnish bowls of it with chopped hard-cooked eggs and green onions.

1-1/2 to 2 pounds boneless pork, cut into 1-inch cubes

4 cups water

1 can (14-1/2 ounces) stewed tomatoes

1 medium onion, chopped

1 medium green pepper, chopped

1/3 cup soy sauce

1 to 2 tablespoons chili powder

1 tablespoon dried celery flakes

1/2 teaspoon garlic powder

1/2 teaspoon pepper

1/3 cup cornstarch

1/3 cup cold water

Hot cooked noodles

1 In a 3-qt. slow cooker, combine the pork, water, tomatoes, onion, green pepper, soy sauce and seasonings. Cover and cook on low for 8 hours.

2 Combine cornstarch and water until smooth; gradually stir into slow cooker. Cover and cook on high for 30 minutes or until slightly thickened. Serve in bowls with noodles.

Yield: 8 servings.

Creole Black Beans 'n' Sausage

(pictured above)

PREP: 25 MIN. ■ COOK: 6 HOURS

Cheryl Landers
LaTour, Missouri
This Louisiana-style entree is so easy, you can make it any day of the week. I brown the meat, cut up veggies and measure spices the night before, and then assemble and start it cooking the next morning. When I get home, I make the rice, and dinner is served!

2 pounds smoked sausage, cut into 1-inch slices

3 cans (15 ounces each) black beans, rinsed and drained

1-1/2 cups each chopped onion, celery and green pepper

1 cup water

1 can (8 ounces) tomato sauce

4 garlic cloves, minced

2 teaspoons dried thyme

1 teaspoon chicken bouillon granules

1 teaspoon white pepper

1/4 teaspoon cayenne pepper

2 bay leaves

Hot cooked rice

1 In a large skillet, brown sausage over medium heat; drain. Transfer to a 5-qt. slow cooker.

2 In a large bowl, combine the beans, onion, celery, green pepper, water, tomato sauce, garlic, thyme, bouillon, white pepper, cayenne and bay leaves; pour over sausage. Cover and cook on low for 6-7 hours or until vegetables are tender. Discard bay leaves. Serve with rice.

Yield: 10 servings.

Creamy Ham And Potatoes

PREP: 20 MIN. ■ COOK: 8 HOURS

Peggy Key
Grant, Alabama
Serve this stick-to-your-ribs dish with a green salad and dessert for a complete meal. The creamy mixture of hearty ham and tender potatoes is brimming with homemade flavor.

4 medium red potatoes, thinly sliced

2 medium onions, finely chopped

1-1/2 cups cubed fully cooked ham

2 tablespoons butter

2 tablespoons all-purpose flour

1 teaspoon ground mustard

1/2 teaspoon salt

1/2 teaspoon pepper

1 can (10-3/4 ounces) condensed cream of celery soup, undiluted

1-1/3 cups water

1 cup (4 ounces) shredded cheddar cheese, optional

1 In a 3-qt. slow cooker, layer potatoes, onions and ham.

2 In a large saucepan, melt butter. Stir in the flour, mustard, salt and pepper until smooth. Combine soup and water; gradually stir into flour mixture. Bring to a boil; cook and stir for 2 minutes or until thickened and bubbly. Pour over ham.

3 Cover and cook on low for 8-9 hours or until potatoes are tender. If desired, sprinkle with cheese before serving.

Yield: 4 servings.

Pork Baby Back Ribs

PREP: 10 MIN. ■ **COOK:** 6 HOURS

LaVerne Parkin
Manitowoc, Wisconsin

These ribs get a touch of sweetness from brown sugar and apricot preserves. It's one slow-cooked recipe that you will surely enjoy time and again.

1 rack pork baby back ribs (2-1/2 pounds)

2 tablespoons canola oil

1 medium onion, thinly sliced

1/2 cup apricot preserves

1/3 cup beef broth

3 tablespoons white vinegar

2 tablespoons Worcestershire sauce

1 tablespoon brown sugar

1 Cut the ribs into five servings. In a Dutch oven, brown ribs in oil in batches. Place onion in a 5-qt. slow cooker; top with ribs.

2 In a small bowl combine the remaining ingredients. Pour over ribs. Cover and cook on low for 6-7 hours or until meat is tender.

Yield: 5 servings.

Slow-Cooked Pork Roast

(pictured above)

PREP: 20 MIN. ■ **COOK:** 4 HOURS + STANDING

Marion Lowery
Medford, Oregon

This pork roast makes a wonderful summer meal, as the oven never needs heating. It's so tender, it just falls apart when cut.

---

2 cans (8 ounces each) unsweetened crushed pineapple, undrained

1 cup barbecue sauce

2 tablespoons unsweetened apple juice

1 tablespoon minced fresh rosemary or 1 teaspoon dried rosemary, crushed

2 teaspoons grated lemon peel

1 teaspoon minced garlic

1 teaspoon Liquid Smoke, optional

1/2 teaspoon salt

1/4 teaspoon pepper

1 boneless pork top loin roast (3 pounds)

1 In a large saucepan, combine the pineapple, barbecue sauce, juice, rosemary, lemon peel, garlic, Liquid Smoke if desired, salt and pepper. Bring to a boil. Reduce heat; simmer, uncovered, for 3 minutes.

2 Cut roast in half. In a nonstick skillet coated with cooking spray, brown the pork roast. Place the roast in a 5-qt. slow cooker.

3 Pour sauce over roast and turn to coat. Cook on high for 4 hours or on low for 6-7 hours. Let stand for 15 minutes before carving.

Yield: 12 servings.

Orange Pork Roast

PREP: 10 MIN. ■ **COOK:** 8 HOURS

Nancy Medeiros
Sparks, Nevada

Overcooking can cause pork roasts to be dry and tough. But this recipe's succulent orange sauce guarantees that the meat turns out absolutely moist and delicious.

- 1 pork shoulder roast (3 to 4 pounds), trimmed
- 1/2 teaspoon salt
- 1/8 teaspoon pepper
- 1 can (6 ounces) frozen orange juice concentrate, thawed
- 1/4 cup honey
- 1/8 teaspoon ground cloves
- 1/8 teaspoon ground nutmeg
- 3 tablespoons all-purpose flour
- 1/4 cup cold water

1 Sprinkle roast with salt and pepper; cut in half. Place in a 5-qt. slow cooker. In a small bowl, combine the orange juice concentrate, honey, cloves and nutmeg; pour over pork. Cover and cook on high for 2 hours. Reduce heat to low and cook 6 hours longer or until meat is tender.

2 Remove meat to a serving platter; cover and keep warm. Skim and discard fat from cooking juices; pour into a small saucepan. Combine the flour and cold water until smooth; stir into the cooking juices. Bring to a boil; cook and stir for 2 minutes or until thickened. Serve with the roast.

Yield: 8 servings.

Mushroom Pork Ragout

(pictured above)

PREP: 20 MIN. ■ **COOK:** 3 HOURS

Connie McDowell
Greenwood, Delaware

A delightful tomato gravy is a tasty complement to this savory pork. It's a nice change from regular pork roast. I serve it with noodles and a side of broccoli or green beans.

- 1 pork tenderloin (3/4 pound)
- 1/8 teaspoon salt
- 1/8 teaspoon pepper
- 1 tablespoon cornstarch
- 3/4 cup canned crushed tomatoes, divided
- 1 tablespoon chopped sun-dried tomatoes (not packed in oil)
- 1-1/4 teaspoons dried savory
- 1-1/2 cups sliced fresh mushrooms
- 1/3 cup sliced onion
- 1-1/2 cups hot cooked egg noodles

1 Rub pork with salt and pepper; cut in half. In a 1-1/2-qt. slow cooker, combine the cornstarch, 1/2 cup crushed tomatoes, sun-dried tomatoes and savory. Top with mushrooms, onion and pork. Pour remaining tomatoes over pork. Cover and cook on low for 3-4 hours or until meat is tender.

2 Remove meat and cut into slices. Stir cooking juices until smooth; serve with pork and noodles.

Yield: 2 servings.

Country Pork Chop Supper

PREP: 10 MIN. ■ COOK: 6 HOURS

Sandy Mullen
Gage, Oklahoma
It doesn't get much easier than this quick and hearty all-in-one slow cooker dinner. And it doesn't get much tastier, either!

> 6 boneless pork loin chops (1/2 inch thick and 4 ounces each)
> 2 jars (12 ounces each) pork gravy
> 1 can (10-3/4 ounces) condensed cream of mushroom soup, undiluted
> 2 tablespoons ketchup
> 1 tablespoon minced chives
> 1 teaspoon pepper
> 1 teaspoon soy sauce
> 1/2 teaspoon seasoned salt
> 3 medium potatoes, peeled and quartered
> 1 package (16 ounces) frozen mixed vegetables

1 Place pork chops in a greased 5-qt. slow cooker. In a large bowl, combine the gravy, soup, ketchup, chives, pepper, soy sauce and seasoned salt; pour over pork. Stir in potatoes and vegetables. Cover and cook on low for 6-7 hours or until meat and potatoes are tender.

Yield: 6 servings.

Dinnertime staples. Country Pork Chop Supper uses many items that are in a well-stocked kitchen. If you don't have chives, toss in some dried parsley flakes. Out of mixed vegetables? Then use 2 to 3 cups of your favorite frozen vegetables. And, other cream soups, like broccoli, celery or chicken, would be great in this dish, too.

Polish Kraut and Apples

(pictured above)
PREP: 10 MIN. ■ COOK: 4 HOURS

Caren Markee
Cary, Illinois
My family loves this satisfying, heartwarming meal on cold winter nights. The tender apples, brown sugar and smoked sausage give this dish fantastic flavor. I like making it because the prep time is very short.

> 1 can (14 ounces) sauerkraut, rinsed and well drained
> 1 package (16 ounces) smoked Polish sausage or kielbasa, cut into chunks
> 3 medium tart apples, peeled and cut into eighths
> 1/2 cup packed brown sugar
> 1/2 teaspoon caraway seeds, optional
> 1/8 teaspoon pepper
> 3/4 cup apple juice

1 Place half of the sauerkraut in a 3-qt. slow cooker. Top with sausage, apples, brown sugar, caraway seeds if desired and pepper. Top with remaining sauerkraut. Pour apple juice over all. Cover and cook on low for 4-5 hours or until the apples are tender.

Yield: 4 servings.

Honey-Glazed Ham

(pictured above)

PREP: 10 MIN. ■ **COOK:** 4-1/2 HOURS

Jacquie Stolz
Little Sioux, Iowa

Here's a great solution for feeding a large group. The simple ham is perfect for family dinners, where time in the kitchen is as valuable as space in the oven.

1 boneless fully cooked ham (4 pounds)

1-1/2 cups ginger ale

1/4 cup honey

1/2 teaspoon ground mustard

1/2 teaspoon ground cloves

1/4 teaspoon ground cinnamon

Sour cream, optional

1 Cut ham in half; place in a 5-qt. slow cooker. Pour ginger ale over ham. Cover and cook on low for 4-5 hours or until ham is heated through.

2 Combine the honey, mustard, cloves and cinnamon; stir until smooth. Spread over ham; cook 30 minutes longer. Garnish with sour cream if desired.

Yield: 14 servings.

Thai-Style Pork

PREP: 15 MIN. ■ **COOK:** 6-1/4 HOURS

Amy Van Orman
Rockford, Michigan
A creamy peanut butter sauce coats moist slices of pork in this delectable dish. This recipe is from a friend in my cooking club, and it's always a favorite.

2 pounds boneless pork loin chops

1/4 cup teriyaki sauce

2 tablespoons rice vinegar

1 teaspoon crushed red pepper flakes

1 teaspoon minced garlic

1 tablespoon cornstarch

1/4 cup cold water

1/4 cup creamy peanut butter

Hot cooked rice

1/2 cup chopped green onions

1/2 cup dry roasted peanuts

Lime juice, optional

1 Place pork chops in a 3-qt. slow cooker. In a small bowl, combine the teriyaki sauce, vinegar, pepper flakes and garlic; pour over meat. Cover and cook on low for 6 hours or until meat is tender.

2 Remove pork and cut into bite-size pieces; keep warm. Skim fat from cooking juices; transfer to a small saucepan. Bring liquid to a boil. Combine cornstarch and water until smooth. Gradually stir into the pan. Bring to a boil; cook and stir for 2 minutes or until thickened. Stir in peanut butter; add meat.

3 Serve with rice. Sprinkle with onions and peanuts. Drizzle with lime juice if desired.

Yield: 6 servings.

Spaghetti Pork Chops

PREP: 20 MIN. ■ **COOK:** 6 HOURS

Ellen Gallavan
Midland, Michigan
These moist chops simmer to perfection in a succlent tangy sauce and are served over a bed of pasta. Your guests will be impressed with this fuss-free dish.

3 cans (8 ounces each) tomato sauce

1 can (10-3/4 ounces) condensed tomato soup, undiluted

1 small onion, finely chopped

1 bay leaf

1 teaspoon celery seed

1/2 teaspoon Italian seasoning

6 bone-in pork loin chops (1 inch thick and 8 ounces each)

2 tablespoons olive oil

Hot cooked spaghetti

1 In a 5-qt. slow cooker, combine the tomato sauce, soup, onion, bay leaf, celery seed and Italian seasoning.

2 In a large skillet, brown pork chops in oil. Add to the slow cooker. Cover and cook on low for 6-8 hours or until meat is tender. Discard bay leaf. Serve chops and sauce over spaghetti.

Yield: 6 servings.

Watching calories? *Use turkey Italian sausage in the Robust Italian Sausage & Pasta recipe. You can save 20 calories and 4 grams of fat per 4-oz. sausage link.*

Robust Italian Sausage & Pasta

(pictured above)
PREP: 15 MIN. ■ **COOK:** 6-1/2 HOURS

LaDonna Reed
Ponca City, Oklahoma
Sit back and let just one appliance do the hard work with this savory main dish. Since you don't cook the pasta separately, there's one less pot to wash after supper.

4 Italian sausage links (4 ounces each), halved

1 jar (25.6 ounces) Italian sausage spaghetti sauce

1 can (10 ounces) diced tomatoes and green chilies, undrained

1 large green pepper, julienned

1 medium onion, diced

2 garlic cloves, minced

1 teaspoon Italian seasoning

2 cups uncooked spiral pasta

1 In a large nonstick skillet, brown sausage links. Transfer to a 3-qt. slow cooker. Add the spaghetti sauce, tomatoes, green pepper, onion, garlic and Italian seasoning. Cover and cook on low for 6 hours.

2 Stir in pasta. Cover and cook on high for 30-40 minutes or until pasta is tender.

Yield: 4 servings.

Pork Roast with Twist of Orange

(pictured above)

PREP: 25 MIN. ■ **COOK:** 4-3/4 HOURS

Janie Canals
West Jordan, Utah

The citrus flavor sets this roast apart. It's my family's favorite! With a nice and easy gravy, this dish is perfect served with rice or mashed potatoes.

4 bacon strips, diced	4-1/2 teaspoons chili powder
1 boneless pork shoulder roast (3 to 4 pounds), trimmed	1 teaspoon salt
	1 teaspoon pepper
1 large onion, thinly sliced	1 cup chicken broth, divided
1-1/2 teaspoons minced garlic	2/3 cup orange juice
1 jalapeno pepper, seeded and finely chopped	1/4 cup all-purpose flour
	Hot mashed potatoes, optional

1 In a large skillet, cook bacon over medium heat until crisp. Remove to paper towels to drain; set aside. Cut roast in half. Brown meat in drippings on all sides. Transfer to a 5-qt. slow cooker, reserving 1 tablespoon drippings.

2 Brown onion in drippings. Add garlic; cook 1 minute longer. Add jalapeno, chili powder, salt and pepper. Stir in 1/2 cup chicken broth, orange juice and bacon; pour over roast. Cover and cook on low for 4-1/2 to 5 hours or until meat is tender.

3 Remove pork and onion; keep warm. Skim fat from cooking juices; transfer to a small saucepan. Bring liquid to a boil. Combine cornstarch and water until smooth. Gradually stir into pan. Bring to a boil; cook and stir for 2 minutes or until thickened. Serve with pork and mashed potatoes if desired.

Yield: 8 servings.

Editor's Note: When cutting hot peppers, disposable gloves are recommended. Avoid touching your face.

Sesame Pork Ribs

PREP: 15 MIN. ■ **COOK:** 5 HOURS

Sandy Alexander
Fayetteville, North Carolina

No one ever believes how little effort it takes to make these juicy ribs. The flavor of the lightly sweet and tangy sauce penetrates through the meat as the ribs simmer for hours.

3/4 cup packed brown sugar
1/2 cup soy sauce
1/2 cup ketchup
1/4 cup honey
2 tablespoons white wine vinegar
3 garlic cloves, minced
1 teaspoon salt
1 teaspoon ground ginger
1/4 to 1/2 teaspoon crushed red pepper flakes
5 pounds country-style pork ribs
1 medium onion, sliced
2 tablespoons sesame seeds, toasted
2 tablespoons chopped green onions

1 In a large bowl, combine the brown sugar, soy sauce, ketchup, honey, vinegar, garlic, salt, ginger and pepper flakes. Add ribs and turn to coat.

2 Place the onion in a 5-qt. slow cooker; top with ribs and sauce. Cover and cook on low for 5-6 hours or until the meat is tender. Place the ribs on a serving platter; sprinkle with the sesame seeds and green onions.

Yield: 6 servings.

Pork and Pinto Beans

PREP: 25 MIN. + STANDING ■ **COOK:** 8-1/4 HOURS

Darlene Brenden
Salem, Oregon

I first tasted this dish at an office get-together, and now I serve it often when company comes. I set out an array of toppings and let everyone fix their own taco salad.

1 pound dried pinto beans
1 boneless pork loin roast (3 to 4 pounds)
1 can (14-1/2 ounces) stewed tomatoes
5 medium carrots, chopped
4 celery ribs, chopped
1-1/2 cups water
2 cans (4 ounces each) chopped green chilies
2 tablespoons chili powder
4 garlic cloves, minced
2 teaspoons ground cumin
1 teaspoon dried oregano
Dash pepper
2 packages (10-1/2 ounces each) corn tortilla chips or 30 flour tortillas (10 inches)
Chopped green onions, sliced ripe olives, chopped tomatoes, shredded cheddar cheese, sour cream and/or shredded lettuce

1 Sort beans and rinse with cold water. Place beans in a Dutch oven; add water to cover by 2 in. Bring to a boil; boil for 2 minutes. Remove from the heat; cover and let stand for 1 to 4 hours or until beans are softened. Drain and rinse beans, discarding liquid.

2 Cut roast in half. Place roast in a 5-qt. slow cooker.

3 In a bowl, combine the beans, tomatoes, carrots, celery, water, chilies, chili powder garlic, cumin, oregano and pepper. Pour over roast. Cover and cook on high for 3 hours. Reduce heat to low; cook 5 hours longer or until beans are tender.

4 Remove meat; cool slightly. Shred with two forks and return to slow cooker; heat through. With a slotted spoon, serve meat mixture over corn chips or in tortillas; serve with toppings of your choice.

Yield: 10 servings.

Shredded Pork Sandwiches

(pictured above)

PREP: 15 MIN. ■ **COOK:** 7-1/2 HOURS

Martha Anne Carpenter
Mesa, Arizona

I like to share this dish at potlucks because it can be made ahead, which I especially appreciate during the busy holiday season. The sweet-and-spicy sauce is always a hit.

1 boneless whole pork loin roast (4 pounds)
1 can (14-1/2 ounces) beef broth
1/3 cup plus 1/2 cup Worcestershire sauce, divided
1/3 cup plus 1/4 cup Louisiana-style hot sauce, divided
1 cup ketchup
1 cup molasses
1/2 cup prepared mustard
10 kaiser rolls, split

1 Cut roast in half; place in a 5-qt. slow cooker. In a small bowl, combine the broth, 1/3 cup Worcestershire sauce and 1/3 cup hot sauce; pour over roast. Cover and cook on low for 7-8 hours or until tender.

2 Remove meat; cool slightly. Shred with two forks. Drain and discard cooking juices. Return to slow cooker.

3 For sauce, combine the ketchup, molasses, mustard and the remaining Worcestershire sauce and hot sauce. Pour over pork. Cover and cook on high for 30 minutes or until heated through. Serve on rolls.

Yield: 10 servings.

Country Cassoulet

PREP: 20 MIN. + STANDING
COOK: 5 HOURS

Suzanne McKinley
Lyons, Georgia
This classic dish goes great with fresh dinner rolls and your favorite green salad.

1 pound (2 cups) dried great northern beans

2 fresh garlic sausage links

3 bacon strips, diced

1-1/2 pounds boneless pork, cut into 1-inch cubes

1 pound boneless lamb, cut into 1-inch cubes

1-1/2 cups chopped onion

3 garlic cloves, minced

2 teaspoons salt

1 teaspoon dried thyme

4 whole cloves

2 bay leaves

2-1/2 cups chicken broth

1 can (8 ounces) tomato sauce

1 Sort beans and rinse with cold water. Place beans in a Dutch oven; add water to cover by 2 in. Bring to a boil; boil for 2 minutes. Remove from the heat; cover and let stand for 1 to 4 hours or until beans are softened. Drain and rinse beans, discarding liquid.

2 In a large skillet over medium-high heat, brown sausage; remove with a slotted spoon to a 5-qt. slow cooker. Add bacon to skillet; cook until crisp. Remove with a slotted spoon to slow cooker.

3 In the bacon drippings, cook pork and lamb until browned on all sides. Using a slotted spoon, remove the pork and lamb to the slow cooker. Stir in the beans and remaining ingredients.

4 Cover and cook on high for 2 hours. Reduce heat to low and cook 3-4 hours longer. Discard cloves and bay leaves. Remove sausage and slice into 1/4-in. pieces; return to the slow cooker and stir gently.

Yield: 8-10 servings.

Smoky Bean Stew

(pictured above)

PREP: 10 MIN. ■ **COOK:** 4 HOURS

Glenda Holmes
Riley, Kansas
I'd rather spend my time reading than cooking. So, I use my slow cooker to make this satisfying sausage-and-bean stew.

1 package (16 ounces) miniature smoked sausage links

1 can (16 ounces) baked beans

2 cups frozen cut green beans

2 cups frozen lima beans

1/2 cup packed brown sugar

1/2 cup thinly sliced fresh carrots

1/2 cup chopped onion

1/2 cup ketchup

1 tablespoon cider vinegar

1 teaspoon prepared mustard

1 In a 3-qt. slow cooker, combine all the ingredients. Cover and cook on high for 4-5 hours or until vegetables are tender.

Yield: 6-8 servings.

Cider-Glazed Ham

PREP: 15 MIN. ■ **COOK:** 4-1/4 HOURS

Jennifer Foos-Furer
Marysville, Ohio
We raise our own pork so I'm always looking for new ways to serve it that'll warm up everyone at the end of a long day. This recipe is always well received.

1 boneless fully cooked ham (3 pounds)

1-3/4 cups apple cider or juice

1/4 cup packed brown sugar

1/4 cup Dijon mustard

1/4 cup honey

2 tablespoons cornstarch

2 tablespoons cold water

1 Place ham in a 5-qt. slow cooker. In a small bowl, combine the cider, brown sugar, mustard and honey; pour over ham. Cover and cook on low for 4-5 hours or until ham is heated through. Remove ham and keep warm.

2 Pour cooking juices into a small saucepan. Combine cornstarch and water until smooth; stir into cooking juices. Bring to a boil; cook and stir for 2 minutes or until thickened. Serve with ham.

Yield: 8 servings.

A tasty combination. Cider-Glazed Ham is a real crowd-pleaser and so easy to make. Also try using orange juice or pineapple juice for the apple cider.

Slow Cooker Pork Chops

(pictured above)

PREP: 15 MIN. ■ **COOK:** 3 HOURS

Sue Bingham
Madisonville, Tennessee
Everyone will enjoy these fork-tender pork chops with a creamy, light gravy. Mashed potatoes, green beans and coleslaw or a salad will nicely round out the meal.

3/4 cup all-purpose flour, divided	4 boneless pork loin chops (1/2 inch thick and 4 ounces each)
1/2 teaspoon ground mustard	
1/2 teaspoon garlic pepper blend	2 tablespoons canola oil
1/4 teaspoon seasoned salt	1 can (14-1/2 ounces) chicken broth

1 In a large resealable plastic bag, combine 1/2 cup flour, mustard, pepper blend and seasoned salt. Add chops, one at a time, and shake to coat. In a large skillet, brown meat in oil on each side. Transfer to a 5-qt. slow cooker.

2 Place remaining flour in a small bowl; whisk in broth until smooth. Pour over chops. Cover and cook on low for 3 to 3-1/2 hours or until meat is tender.

3 Remove pork to a serving plate and keep warm. Whisk pan juices until smooth; serve with pork.

Yield: 4 servings.

Sweet 'n' Sour Sausage

PREP: 15 MIN. ■ **COOK:** 4-1/2 HOURS

Barbara Schutz
Pandora, Ohio
Carrots, green pepper and pineapple lend gorgeous color to this sausage supper. Serve this combination stir-fry style over rice or chow mein noodles.

1 pound smoked kielbasa or Polish sausage, sliced

1 can (20 ounces) unsweetened pineapple chunks, undrained

1-1/2 cups fresh baby carrots, quartered lengthwise

1 large green pepper, cut into 1-inch pieces

1 medium onion, cut into chunks

1/3 cup packed brown sugar

1 tablespoon soy sauce

1/2 teaspoon chicken bouillon granules

1/4 teaspoon garlic powder

1/4 teaspoon ground ginger

2 tablespoons cornstarch

1/4 cup cold water

Hot cooked rice or chow mein noodles

1 In a 3-qt. slow cooker, combine the sausage, pineapple, vegetables, brown sugar, soy sauce, bouillon granules, garlic powder and ginger. Cover and cook on low for 4-5 hours.

2 Mix cornstarch and water until smooth; stir into sausage mixture. Cover and cook on high for 30 minutes or until gravy is thickened. Serve with rice.

Yield: 6 servings.

Tuscan Pork Stew

(pictured above)
PREP: 15 MIN. ■ **COOK:** 8-1/2 HOURS

Penny Hawkins
Mebane, North Carolina
Tender chunks of pork slowly cook in a nicely seasoned, wine-infused sauce. Add some crushed red pepper flakes for a little extra kick.

1 boneless whole pork loin roast (1-1/2 pounds), cut into 1-inch cubes

2 tablespoons olive oil

2 cans (14-1/2 ounces each) Italian diced tomatoes, undrained

2 cups reduced-sodium chicken broth

2 cups frozen pepper stir-fry vegetable blend, thawed

1/2 cup dry red wine or additional reduced-sodium chicken broth

1/4 cup orange marmalade

2 garlic cloves, minced

1 teaspoon dried oregano

1/2 teaspoon fennel seed

1/2 teaspoon pepper

1/8 teaspoon crushed red pepper flakes, optional

2 tablespoons cornstarch

2 tablespoons cold water

Hot cooked fettuccine, optional

1 In a large skillet, brown pork in oil until no longer pink; drain. Place pork in a 5-qt. slow cooker.

2 In a large bowl, combine the tomatoes, broth, vegetable blend, wine, marmalade, garlic, oregano, fennel seed, pepper and pepper flakes if desired; pour over pork. Cover and cook on low for 8 hours or until meat is tender.

3 Mix cornstarch and water until smooth; stir into stew. Cover and cook on high for 30 minutes or until gravy is thickened. Serve with fettuccine if desired.

Yield: 8 servings.

Slow-Cooked Pork Tacos

PREP: 20 MIN. ■ **COOK:** 4-1/4 HOURS

Kathleen Wolf
Naperville, Illinois
Sometimes I'll substitute Bibb lettuce leaves for the tortillas to make crunchy lettuce wraps, and I find that leftovers are perfect for burritos.

1 boneless pork sirloin roast (2 pounds), cut into 1-inch pieces

1-1/2 cups salsa verde

1 medium sweet red pepper, chopped

1 medium onion, chopped

1/4 cup chopped dried apricots

2 tablespoons lime juice

2 garlic cloves, minced

1 teaspoon ground cumin

1/2 teaspoon salt

1/4 teaspoon white pepper

Dash hot pepper sauce

10 flour tortillas (8 inches), warmed

Reduced-fat sour cream, thinly sliced green onions, cubed avocado, shredded reduced-fat cheddar cheese and chopped tomato, optional

1 In a 3-qt. slow cooker, combine the pork, salsa, red pepper, onion, apricots, lime juice, garlic, cumin, salt, white pepper and hot pepper sauce. Cover and cook on high for 4-5 hours or until meat is very tender.

2 Remove meat; cool slightly. Shred with two forks and return to slow cooker; heat through. Place about 1/2 cup pork mixture down the center of each tortilla. Serve with toppings if desired.

Yield: 10 tacos.

Slow-Cooked Pork Loin

PREP: 20 MIN. ■ **COOK:** 5 HOURS

Kathleen Hendrick
Alexandria, Kentucky

Sweet apple undertones lend special flair to this pork loin.
It's topped with gravy for down-home appeal, creating a
slimmed-down dish that'll keep them coming back for more.

1 boneless whole pork loin roast (3-1/2 to 4 pounds)

1 tablespoon canola oil

1 medium onion, chopped

1 celery rib, cut into 1-inch pieces

1 envelope brown gravy mix

1 cup water

1 cup unsweetened apple juice

1/2 cup unsweetened applesauce

2 teaspoons Worcestershire sauce

1/2 teaspoon seasoned salt

1/2 teaspoon pepper

1 Cut roast in half. In a large skillet, brown roast in
oil on all sides. Transfer to a 5-qt. slow cooker.

2 In the same skillet, saute onion and celery until
tender; add to slow cooker. In a small bowl,
combine gravy mix and water. Stir in the remaining
ingredients; pour over pork. Cover and cook on low
for 5-6 hours or until a meat thermometer reads
160°. Skim fat from cooking juices; thicken
if desired. Serve with roast.

Yield: 12 servings.

Southwestern Stew

PREP: 10 MIN. ■ **COOK:** 6 HOURS

Virginia Price
Cheyenne, Wyoming
Slow cooking allows the flavors in this recipe to blend beautifully. Over the past few years, it's become our traditional meal during big football games.

- 1-1/2 pounds boneless pork, cut into 1/2-inch cubes
- 2 tablespoons canola oil
- 1 medium onion, chopped
- 1 can (15-1/2 ounces) yellow hominy, drained
- 1 can (14-1/2 ounces) diced tomatoes, undrained
- 1 can (4 ounces) chopped green chilies
- 1/2 cup water
- 1/2 teaspoon chili powder
- 1/4 teaspoon garlic powder
- 1/4 teaspoon salt
- 1/4 teaspoon ground cumin
- 1/4 teaspoon pepper

1 In a large skillet over medium-high heat, brown pork in oil. Add onion and cook for 2 minutes or until tender. Transfer to a 3-qt. slow cooker.

2 Add the remaining ingredients. Cover and cook on high for 2 hours. Reduce heat to low and cook 4 hours longer or until meat is tender.

Yield: 4-6 servings.

Some like it hot. *If your crowd likes their meals with tongue-tingling heat, add some chopped jalapeno or serrano chilies to the stew. Using the seeds will add even more heat. You can also increase the chili powder and add a touch of cayenne pepper.*

Sweet 'n' Sour Pork Chops

(pictured above)

PREP: 5 MIN. ■ **COOK:** 4-1/4 HOURS

Laurie Stafford
Waterville, New York
These tangy pork chops are simply delicious. And they couldn't be much easier to make with only five ingredients.

- 1 can (8 ounces) crushed pineapple, undrained
- 1 cup honey barbecue sauce
- 1/3 cup finely chopped onion
- 2 tablespoons chili sauce
- 4 bone-in pork loin chops (3/4 inch thick and 8 ounces each)

1 In a small bowl, combine the pineapple, barbecue sauce, onion and chili sauce. Pour half into a greased 3-qt. slow cooker. Top with pork chops and remaining sauce. Cover and cook on low for 4-1/4 to 5-1/4 hours or until meat is tender.

Yield: 4 servings.

Mushroom Pork Tenderloin

PREP: 5 MIN. ■ **COOK:** 4 HOURS

Donna Hughes
Rochester, New Hampshire
This pork simmers in a savory gravy, which is prepared with canned soups...it couldn't be easier.

　　2 pork tenderloins (1 pound each)
　　1 can (10-3/4 ounces) condensed cream of mushroom soup, undiluted
　　1 can (10-3/4 ounces) condensed golden mushroom soup, undiluted
　　1 can (10-1/2 ounces) condensed French onion soup, undiluted
　　Hot mashed potatoes, optional

1 Place pork in a 3-qt. slow cooker. Combine soups; stir until smooth. Pour over pork. Cover and cook on low for 4-5 hours or until meat is tender. Serve with mashed potatoes if desired.

Yield: 6 servings.

Slow-Cooked Pork Roast Dinner

(pictured above)

PREP: 25 MIN. ■ **COOK:** 6 HOURS

Jane Montgomery
Piqua, Ohio
This easy and delicious recipe will give you the juiciest pork you have ever tasted! You can cut it with a fork, and it's just as moist and tender the next day, that is if there are any leftovers.

　　1 large onion, halved and sliced
　　1 boneless pork loin roast (2-1/2 pounds)
　　4 medium potatoes, peeled and cubed
　　1 package (16 ounces) frozen sliced carrots
　　1 cup hot water
　　1/4 cup sugar
　　3 tablespoons cider vinegar
　　2 tablespoons reduced-sodium soy sauce
　　1 tablespoon ketchup
　　1/2 teaspoon salt
　　1/2 teaspoon pepper
　　1/4 teaspoon garlic powder
　　1/4 teaspoon chili powder
　　2 tablespoons cornstarch
　　2 tablespoons cold water

1 Place onion in the bottom of a 5-qt. slow cooker. Add the pork, potatoes and carrots. Whisk the hot water, sugar, vinegar, soy sauce, ketchup, salt, pepper, garlic powder and chili powder; pour over pork and vegetables. Cover and cook on low for 6-8 hours or until a meat thermometer reads 160°.

2 Remove pork and vegetables to a serving platter; keep warm. Skim fat from cooking juices; transfer to a small saucepan. Bring liquid to a boil. Combine cornstarch and water until smooth. Gradually stir into the pan. Bring to a boil; cook and stir for 2 minutes or until thickened. Serve with meat and vegetables.

Yield: 8 servings.

Chinese Pork Chops

PREP: 15 MIN. ■ **COOK:** 3 HOURS

Sharon Crider
Junction City, Kansas
They are so saucy and tender that these tasty chops became a family favorite the first time I served them.

　　6 boneless pork loin chops (4 ounces each)
　　1 small onion, finely chopped
　　1/3 cup ketchup
　　3 tablespoons brown sugar
　　3 tablespoons water
　　3 tablespoons reduced-sodium soy sauce
　　1 garlic clove, minced
　　1 teaspoon ground ginger
　　3 cups hot cooked rice

1 Place pork chops in a 3-qt. slow cooker coated with cooking spray. In a small bowl, combine the onion, ketchup, brown sugar, water, soy sauce, garlic and ginger. Pour over chops. Cover and cook on low for 3-4 hours or until meat is tender. Serve with rice and cooking juices.

Yield: 6 servings.

Tasty Pork Ribs

PREP: 10 MIN. ■ **COOK:** 6 HOURS

Michelle Rominger
Albia, Iowa
I like to serve these tender, country-style ribs over rice.
The tantalizing aroma and zippy Cajun barbecue sauce
are sure to make them a favorite at your house.

8 bone-in country-style pork ribs
(8 ounces each)
1 cup ketchup
1 cup barbecue sauce
1/4 cup packed brown sugar
1/4 cup Worcestershire sauce
1 tablespoon balsamic vinegar
1 tablespoon molasses
1 garlic clove, minced
2 tablespoons dried minced onion
1 teaspoon Cajun seasoning
1 teaspoon ground mustard
1/2 teaspoon salt
1/4 teaspoon pepper

1 Place ribs in a 5-qt. slow cooker. Combine the
   remaining ingredients; pour over ribs. Cover and
   cook on low for 6-7 hours or until meat is tender.

Yield: 8 servings.

Cranberry Pork Chops

PREP: 15 MIN. ■ **COOK:** 7-1/4 HOURS

Robin Czachor
Appleton, Wisconsin
My husband and two kids rave over these moist chops. Use the mild sweet-and-sour sauce to make a gravy that can be served over mashed potatoes or rice. Then add a salad and you have a very satisfying meal that doesn't keep you in the kitchen for hours.

6 bone-in pork loin chops (8 ounces each)
1 can (14 ounces) jellied cranberry sauce
1/2 cup cranberry or apple juice
1/4 cup sugar
2 tablespoons spicy brown mustard
2 tablespoons cornstarch
1/4 cup cold water
1/2 teaspoon salt
Dash pepper

1 Place pork chops in a 3-qt. slow cooker. In a small bowl, combine the cranberry sauce, juice, sugar and mustard until smooth; pour over chops. Cover and cook on low for 7-8 hours or until meat is tender. Remove chops; keep warm.

2 In a small saucepan, combine cornstarch and cold water until smooth; gradually stir in cooking juices. Bring to a boil; cook and stir for 2 minutes or until thickened. Stir in salt and pepper. Serve with chops.

Yield: 6 servings.

> **Budget saver.** If you're on a limited grocery budget, try the less-costly pork arm or blade chops for this recipe. Trim the fat from the edge of the chops before cooking. Once the chops are done, skim the fat from the cooking juices before making the sauce.

Slow-Cooked Pork Barbecue

(pictured above)
PREP: 15 MIN. ■ **COOK:** 5 HOURS

Connie Johnson
Springfield, Missouri
I need only five ingredients to fix this fantastic pork for sandwiches. I think it's perfect just the way it is, but feel free to adjust the sauce ingredients to suit your family's tastes.

1 boneless pork loin roast (3 to 4 pounds)
1-1/2 teaspoons seasoned salt
1 teaspoon garlic powder
1 cup barbecue sauce
1 cup cola
8 to 10 sandwich rolls, split

1 Cut roast in half; place in a 5-qt. slow cooker. Sprinkle with seasoned salt and garlic powder. Cover and cook on low for 4 hours or until meat is tender.

2 Remove meat; cool slightly. Skim fat from cooking juices. Shred meat with two forks and return to the slow cooker. Combine barbecue sauce and cola; pour over meat. Cover and cook on high for 1-2 hours or until sauce is thickened. Serve on rolls.

Yield: 8-10 servings.

Glazed Pork Roast

PREP: 30 MIN. ■ **COOK:** 4 HOURS

Radelle Knappenberger
Oviedo, Florida
This light recipe is always popular with adults and children alike. It's an excellent take-along meal for potlucks.

1 boneless whole pork loin roast
(4 pounds), trimmed
1 tablespoon olive oil
1 tablespoon butter, melted
2/3 cup thawed orange juice concentrate
1/3 cup water
3 garlic cloves, minced
1-1/2 teaspoons salt
1/2 teaspoon pepper

GLAZE:

1/4 cup packed brown sugar
2 tablespoons balsamic vinegar
1 tablespoon thawed orange juice concentrate
1 garlic clove, minced
1 can (11 ounces) mandarin oranges, drained, optional

1 Cut roast in half. In a large skillet, brown roast in oil and butter on all sides. Transfer to a 5-qt. slow cooker.

2 Add the orange juice concentrate, water, garlic, salt and pepper. Cover and cook on low for 4-6 hours or until a meat thermometer reads 160°.

3 For glaze, in a small saucepan, combine the brown sugar, vinegar, orange juice concentrate and garlic. Bring to a boil. Reduce heat; simmer, uncovered, for 3-5 minutes or until reduced to about 1/4 cup. Brush over roast. Garnish with oranges if desired.

Yield: 16 servings.

Creamy Cabbage-Pork Stew

(pictured above)

PREP: 20 MIN. ■ **COOK:** 6 HOURS

Ruth Ann Stelfox
Raymond, Alberta
Savory flavors blend beautifully in this hearty recipe. In a pinch, I use a ring of garlic bologna cut into chunks in place of the pork shoulder.

1 pound boneless pork shoulder, cut into 3/4-inch cubes
1 tablespoon canola oil
2 cans (10-3/4 ounces each) condensed cream of celery soup, undiluted
1-1/2 cups apple juice
2 medium red potatoes, cut into 1-inch chunks
3 medium carrots, sliced
1/4 teaspoon caraway seeds
1/4 teaspoon pepper
3 cups coarsely chopped cabbage
1/2 cup 2% milk

1 In a large skillet over medium-high heat, brown pork in oil on all sides; drain. Transfer to a 3-qt. slow cooker.

2 Stir in the soup, apple juice, potatoes, carrots, caraway and pepper. Cover and cook on high for 3-1/2 hours.

3 Add the cabbage and milk. Cover and cook 2-1/2 hours longer or until meat and vegetables are tender.

Yield: 6 servings.

Pulled Pork Sandwiches

(pictured above)

PREP: 20 MIN. ■ **COOK:** 6-1/4 HOURS

Tiffany Martinez
Aliso Viejo, California
The sourdough bread, chipotle mayonnaise, cheese and tomato make this pulled pork sandwich something special.

1 boneless pork sirloin roast (2 pounds), trimmed	1/8 teaspoon pepper
1 cup barbecue sauce	16 slices sourdough bread
1/4 cup chopped onion	1 chipotle pepper in adobo sauce, chopped
2 garlic cloves, minced	3/4 cup mayonnaise
1/2 teaspoon ground cumin	8 slices cheddar cheese
1/4 teaspoon salt	2 plum tomatoes, thinly sliced

1 Place pork in a 3-qt. slow cooker. Combine the barbecue sauce, onion, garlic, cumin, salt and pepper; pour over pork. Cover and cook on low for 6-7 hours or until meat is tender.

2 Remove meat; cool slightly. Shred with two forks and return to slow cooker; heat through.

3 Place bread on an ungreased baking sheet. Broil 4-6 in. from the heat for 2-3 minutes on each side or until golden brown. Meanwhile, in a small bowl, combine chipotle pepper and mayonnaise; spread over toast. Spoon 1/2 cup meat mixture onto each of eight slices of toast. Top with cheese, tomatoes and remaining toast.

Yield: 8 servings.

Easy and Elegant Ham

PREP: 5 MIN. ■
COOK: 6 HOURS + STANDING

Denise DiPace
Medford, New Jersey
This ham takes only a few minutes in the morning to prep, frees up my oven, tastes outstanding and feeds a crowd.

2 cans (20 ounces each) sliced pineapple

1 fully cooked boneless ham (about 6 pounds)

1 jar (6 ounces) maraschino cherries, well drained

1 jar (12 ounces) orange marmalade

1 Drain pineapple, reserving juice; set juice aside. Place half of the pineapple in an ungreased 5-qt. slow cooker. Cut ham in half; place over pineapple. Add cherries, remaining pineapple and reserved pineapple juice. Spoon marmalade over ham. Cover and cook on low for 6-7 hours or until heated through.

2 Remove to a warm serving platter. Let stand for 10-15 minutes before slicing. Serve pineapple and cherries with sliced ham.

Yield: 18-20 servings.

Hot Dogs 'n' Beans

PREP: 10 MIN. ■ **COOK:** 7 HOURS

June Formanek
Belle Plaine, Iowa
You'll please kids of all ages with this tasty combination that's good for casual get-togethers.

3 cans (two 28 ounces, one 16 ounces) pork and beans

1 package (1 pound) hot dogs, halved lengthwise and cut into 1-inch pieces

1 large onion, chopped

1/2 cup packed brown sugar

3 tablespoons prepared mustard

4 bacon strips, cooked and crumbled

1 In a 5-qt. slow cooker, combine all the ingredients. Cover and cook on low for 7-8 hours.

Yield: 10 servings.

Mexican Pork Roast

PREP: 15 MIN. ■ **COOK:** 8-1/4 HOURS

Chuck Allen
Dana Point, California
A friend who lives in Mexico shared this recipe with me a few years ago. They cooked the roast in a clay pot in a slow oven, but I found it works well in a slow cooker. The leftovers make great burritos and tacos.

- 2 medium onions, sliced
- 2 medium carrots, sliced
- 2 jalapeno peppers, seeded and chopped
- 3 garlic cloves, minced
- 2 tablespoons olive oil
- 1/2 cup water
- 1/2 cup chicken broth
- 1 teaspoon ground coriander
- 1/2 teaspoon salt
- 1/2 teaspoon ground cumin
- 1/2 teaspoon dried oregano
- 1/4 teaspoon pepper
- 1 boneless pork shoulder roast (3 pounds)

1 In a large skillet, saute the onions, carrots, jalapenos and garlic in oil for 3 minutes. Transfer to a 5-qt. slow cooker; add water and broth.

2 In a small bowl, combine the coriander, salt, cumin, oregano and pepper; rub over roast. Cut roast in half; place in the slow cooker. Cover and cook on low for 8-9 hours or until meat is tender.

3 Transfer roast and vegetables to a serving platter; keep warm. Strain cooking juices and skim fat. Pour into a small saucepan. Bring to a boil; cook until the liquid is reduced to about 1 cup. Serve with roast and vegetables.

Yield: 8 servings.

Editor's Note: When cutting hot peppers, disposable gloves are recommended. Avoid touching your face.

All-Day Red Beans & Rice

(pictured above)

PREP: 20 MIN. + SOAKING ■ **COOK:** 8-1/2 HOURS

Celinda Dahlgren
Napa, California
My family loves New Orleans-style cooking, so I make this authentic dish often. Being a busy working mom, I appreciate how simple it is. And its smoky ham flavor is scrumptious.

- 1 cup dried red beans
- 7 cups water, divided
- 2 smoked ham hocks
- 1 medium onion, chopped
- 1-1/2 teaspoons minced garlic
- 1 teaspoon ground cumin
- 1 medium tomato, chopped
- 1 medium green pepper, chopped
- 1 teaspoon salt
- 4 cups hot cooked rice

1 Sort beans and rinse in cold water. Place beans in a 3-qt. slow cooker. Add 4 cups water; cover and let stand overnight.

2 Drain and rinse beans, discarding liquid. Return beans to slow cooker; add the ham hocks, onion, garlic, cumin and remaining 3 cups water. Cover and cook on low for 8-10 hours or until beans are tender.

3 Remove ham hocks; cool slightly. Remove meat from bones. Finely chop meat and return to slow cooker; discard bones. Stir in the tomato, pepper and salt; cover and cook on high for 30 minutes or until pepper is tender. Serve with rice.

Yield: 6 servings.

Old-Fashioned Pork Chops

PREP: 20 MIN. ■ **COOK:** 5 HOURS

Loy Acerra Crane
Jackson, Tennessee
Tender chops simmer to fork-tender perfection in this classic dish. The savory sauce comes together easily with a can of soup, an onion and a few parsley flakes. I serve this regularly for an easy weeknight meal, but it goes over well as a company dinner, too.

1/2 cup all-purpose flour

1-1/2 teaspoons ground mustard

1/2 teaspoon garlic salt

1/2 teaspoon pepper

6 boneless pork loin chops (5 ounces each)

2 tablespoons canola oil

1 can (10-1/2 ounces) condensed chicken with rice soup, undiluted

1 medium onion, quartered

1-1/2 teaspoons dried parsley flakes

1 In a large resealable plastic bag, combine the flour, mustard, garlic salt and pepper. Add pork, a few pieces at a time, and shake to coat. In a large skillet, brown chops in oil on each side. Transfer to a 3-qt. slow cooker.

2 Top with soup, onion and parsley. Cover and cook on low for 5-6 hours or until meat is tender.

Yield: 6 servings.

Busy-Day Barbecued Ribs

PREP: 5 MIN. ■ COOK: 5 HOURS

Sherry Smalley
South Milwaukee, Wisconsin
I don't have a lot of time on weekends to spend in the kitchen. That's when this recipe comes in handy. I put all the ingredients in the slow cooker, and before I know it, dinner is ready!

3-1/2 to 4 pounds country-style pork ribs

1 can (10-3/4 ounces) condensed tomato soup, undiluted

1/2 cup packed brown sugar

1/3 cup cider vinegar

1 tablespoon soy sauce

1 teaspoon celery seed

1 teaspoon chili powder

1 Place ribs in a 5-qt. slow cooker. Combine remaining ingredients; pour over ribs. Cover and cook on high for 1 hour. Reduce heat to low and cook 4-5 hours longer. Thicken sauce for gravy if desired.

Yield: 6-8 servings.

Switch-and-Go Ribs

PREP: 10 MIN. ■ COOK: 6 HOURS

Lil Neuls
Caballo, New Mexico
A slightly sweet sauce gives these boneless ribs mild teriyaki flavor.

1-1/2 pounds boneless country-style pork ribs

1 tablespoon canola oil

1/3 cup orange marmalade

1/3 cup teriyaki sauce

1 teaspoon minced garlic

1 In a large skillet, brown ribs in oil on both sides. In a small bowl, combine the marmalade, teriyaki sauce and garlic.

2 Pour half of the sauce into a 3-qt. slow cooker; top with ribs. Drizzle with the remaining sauce. Cover and cook on low for 6-8 hours or until meat is tender.

Yield: 4 servings.

Bandito Chili Dogs

(pictured above)

PREP: 15 MIN. ■ COOK: 4 HOURS

Marion Lowery
Medford, Oregon
I've brought these beefy chili dogs to family functions for years. Adults and children alike love the cheesy chili sauce that's a snap to make.

1 package (1 pound) hot dogs

2 cans (15 ounces each) chili without beans

1 can (10-3/4 ounces) condensed cheddar cheese soup, undiluted

1 can (4 ounces) chopped green chilies

10 hot dog buns, split

1 medium onion, chopped

1 to 2 cups corn chips, coarsely crushed

1 cup (4 ounces) shredded cheddar cheese

1 Place hot dogs in a 3-qt. slow cooker. In a large bowl, combine the chili, soup and green chilies; pour over hot dogs. Cover and cook on low for 4-5 hours.

2 Serve hot dogs in buns; top with chili mixture, onion, corn chips and cheese.

Yield: 10 servings.

Sweet & Sour Pork Ribs

PREP: 30 MIN. ■ **COOK:** 8 HOURS

Merle Dyck
Elkford, British Columbia
For years I wondered why people raved about ribs. I didn't have the patience or energy to bother with them...until I made this recipe. Now I'm a believer, too.

> 2 cups packed brown sugar
> 1/4 cup all-purpose flour
> 1/2 cup cider vinegar
> 1/3 cup water
> 2 tablespoons soy sauce
> 2 tablespoons ketchup
> 3 garlic cloves, minced
> 8 bone-in country-style pork ribs
> (3 inches thick and 8 ounces each)

1 In a small saucepan, combine brown sugar and flour. Stir in the vinegar, water, soy sauce, ketchup and garlic. Bring to a boil; cook and stir for 2 minutes or until thickened.

2 Place ribs in a 5-qt. slow cooker. Top with sauce. Cover and cook on low for 8-10 hours or until meat is tender. Skim fat from sauce. Serve ribs with sauce.

Yield: 8 servings.

What to do with rock-hard brown sugar.
To soften brown sugar, place a slice of bread or an apple wedge with the brown sugar in a covered container for a few days. If you're in a hurry, microwave on high for 20-30 seconds. Repeat if necessary, but watch carefully, because the sugar will begin to melt. Always store brown sugar in an airtight container.

Italian Pork Chops

(pictured above)
PREP: 15 MIN. ■ **COOK:** 5-1/2 HOURS

Bonnie Marlow
Ottoville, Ohio
Not only is it easy to use my slow cooker, but the results are fabulous. Meat cooked this way is always so tender and juicy. These pork chops in a thick tomato sauce turn out great.

> 6 boneless pork loin chops (1/2 inch thick and 6 ounces each)
> 1 tablespoon canola oil
> 1 medium green pepper, diced
> 1 can (6 ounces) tomato paste
> 1 jar (4-1/2 ounces) sliced mushrooms, drained
> 1/2 cup water
> 1 envelope spaghetti sauce mix
> 1/2 to 1 teaspoon hot pepper sauce

1 In a large skillet, brown pork chops in oil over medium heat for 3-4 minutes on each side; drain. In a 5-qt. slow cooker, combine the remaining ingredients. Top with pork chops. Cover and cook on low for 5-1/2 to 6 hours or until a meat thermometer reads 160°.

Yield: 6 servings.

Country-Style Pork Loin

(pictured above)

PREP: 20 MIN. ■ **COOK:** 5-1/4 HOURS

Corina Flansberg
Carson City, Nevada

This pork roast is so juicy, it melts in your mouth. My son puts it at the top of his list of favorite foods. We like it with mashed potatoes.

---

1 boneless whole pork loin roast (3 pounds)

1/2 cup all-purpose flour

1 teaspoon onion powder

1 teaspoon ground mustard

2 tablespoons canola oil

2 cups chicken broth

1/4 cup cornstarch

1/4 cup cold water

Hot mashed potatoes, optional

1 Cut pork roast in half. In a large resealable plastic bag, combine the flour, onion powder and mustard. Add pork, one portion at a time, and shake to coat.

2 In a large skillet, brown pork on all sides in oil over medium-high heat. Transfer to a 5-qt. slow cooker. Pour broth over pork. Cover and cook on low for 5-6 hours or or until a meat thermometer reads 160°. Remove pork and keep warm.

3 For gravy, strain cooking juices and skim fat; pour 2-1/2 cups cooking juices into a large saucepan. Combine cornstarch and water until smooth; stir into juices. Bring to a boil; cook and stir for 2 minutes or until thickened. Slice pork; serve with gravy and mashed potatoes if desired.

Yield: 8 servings.

Pork Chops with Sauerkraut

(pictured above)

PREP: 15 MIN. ■ **COOK:** 3 HOURS

Stephanie Miller
Omaha, Nebraska

I pair tender pork chops with tangy sauerkraut in this filling main dish. It's so quick and easy to put together.

**4 bone-in center-cut pork loin chops
(1/2 inch thick and 8 ounces each)**

2 tablespoons canola oil

1 jar (32 ounces) sauerkraut, undrained

3/4 cup packed brown sugar

1 medium green pepper, sliced

1 medium onion, sliced

1 In a large skillet over medium heat, brown pork chops in oil for 3-4 minutes on each side; drain. In a 5-qt. slow cooker, combine the sauerkraut and brown sugar. Top with the pork chops, green pepper and onion.

2 Cover and cook on low for 3 to 3-1/2 hours or until meat is tender. Serve with a slotted spoon.

Yield: 4 servings.

Teriyaki Pork Roast

PREP: 10 MIN. ■ **COOK:** 7-1/4 HOURS

Roxanne Hulse
Gainsville, Georgia

Since my husband works full-time and attends school, I do a great deal around the house, including getting our three children to where they need to go. I'm always looking for no-fuss recipes, so I was thrilled to find this one. The teriyaki seasoned pork roast has become a family favorite.

3/4 cup unsweetened apple juice

2 tablespoons sugar

2 tablespoons soy sauce

1 tablespoon white vinegar

1 teaspoon ground ginger

1/4 teaspoon garlic powder

1/8 teaspoon pepper

1 boneless pork loin roast (about 3 pounds)

7-1/2 teaspoons cornstarch

3 tablespoons cold water

1 In a greased 3-qt. slow cooker, combine the apple juice, sugar, soy sauce, vinegar, ginger, garlic powder and pepper. Cut roast in half; add to slow cooker and turn to coat. Cover and cook on low for 7-8 hours or until a meat thermometer reads 160°.

2 Remove meat to a serving platter; keep warm. Skim fat from cooking juices; transfer to a small saucepan. Bring liquid to a boil. Combine cornstarch and water until smooth. Gradually stir into the pan. Bring to a boil; cook and stir for 2 minutes or until thickened. Serve with meat.

Yield: 8 servings.

Slow-Cooked Ham 'n' Broccoli

(pictured above)

PREP: 10 MIN. ■ **COOK:** 2 HOURS + STANDING

Jill Pennington
Jacksonville, Florida

Ham and broccoli cook up into a creamy delight in this dish. This recipe is a complete meal-in-one so you don't need to fuss with side dishes.

3 cups cubed fully cooked ham

3 cups frozen chopped broccoli, thawed

1 can (10-3/4 ounces) condensed cream of mushroom soup, undiluted

1 jar (8 ounces) process cheese sauce

1 can (8 ounces) sliced water chestnuts, drained

1-1/4 cups uncooked instant rice

1 cup 2% milk

1 celery rib, chopped

1 medium onion, chopped

1/8 to 1/4 teaspoon pepper

1/2 teaspoon paprika

1 In a 3-qt. slow cooker, combine the ham, broccoli, soup, cheese sauce, water chestnuts, rice, milk, celery, onion and pepper. Cover and cook on high for 2-3 hours or until the rice is tender. Let stand for 10 minutes before serving. Sprinkle with paprika.

Yield: 6-8 servings.

Tender Pork Chops

PREP: 20 MIN. ■ COOK: 6 HOURS

Patricia Dick
Anderson, Indiana
My family has enjoyed these simple pork chops for years. The meat falls right off the bone!

> 1/2 cup all-purpose flour
> 1-1/2 teaspoons ground mustard
> 1 teaspoon seasoned salt
> 1/2 teaspoon garlic powder
> 6 bone-in pork loin chops (1 inch thick and 8 ounces each)
> 2 tablespoons canola oil
> 1 can (10-1/2 ounces) condensed chicken with rice soup, undiluted

1 In a large resealable plastic bag, combine the flour, mustard, seasoned salt and garlic powder. Add pork chops, one at a time, and shake to coat.

2 In a large skillet, brown chops in oil on both sides. Place in a 3-qt. slow cooker. Pour soup over pork. Cover and cook on low for 6-7 hours or until meat is tender.

Yield: 6 servings.

Pulled Pork Subs

(pictured above)

PREP: 15 MIN. ■ COOK: 5-1/4 HOURS

Denise Davis
Porter, Maine
Honey and ground ginger are the flavor boosters behind my no-stress subs. A bottle of barbecue sauce ties it all together in a pinch.

> 1 small onion, finely chopped
> 1 boneless pork shoulder roast (2-1/2 pounds)
> 1 bottle (18 ounces) barbecue sauce
> 1/2 cup water
> 1/4 cup honey
> 6 garlic cloves, minced
> 1 teaspoon seasoned salt
> 1 teaspoon ground ginger
> 8 submarine buns, split

1 Place onion and roast in a 5-qt. slow cooker. In a small bowl, combine the barbecue sauce, water, honey, garlic, seasoned salt and ginger; pour over meat. Cover and cook on high for 5-6 hours or until meat is tender.

2 Remove meat; cool slightly. Shred meat with two forks and return to the slow cooker; heat through. Serve on buns. Cut sandwiches in half.

Yield: 16 servings.

Pork Spareribs

PREP: 5 MIN. ■ COOK: 6 HOURS

Shari Sieg
Silver Springs, Florida
Who knew that five ingredients could be so delicious? These ribs are so tender.

> 3 pounds pork spareribs
> 2 cans (28 ounces each) diced tomatoes, undrained
> 2 cups barbecue sauce
> 1/4 cup packed brown sugar
> 1/4 cup white wine vinegar

1 Cut ribs into serving-size portions. Place ribs in a 5-qt. slow cooker. Combine all the remaining ingredients; pour over ribs. Cover and cook on low for 6-7 hours or until meat is tender. Serve with a slotted spoon.

Yield: 6 servings.

Hot Ham Sandwiches

PREP: 10 MIN. ■ **COOK:** 4 HOURS

Susan Rehm
Grahamsville, New York
I came up with this crowd-pleasing recipe when trying to re-create a favorite sandwich from a restaurant near my hometown. Flavored with sweet relish, the ham sandwiches are oh-so-easy.

> **3 pounds thinly sliced deli ham
> (about 40 slices)**
>
> **2 cups apple juice**
>
> **2/3 cup packed brown sugar**
>
> **1/2 cup sweet pickle relish**
>
> **2 teaspoons prepared mustard**
>
> **1 teaspoon paprika**
>
> **12 kaiser rolls, split**
>
> **Additional sweet pickle relish, optional**

1 Separate ham slices and place in a 3-qt. slow cooker. In a small bowl, combine the apple juice, brown sugar, relish, mustard and paprika. Pour over the ham. Cover and cook on low for 4-5 hours or until heated through. Place 3-4 slices of ham on each roll. Serve with additional relish if desired.

Yield: 12 servings.

Storing maple syrup. Unopened containers of maple syrup can be stored in a cool, dry place. Real maple syrup contains no preservatives. So even though it has a high sugar content, an open container can spoil if stored at room temperature. Once the container has been opened, store it in the refrigerator.

Maple Pork Ribs

(pictured above)

PREP: 10 MIN. ■ **COOK:** 5 HOURS

Phyllis Eismann Schmalz
Kansas City, Kansas
These mouthwatering ribs are draped in a luscious maple-mustard sauce.

> **1 pound boneless country-
> style pork ribs, trimmed and
> cut into 3-inch pieces**
>
> **2 teaspoons canola oil**
>
> **1 medium onion, cut into**
>
> **1/4-inch slices and separated
> into rings**
>
> **3 tablespoons maple syrup**
>
> **2 tablespoons spicy brown
> or Dijon mustard**

1 In a large skillet, brown ribs in oil on all sides; drain. Place ribs and onion in a 1-1/2-qt. slow cooker. Combine syrup and mustard; pour over ribs. Cover and cook on low for 5-7 hours or until meat is tender.

Yield: 2 servings.

Asian Pork Roast

PREP: 25 MIN. ■ **COOK:** 4-1/2 HOURS

Sheree Shown
Junction City, Oregon
Slow-cooked dishes are a favorite in our home, and this one is perfect for fall and winter evenings. A pork roast cooks all afternoon with sweet onions, honey, soy sauce and ginger for fabulous flavor.

- 2 large onions, thinly sliced
- 3 garlic cloves, minced
- 1/2 teaspoon salt
- 1/2 teaspoon pepper
- 1 boneless whole pork loin roast (3 pounds)
- 1 tablespoon canola oil
- 3 bay leaves
- 1/4 cup hot water
- 1/4 cup honey
- 1/4 cup reduced-sodium soy sauce
- 2 tablespoons rice vinegar
- 1 teaspoon ground ginger
- 1/2 teaspoon ground cloves
- 3 tablespoons cornstarch
- 1/4 cup cold water
- 2 tablespoons sesame seeds, toasted
- **Hot cooked rice and sliced green onion tops, optional**

1 Place onions in a 5-qt. slow cooker. In a small bowl, combine the garlic, salt and pepper. Cut roast in half; rub with garlic mixture. In a large nonstick skillet coated with cooking spray, brown pork in oil on all sides. Transfer to slow cooker; add the bay leaves.

2 In a small bowl, combine hot water and honey; stir in the soy sauce, vinegar, ginger and cloves. Pour over pork. Cover and cook on low for 4-5 hours or until a meat thermometer reads 160°.

3 Remove meat and onions from slow cooker; keep warm. Discard bay leaves. In a small bowl, combine cornstarch and cold water until smooth. Gradually stir into slow cooker. Cover and cook on high for 30 minutes or until thickened, stirring twice. Slice pork; top with onions, sauce and sesame seeds. Serve with rice and garnish with green onion tops if desired.

Yield: 12 servings.

Slow-Cooked Pork and Beans

(pictured above)

PREP: 15 MIN. ■ **COOK:** 6 HOURS

Patricia Hager
Nicholasville, Kentucky
I like to get this dish started before leaving for work in the morning. When I get home, my supper's ready. It's a hearty meal that is also good for a potluck. A generous helping of tender pork and beans is wonderful alongside a slice of warm corn bread.

- 1 boneless whole pork loin roast (3 pounds)
- 1 medium onion, sliced
- 3 cans (15 ounces each) pork and beans
- 1-1/2 cups barbecue sauce
- 1/4 cup packed brown sugar
- 1 teaspoon garlic powder

1 Cut roast in half; place in a 5-qt. slow cooker. Top with onion. Combine the beans, barbecue sauce, brown sugar and garlic powder; pour over meat. Cover and cook on low for 6 hours or until meat is tender.

2 Remove roast; cool slightly. Shred with two forks and return meat to slow cooker; heat through.

Yield: 12 servings.

Fruity Pork Chops

PREP: 20 MIN. ■ **COOK:** 7-1/4 HOURS

Bonnie Baumgardner
Sylva, North Carolina
Pork chops are simmered in fruit juice seasoned with orange peel, mustard and red wine vinegar. Then a delightful sauce is made with a can of handy fruit cocktail.

4 bone-in pork loin chops (1 inch thick and 8 ounces each)

1/2 teaspoon salt

1/4 teaspoon pepper

1/8 teaspoon dried rosemary, crushed

1/8 teaspoon dill weed

1/8 teaspoon ground ginger

2 tablespoons canola oil

1 can (15 ounces) fruit cocktail

2 tablespoons red wine vinegar

1 tablespoon prepared mustard

1/4 teaspoon grated orange peel

2 tablespoons cornstarch

2 tablespoons cold water

1 Sprinkle pork chops with salt, pepper, rosemary, dill and ginger. In a large skillet, brown chops on both sides in oil. Transfer to a 3-qt. slow cooker.

2 Drain fruit cocktail. In a small bowl, combine the vinegar, mustard, orange peel and reserved fruit juice. Pour over pork. Cover and cook on low for 7-8 hours or until meat is tender.

3 Remove chops and keep warm. Strain the cooking juices into a small saucepan. Combine the cornstarch and water until smooth; stir into the cooking juices. Bring to a boil; cook and stir for 2 minutes until thickened and bubbly. Add the fruit cocktail; heat through. Serve with the pork chops.

Yield: 4 servings.

Pork Chili Verde

(pictured above)

PREP: 25 MIN. ■ **COOK:** 6-1/2 HOURS

Kimberly Burke
Chico, California
Pork gently stews with jalapenos, onion, green enchilada sauce and spices in this flavor-packed Mexican dish. It's great on its own or stuffed in a warm tortilla with sour cream, grated cheese or olives on the side.

1 boneless pork sirloin roast (3 pounds), cut into 1-inch cubes

4 medium carrots, sliced

1 medium onion, thinly sliced

1 cup minced fresh cilantro

4 garlic cloves, minced

3 tablespoons canola oil

1 can (28 ounces) green enchilada sauce

2 jalapeno peppers, seeded and chopped

1 tablespoon cornstarch

1/4 cup cold water

Hot cooked rice

Flour tortillas, warmed

1 In a large skillet, saute the pork, carrots, onion, cilantro and garlic in oil in batches until pork is browned. Transfer to a 5-qt. slow cooker.

2 Add the enchilada sauce and jalapenos. Cover and cook on low for 6 hours or until meat is tender.

3 In a small bowl, combine cornstarch and water until smooth; stir into pork mixture. Cover and cook on high for 30 minutes or until thickened. Serve with rice and tortillas.

Yield: 8 servings.

Editor's Note: When cutting hot peppers, disposable gloves are recommended. Avoid touching your face.

Fiesta Pork Sandwiches

PREP: 20 MIN. + MARINATING
COOK: 8 HOURS

Yvette Massey
La Luz, New Mexico
This is an easy and flavorful dish that my family really enjoys. When I fix it for company, I usually prepare the meat the day before so I can concentrate on side dishes and relaxing with my guests on the day of the party.

1 boneless pork shoulder roast
(3 to 4 pounds)

2/3 cup lime juice

1/4 cup grapefruit juice

1/4 cup water

2 bay leaves

12 garlic cloves, minced

1 teaspoon salt

1 teaspoon dried oregano

1 teaspoon chili powder

2 tablespoons olive oil

1 large onion, thinly sliced

12 to 14 sandwich rolls, split

1 Cut the roast in half; pierce several times with a fork. In a large bowl, combine the juices, water, bay leaves, garlic, salt, oregano and chili powder. Pour half of marinade into a large resealable plastic bag; add the pork. Seal bag and turn to coat; refrigerate overnight, turning occasionally. Cover and refrigerate remaining marinade.

2 Drain and discard marinade from pork. In a Dutch oven over medium heat, brown roast in oil on all sides.

3 Place the onion, roast and reserved marinade in a 5-qt. slow cooker. Cover and cook on high for 2 hours. Reduce heat to low; cook 6-8 hours longer or until the meat is tender. Remove the roast; shred or thinly slice. Discard the bay leaf. Skim the fat from cooking juices and serve pork on rolls with the juices as a dipping sauce.

Yield: 12-14 servings.

Bavarian Pork Loin

(pictured above)

PREP: 25 MIN. ■ **COOK:** 6 HOURS

Edie DeSpain
Logan, Utah
I got the recipe for this tender pork roast from an aunt, who made it all the time. What a delicious taste sensation with sauerkraut and apples.

1 boneless whole pork loin roast (3 to 4 pounds)

1 can (14 ounces) Bavarian sauerkraut, rinsed and drained

1-3/4 cups chopped carrots

1 large onion, finely chopped

1/2 cup unsweetened apple juice

2 teaspoons dried parsley flakes

3 large tart apples, peeled and quartered

1 Cut roast in half; place in a 5-qt. slow cooker. In a small bowl, combine the sauerkraut, carrots, onion, apple juice and parsley; spoon over roast. Cover and cook on low for 4 hours.

2 Add apples to slow cooker. Cover and cook 2 to 2-1/2 hours longer or until a meat thermometer reads 160°. Remove the roast; let stand for 5 minutes before slicing. Serve with sauerkraut mixture.

Yield: 10 servings.

Pork Roast Dinner

(pictured above)

PREP: 30 MIN. + MARINATING ■ **COOK:** 8 HOURS

Lisa Chamberlain
St. Charles, Illinois
I am single and love to cook, so I often entertain family
and friends. They love new recipes, and this was one of
their favorites. The leftover meat makes great barbecue pork
sandwiches the next day.

- 1 boneless whole pork loin roast (3 to 4 pounds)
- 2 teaspoons minced garlic
- 2 teaspoons fennel seed, crushed
- 1-1/2 teaspoons dried rosemary, crushed
- 1 teaspoon dried oregano
- 1 teaspoon paprika
- 3/4 teaspoon salt
- 1/4 teaspoon pepper
- 1-1/2 pounds medium potatoes, peeled and cut into chunks
- 1-1/2 pounds large sweet potatoes, peeled and cut into chunks
- 2 large sweet onions, cut into eighths
- 1/2 cup chicken broth

1 Cut roast in half. Combine the garlic, fennel,
rosemary, oregano, paprika, salt and pepper; rub
over pork. Cover and refrigerate for 8 hours.

2 Place potatoes and onions in a 5-qt. slow cooker.
Top with pork. Pour broth over meat. Cover and cook
on low for 8-10 hours or until a meat thermometer
reads 160° and vegetables are tender.

Yield: 8 servings.

Chinese Pork Ribs

(pictured above)

PREP: 10 MIN. ■ **COOK:** 6 HOURS

June Ross
Belmont, North Carolina

Add an Asian flair to an all-American dish like ribs. This recipe has a wonderful flavor with the saltiness of the soy and sweetness of the orange marmalade.

1/4 cup reduced-sodium soy sauce

1/3 cup reduced-sugar orange marmalade

3 tablespoons ketchup

2 garlic cloves, minced

3 to 4 pounds bone-in country-style pork ribs

1 In a small bowl, combine the soy sauce, marmalade, ketchup and garlic. Pour half into a 5-qt. slow cooker. Top with ribs; drizzle with remaining sauce. Cover and cook on low for 6 hours or until tender. Thicken cooking juices if desired.

Yield: 6 servings.

Sticky ribs. The sweet-savory sauce on these ribs is delicious, but can be messy. As a special touch, have some hot, moist washcloths at the table to wipe off sticky fingers.

Cranberry-Apricot Pork Roast with Potatoes

PREP: 15 MIN. ■ **COOK:** 5 HOURS

Patricia Trench
Panama City, Florida
Here's a delightful meal-in-one that makes weeknight dining a snap. The apricots blend well with the whole-berry cranberry sauce for a delightful sweet-and-tart taste. Cayenne pepper adds just the right touch of zing to this meat-and-potatoes meal.

1 boneless whole pork loin roast (3 pounds)

4 medium potatoes, peeled and quartered

1 can (14 ounces) whole-berry cranberry sauce

1 can (15 ounces) apricot halves, drained

1 medium onion, quartered

1/2 cup chopped dried apricots

1 tablespoon sugar

1/2 teaspoon ground mustard

1/4 teaspoon cayenne pepper

1 Cut roast in half. Place potatoes in a 5-qt. slow cooker. Add the pork.

2 In a blender, combine the cranberry sauce, apricots, onion, dried apricots, sugar, mustard, and cayenne. Cover and process for 30 seconds or until almost smooth. Pour over pork. Cover and cook on low for 5-6 hours or until a meat thermometer reads 160°.

3 Remove pork and potatoes to a serving platter and bowl. Pour cooking juices into a pitcher; serve with meat and potatoes.

Yield: 8 servings.

Brats with Sauerkraut

(pictured above)

PREP: 10 MIN. ■ **COOK:** 6 HOURS

Darlene Dixon
Hanover, Minnesota
I've made many variations of this excellent main dish. The bratwurst can be plain, smoked or cheese-flavored, served whole or cut in slices, with a bun or without. It would be popular at a party or potluck.

8 uncooked bratwurst links

1 can (14 ounces) sauerkraut, rinsed and well drained

2 medium apples, peeled and finely chopped

3 bacon strips, cooked and crumbled

1/4 cup packed brown sugar

1/4 cup finely chopped onion

1 teaspoon ground mustard

8 brat buns, split

1 Place the bratwurst in a 5-qt. slow cooker. In a large bowl, combine the sauerkraut, apples, bacon, brown sugar, onion and mustard; spoon over bratwurst. Cover and cook on low for 6-7 hours or until sausage is no longer pink.

2 Place the brats in the buns; using a slotted spoon, top with the sauerkraut mixture.

Yield: 8 servings.

poultry

Lemon Chicken Breasts With Veggies

(pictured at left)

PREP: 25 MIN. ■ **COOK:** 8 HOURS

Amber Otis
Morris, Oklahoma
Try this recipe for a hearty, comforting dish with a subtle lemon flavor. It has everything you need for a satisfying meal.

1 pound fresh baby carrots

3 cups cubed red potatoes

1 package (14 ounces) frozen pearl onions, thawed

2 celery ribs, thinly sliced

6 bone-in chicken breast halves (10 ounces each), skin removed

1 can (10-3/4 ounces) condensed cream of chicken soup, undiluted

1/2 cup water

1/2 cup lemon juice

1 teaspoon dried parsley flakes

1 teaspoon dried thyme

1/2 teaspoon pepper

1/4 teaspoon salt

1 In a 5- or 6-qt. slow cooker, combine the carrots, potatoes, onions and celery. Top with chicken. In a small bowl, combine the soup, water, lemon juice, parsley, thyme, pepper and salt. Pour soup mixture over chicken. Cover and cook on low for 8-9 hours or until chicken is tender.

Yield: 6 servings.

Slow-Cooked White Chili

(pictured at right)

PREP: 25 MIN. ■ **COOK:** 5 HOURS

Lori Weber
Wentzville, Missouri
This mouthwatering slow-simmered chili features chicken, two kinds of beans and crunchy corn. It's quick, easy and tastes great. It's a family favorite that we enjoy with corn bread.

3/4 pound boneless skinless chicken breasts, cubed

1 medium onion, chopped

1 tablespoon canola oil

1 garlic clove, minced

1-1/2 cups water

1 can (15 ounces) white kidney or cannellini beans, rinsed and drained

1 can (15 ounces) garbanzo beans or chickpeas, rinsed and drained

1 can (11 ounces) whole kernel white corn, drained or 1-1/4 cups frozen shoepeg corn

1 can (4 ounces) chopped green chilies

1 to 2 teaspoons chicken bouillon granules

1 teaspoon ground cumin

1 In a large skillet, saute chicken and onion in oil until onion is tender. Add garlic; cook 1 minute longer. Transfer to a 3-qt. slow cooker.

2 Stir in the remaining ingredients. Cover and cook on low for 5-6 hours or until chicken is no longer pink.

Yield: 8 servings (2 quarts).

Corsican Chicken

PREP: 20 MIN. ■ COOK: 4-3/4 HOURS

Mary Bergfeld
Eugene, Oregon
Moist and tender chicken thighs make a delicious hot entree for winter months. Just add a salad and a dessert for a complete meal.

> 3 tablespoons butter, softened
>
> 2 tablespoons herbes de Provence
>
> 1 teaspoon salt
>
> 2 garlic cloves, minced
>
> 1/2 teaspoon coarsely ground pepper
>
> 2 pounds boneless skinless chicken thighs
>
> 1 large onion, chopped
>
> 1/2 cup oil-packed sun-dried tomatoes, julienned
>
> 1 can (10-1/2 ounces) condensed beef consomme, undiluted
>
> 1/2 cup dry vermouth or orange juice
>
> 1/2 cup pitted Greek olives, quartered
>
> 1 teaspoon grated orange peel
>
> 2 teaspoons cornstarch
>
> 1 tablespoon cold water
>
> 2 tablespoons minced fresh basil
>
> 2 tablespoons diced pimientos
>
> 2 tablespoons minced fresh parsley

1 In a small bowl, combine the butter, herbes de Provence, salt, garlic and pepper; rub over chicken. Place in a 5-qt. slow cooker.

2 Add the onion, tomatoes, consomme and vermouth. Cover and cook on low for 4-5 hours or until chicken juices run clear. Add olives and orange peel. Cover and cook on high for 30 minutes.

3 Remove chicken and vegetables to a serving platter; keep warm. Skim fat from cooking juices; transfer to a small saucepan. Bring liquid to a boil. Combine cornstarch and water until smooth. Gradually stir into the pan. Bring to a boil; cook and stir for 2 minutes or until thickened. Pour over chicken. Sprinkle with basil, pimientos and parsley.

Yield: 6-8 servings.

Editor's Note: Look for herbes de Provence in the spice aisle.

Simple Chicken Stew

(pictured above)

PREP: 20 MIN. ■ COOK: 6 HOURS

Amy Dulling
Rockwood, Tennessee
This comforting stew was one of my husband's experiments that turned out to be one of our favorite Sunday dinners.

> 1 can (10-3/4 ounces) condensed cream of chicken soup, undiluted
>
> 1 cup water
>
> 1/2 pound boneless skinless chicken breasts, cut into cubes
>
> 1 large potato, peeled and cut into 3/4-inch cubes
>
> 2 medium carrots, cut into 1/4-inch slices
>
> 1/2 cup sliced fresh mushrooms
>
> 1/4 cup chopped onion
>
> 1 teaspoon chicken bouillon granules
>
> 1/4 teaspoon poultry seasoning

1 In a 3-qt. slow cooker, combine all the ingredients. Cover and cook on low for 6-7 hours or until chicken and vegetables are tender.

Yield: 2 servings.

Italian Chicken

PREP: 20 MIN. ■ **COOK:** 3-1/4 HOURS

Judi Guizado
Rancho Cucamonga, California
A friend gave me this easy, low-fat recipe years ago, and
I've tweaked the spices to my family's tastes. I'm requested
to make it at least twice a month.

  6 boneless skinless chicken breast halves
  (about 8 ounces each)
  1 can (14-1/2 ounces) Italian stewed tomatoes
  3/4 cup plus 3 tablespoons water, divided
  2 tablespoons dried minced onion
  2 teaspoons chicken bouillon granules
  2 teaspoons chili powder
  1/2 teaspoon dried tarragon

  1/2 teaspoon Italian seasoning
  1/4 teaspoon garlic powder
  3 tablespoons cornstarch
  Hot cooked rice

1 Place chicken in a 5-qt. slow cooker. In a small bowl,
  combine the tomatoes, 3/4 cup water, onion, bouillon
  and seasonings; pour over chicken. Cover and cook
  on low for 3-4 hours or until chicken is tender.

2 Transfer chicken to a serving platter; keep warm.
  Skim fat from cooking juices; transfer to a small
  saucepan. Bring liquid to a boil. Combine cornstarch
  and remaining water until smooth. Gradually stir into
  the pan. Bring to a boil; cook and stir for 2 minutes
  or until thickened. Serve with chicken and rice.

Yield: 6 servings.

Turkey with Cranberry Sauce

PREP: 15 MIN. ■ **COOK:** 4-1/4 HOURS

Marie Ramsden
Fairgrove, Michigan
This is a very tasty and easy way to cook a turkey breast in the slow cooker. Ideal for large potlucks, the sweet cranberry sauce complements the turkey nicely.

> 2 boneless skinless turkey breast halves (4 pounds each)
> 1 can (14 ounces) jellied cranberry sauce
> 1/2 cup plus 2 tablespoons water, divided
> 1 envelope onion soup mix
> 2 tablespoons cornstarch

1 Cut each turkey breast in half; place in two 5-qt. slow cookers. In a large bowl, combine the cranberry sauce, 1/2 cup water and soup mix. Pour half over each turkey. Cover and cook on low for 4-6 hours or until a meat thermometer reads 170°. Remove turkey and keep warm.

2 Transfer both cranberry mixtures to a large saucepan. Combine the cornstarch and remaining water until smooth. Bring cranberry mixture to a boil; gradually stir in cornstarch mixture until smooth. Cook and stir for 2 minutes or until thickened. Slice turkey; serve with cranberry sauce.

Yield: 20-25 servings.

Pepper Jack Chicken
(pictured above)

PREP: 20 MIN. ■ **COOK:** 5 HOURS

Linda Foreman
Locust Grove, Oklahoma
Simmer up a delicious meal with just a few basic ingredients. Your family is sure to love this colorful medley with tender chicken and a zippy cheese sauce.

> 6 boneless skinless chicken breast halves (5 ounces each), cut into chunks
> 1 each small green, sweet red and orange pepper, cut into thin strips
> 1 can (10-3/4 ounces) condensed nacho cheese soup, undiluted
> 1/2 cup chunky salsa
> 1/8 teaspoon chili powder
> 4-1/2 cups hot cooked rice

1 In a 3-qt. slow cooker, combine the chicken, peppers, soup, salsa and chili powder. Cover and cook on low for 5-6 hours or until chicken is no longer pink. Serve with rice.

Yield: 6 servings.

Cutting sweet pepper. *Here's an easy way to cut sweet pepper into strips. Place the washed pepper stem side up on a cutting board. Using a sharp knife, cut a side off the pepper. Rotate the pepper and continue to cut off the sides, leaving the center top intact. When you are finished, most of the seeds will be clinging to the top and can be discarded. Rinse off any stray seeds, then cut each pepper piece into strips.*

Slow-Cooked Goose

PREP: 20 MIN. + MARINATING
COOK: 4 HOURS

Edna Ylioja
Lucky Lake, Saskatchewan
My husband, Willard, and I own a hunting lodge and host about 16 hunters a week at our camp. The slow cooker makes easy work of fixing this flavorful goose dish, which is a favorite of our guests. The recipe makes lots of savory gravy to serve over mashed potatoes.

1/2 cup soy sauce

4 teaspoons canola oil

4 teaspoons lemon juice

2 teaspoons Worcestershire sauce

1 teaspoon garlic powder

2 pounds cubed goose breast

3/4 to 1 cup all-purpose flour

1/4 cup butter, cubed

1 can (10-3/4 ounces) condensed golden mushroom soup, undiluted

1-1/3 cups water

1 envelope onion soup mix

Hot cooked mashed potatoes, noodles or rice

1 In a large resealable plastic bag, combine the soy sauce, oil, lemon juice, Worcestershire sauce and garlic powder; add goose. Seal and turn to coat. Refrigerate for 4 hours or overnight.

2 Drain and discard marinade from goose. Place flour in another large resealable plastic bag; add goose in batches and shake to coat. In a large skillet over medium heat, brown goose in butter on all sides. Transfer to a 3-qt. slow cooker.

3 Add the soup, water and soup mix. Cover and cook on high for 4-5 hours or until chicken is tender. Serve with potatoes, noodles or rice.

Yield: 4 servings.

Herbed Chicken with Wild Rice

(pictured above)

PREP: 20 MIN. ■ **COOK:** 4 HOURS

Becky Gifford
Conway, Arkansas
We always are very busy. With three kids involved in many different after-school and evening activities, it's nice to come home to a meal that's already prepared and ready to eat!

1 package (6 ounces) long grain and wild rice mix

6 boneless skinless chicken breast halves (5 ounces each)

1 tablespoon canola oil

1 teaspoon butter

1/2 pound sliced fresh mushrooms

1 can (10-3/4 ounces) condensed cream of chicken soup, undiluted

1 cup water

3 bacon strips, cooked and crumbled

1 teaspoon dried parsley flakes

1/2 teaspoon dried thyme

1/4 teaspoon dried tarragon

1 Place rice in a 5-qt. slow cooker; set aside seasoning packet. In a large skillet, brown chicken in oil and butter. Add to slow cooker. In the same skillet, saute mushrooms until tender; place over chicken.

2 In a small bowl, combine the soup, water, bacon, herbs and contents of seasoning packet. Pour over top. Cover and cook on low for 4 hours or until chicken is tender.

Yield: 6 servings.

Saucy Chicken with Veggies and Rice

PREP: 15 MIN. ■ **COOK:** 4-1/2 HOURS

Teri Lindquist
Gurnee, Illinois
I'm proud to share this recipe. I created it many years ago for a slow cooker contest and won first place! It's rich and flavorful, yet so easy.

3 cups sliced celery

3 cups sliced fresh carrots

2 cups sliced onion

6 boneless skinless chicken breast halves
(5 ounces each)

1 can (10-3/4 ounces) condensed cream of mushroom soup, undiluted

1 envelope onion soup mix

1 teaspoon dried thyme

1 teaspoon pepper

1/2 teaspoon dried tarragon

2 tablespoons cornstarch

1/3 cup white wine or chicken broth

Hot cooked rice

1 Place the celery, carrots, onion and chicken in a 5-qt. slow cooker. In a small bowl, combine the soup, soup mix, thyme, pepper and tarragon; pour over chicken. Cover and cook on low for 4-5 hours or until chicken is tender.

2 Mix cornstarch and wine until smooth; stir into slow cooker. Cover and cook on high for 30 minutes or until gravy is thickened. Serve with rice.

Yield: 6 servings.

Tropical BBQ Chicken

PREP: 15 MIN. ■ **COOK:** 5-1/4 HOURS

Yvonne McKim
Vancouver, Washington
This is my favorite slow cooker recipe. The delicious, slightly spicy sauce will win you over, too!

6 chicken leg quarters

3/4 cup ketchup

1/2 cup orange juice

1/4 cup packed brown sugar

1/4 cup red wine vinegar

1/4 cup olive oil

4 teaspoons minced fresh parsley

2 teaspoons Worcestershire sauce

1 teaspoon garlic salt

1/2 teaspoon pepper

2 tablespoons plus 2 teaspoons cornstarch

1/4 cup water

1 With a sharp knife, cut leg quarters at the joints. Place chicken in a 4-qt. slow cooker. In a small bowl, combine the ketchup, orange juice, brown sugar, vinegar, oil, parsley, Worcestershire sauce, garlic salt and pepper; pour over chicken. Cover and cook on low for 5-6 hours or until chicken juices run clear.

2 Remove chicken to a serving platter; keep warm. Skim fat from cooking juices; transfer 2 cups to a small saucepan. Bring liquid to a boil. Combine cornstarch and water until smooth. Gradually stir into the pan. Bring to a boil; cook and stir for 2 minutes or until thickened. Serve with chicken.

Yield: 12 servings.

Get that last bit of ketchup from the bottle. It's hard to get the last of the ketchup from the bottle. When you're making a sauce like the one in Tropical BBQ Chicken, pour a measured amount of the other liquid ingredients into the bottle, such as the orange juice and vinegar and shake the ketchup bottle. When you pour the ketchup mixture into a measuring cup, just subtract the amount of the first liquid to determine the amount of the ketchup.

Maple Mustard Chicken

(pictured above)

PREP: 5 MIN. ■ **COOK:** 3 HOURS

Jennifer Seidel
Midland, Michigan
This recipe is one of my husband's favorites. It only calls for four ingredients, and we try to have them on hand all the time for a delightful and cozy dinner anytime!

6 boneless skinless chicken breast halves (6 ounces each)

1/2 cup maple syrup

1/3 cup stone-ground mustard

2 tablespoons quick-cooking tapioca

Hot cooked brown rice

1 Place chicken in a 3-qt. slow cooker. In a small bowl, combine the syrup, mustard and tapioca; pour over chicken. Cover and cook on low for 3-4 hours or until the chicken is tender. Serve with the rice.

Yield: 6 servings.

Busy Mom's Chicken Fajitas

PREP: 15 MIN. ■ **COOK:** 5 HOURS

Sarah Newman
Brooklyn Center, Minnesota
Staying at home with a young child makes preparing dinner a challenge, but a slow cooker makes it easy. The savory meat in these fajitas is a hit.

1 pound boneless skinless chicken breast halves

1 can (16 ounces) kidney beans, rinsed and drained

1 can (14-1/2 ounces) diced tomatoes with mild green chilies, drained

1 each medium green, sweet red and yellow peppers, julienned

1 medium onion, halved and sliced

2 teaspoons ground cumin

2 teaspoons chili powder

1 garlic clove, minced

1/4 teaspoon salt

6 flour tortillas (8 inches), warmed

Shredded lettuce and chopped tomatoes, optional

1 In a 3-qt. slow cooker, combine the chicken, beans, tomatoes, peppers, onion and seasonings. Cover and cook on low for 5-6 hours or until chicken is tender.

2 Remove chicken; cool slightly. Shred chicken and return to the slow cooker; heat through.

3 Spoon about 3/4 cup chicken mixture down the center of each tortilla. Top with lettuce and tomatoes if desired.

Yield: 6 servings.

Spicy Beans with Turkey Sausage

(pictured above)

PREP: 25 MIN. ■ **COOK:** 5 HOURS

Dorothy Jordan
College Station, Texas
Here's a jambalaya-type supper that comes together quickly. It's a wonderful way to warm up cold winter nights and works equally well for casual get-togethers or family dinners. For extra pizzazz, top with sour cream or shredded cheese, or try it with a loaf of crusty bread.

1 pound smoked turkey sausage, halved lengthwise and cut into 1/2-inch slices

1 can (16 ounces) kidney beans, rinsed and drained

1 can (15-1/2 ounces) great northern beans, rinsed and drained

1 can (15 ounces) black beans, rinsed and drained

1-1/2 cups frozen corn

1-1/2 cups salsa

1 large green pepper, chopped

1 large onion, chopped

1/2 to 1 cup water

3 garlic cloves, minced

1 teaspoon ground cumin

1 In a 5-qt. slow cooker, combine all the ingredients. Cover and cook on low for 5-6 hours or until sausage is cooked through. Stir before serving.

Yield: 6 servings.

King-Size Drumsticks

PREP: 15 MIN. ■ **COOK:** 8-1/4 HOURS

Taste of Home Test Kitchen
Let your slow cooker do the work for you when these tender turkey legs make an appearance at supper. Canned enchilada sauce, green chilies and cumin give this lip-smacking entree a zesty treatment.

1 can (10 ounces) enchilada sauce

1 can (4 ounces) chopped green chilies, drained

1 teaspoon dried oregano

1/2 teaspoon garlic salt

1/2 teaspoon ground cumin

6 turkey drumsticks (12 ounces each), skin removed

3 tablespoons cornstarch

3 tablespoons cold water

1 In a large bowl, combine the enchilada sauce, chilies, oregano, garlic salt and cumin. Place the drumsticks in a 5-qt. slow cooker; top with sauce. Cover and cook on low for 8-10 hours or until a meat thermometer reads 180°.

2 Remove turkey to a serving platter; keep warm. Skim fat from cooking juices; transfer to a small saucepan. Bring liquid to a boil. Combine cornstarch and water until smooth. Gradually stir into the pan. Bring to a boil; cook and stir for 2 minutes or until thickened. Serve with turkey drumsticks.

Yield: 6 servings.

Add a splash of spiciness. If you would like to make the drumsticks a bit spicier, use a hot enchilada sauce. Or add a few drops of hot pepper sauce or a sprinkle of chili powder or cayenne pepper to the dish.

Tangy Chicken Thighs

(pictured above)

PREP: 25 MIN. ■ **COOK:** 4-3/4 HOURS

dutchmom4MI
Taste of Home Online Community
I love this recipe because it turns affordable chicken thighs into a rich and delicious meal. The sauce is what makes this dish, because it's creamy and tangy. A crisp salad or fresh vegetable rounds out the meal.

1 envelope Italian salad dressing mix

1/2 teaspoon pepper

6 boneless skinless chicken thighs (about 1-1/2 pounds)

2 tablespoons butter, melted

1 large onion, chopped

2 garlic cloves, minced

1 can (10-3/4 ounces) condensed cream of chicken soup, undiluted

1 package (8 ounces) cream cheese, softened and cubed

1/4 cup chicken broth

Hot cooked noodles or rice, optional

1 Combine salad dressing mix and pepper. In a 3-qt. slow cooker, layer half of the chicken, butter, salad dressing mixture, onion and garlic. Repeat layers. Cover and cook on low for 4-5 hours or until chicken is tender. Skim fat from cooking juices.

2 In a small bowl, combine the soup, cream cheese and broth until blended; add to slow cooker. Cover and cook for 45 minutes or until heated through.

3 Remove chicken to a serving platter; stir sauce until smooth. Serve chicken with sauce and noodles or rice if desired.

Yield: 6 servings.

Chicken Merlot with Mushrooms

(pictured above)

PREP: 10 MIN. ■ **COOK:** 5 HOURS

Shelli McWilliam
Salem, Oregon

This dish is perfect for any night of the week. It is sure to become a staple in your home.

3/4 pound sliced fresh mushrooms

1 large onion, chopped

2 garlic cloves, minced

3 pounds boneless skinless chicken thighs

1 can (6 ounces) tomato paste

3/4 cup chicken broth

1/4 cup merlot or additional chicken broth

2 tablespoons quick-cooking tapioca

2 teaspoons sugar

1-1/2 teaspoons dried basil

1/2 teaspoon salt

1/4 teaspoon pepper

2 tablespoons grated Parmesan cheese

Hot cooked pasta, optional

1 Place the mushrooms, onion and garlic in a 5-qt. slow cooker. Top with chicken.

2 In a small bowl, combine the tomato paste, broth, wine, tapioca, sugar, basil, salt and pepper. Pour over chicken. Cover and cook on low for 5-6 hours or until chicken is tender. Sprinkle with cheese. Serve with pasta if desired.

Yield: 5 servings.

Fiesta Chicken Burritos

PREP: 30 MIN. ■ **COOK:** 4-1/4 HOURS

Margaret Latta
Paducah, Kentucky

Looking for some heat with supper but still want a cool kitchen? Try these slow cooker burritos with a spicy touch the whole family will love! And for those who prefer a spicier dish, add a teaspoon of cayenne pepper.

1-1/2 pounds boneless skinless chicken breasts

1 can (15-1/4 ounces) whole kernel corn, drained

1 can (15 ounces) black beans, rinsed and drained

1 can (10 ounces) diced tomatoes and green chilies, undrained

1 jalapeno pepper, seeded and finely chopped

3 tablespoons ground cumin

1 teaspoon salt

1 teaspoon paprika

1/2 teaspoon pepper

Dash cayenne pepper

Dash crushed red pepper flakes

1 package (8 ounces) reduced-fat cream cheese

8 flour tortillas (8 inches), warmed

Optional toppings: sour cream, shredded cheddar cheese, shredded lettuce and chopped tomatoes

1 Place chicken in a greased 4-qt. slow cooker. In a large bowl, combine the corn, beans, tomatoes, jalapeno and seasonings; pour over chicken. Cover and cook on low for 4-5 hours or until chicken is tender.

2 Remove chicken; cool slightly. Shred meat with two forks and return to the slow cooker. Stir in cream cheese. Cover and cook 15 minutes longer or until heated through.

3 Spoon 3/4 cup chicken mixture down the center of each tortilla; add toppings of your choice. Fold sides and ends over filling and roll up.

Yield: 8 servings.

Editor's Note: When cutting hot peppers, disposable gloves are recommended. Avoid touching your face.

Southwest Chicken Chili

PREP: 15 MIN. ■ **COOK:** 6 HOURS

Phyllis Beatty
Chandler, Arizona
Chicken thighs are a nice change-of-pace in this easy chili. I also add a smoked ham hock and fresh cilantro to give the quick-to-fix entree an interesting taste.

1-1/2 pounds boneless skinless chicken thighs, cut into 1-inch cubes
1 tablespoon olive oil
1 smoked ham hock
1 can (15-1/2 ounces) great northern beans, rinsed and drained
1 can (14-1/2 ounces) chicken broth
1 can (4 ounces) chopped green chilies
1/4 cup chopped onion
2 tablespoons minced fresh cilantro
1 teaspoon garlic powder
1 teaspoon ground cumin
1/2 teaspoon dried oregano
1/8 to 1/4 teaspoon crushed red pepper flakes
Sour cream, optional

1 In a large skillet, brown chicken in oil. Transfer to a 3-qt. slow cooker.

2 Add the ham hock, beans, broth, chilies, onion and seasonings. Cover and cook on low for 6 to 8 hours or until the ham is tender.

3 Remove ham bone. When cool enough to handle, remove meat from bone; discard bone. Cut meat into bite-size pieces and return to slow cooker. Serve with sour cream if desired.

Yield: 5 servings.

Chicken Cacciatore

(pictured above)

PREP: 20 MIN. ■ **COOK:** 4 HOURS

Denise Hollebeke
Penhold, Alberta
Here's an all-time favorite Italian dish. Dried herbs and fresh garlic give it an aromatic flavor. Green pepper, sliced mushrooms and diced tomatoes do a fine job of rounding out the juicy chicken entree.

1/3 cup all-purpose flour
1 broiler/fryer chicken (3 to 4 pounds), cut up
2 tablespoons canola oil
2 medium onions, cut into wedges
1 medium green pepper, cut into strips
1 jar (6 ounces) sliced mushrooms, drained
1 can (14-1/2 ounces) diced tomatoes, undrained
2 garlic cloves, minced
1/2 teaspoon salt
1/2 teaspoon dried oregano
1/4 teaspoon dried basil
1/2 cup shredded Parmesan cheese

1 Place flour in a large resealable plastic bag. Add chicken, a few pieces at a time, and shake to coat. In a large skillet, brown chicken in oil on all sides. Transfer to a 5-qt. slow cooker.

2 Top with onions, green pepper and mushrooms. In a small bowl, combine the tomatoes, garlic, salt, oregano and basil; pour over vegetables. Cover and cook on low for 4-5 hours or until chicken juices run clear and vegetables are tender. Serve with cheese.

Yield: 6 servings.

Turkey Sloppy Joes

(pictured above)

PREP: 15 MIN. ■ **COOK:** 4 HOURS

Marylou LaRue
Freeland, Michigan

This tangy sandwich filling is so easy to prepare, and it goes over well at gatherings large and small. I frequently take it to potlucks, and I'm always asked for the recipe.

1 pound ground turkey breast
1 small onion, chopped
1/2 cup chopped celery
1/4 cup chopped green pepper
1 can (10-3/4 ounces) reduced-sodium condensed tomato soup, undiluted
1/2 cup ketchup
1 tablespoon brown sugar
2 tablespoons prepared mustard
1/4 teaspoon pepper
8 hamburger buns, split

1 In a large saucepan coated with cooking spray, cook the turkey, onion, celery and green pepper over medium heat until meat is no longer pink; drain if necessary. Stir in the soup, ketchup, brown sugar, mustard and pepper. Transfer to a 3-qt. slow cooker. Cover and cook on low for 4 hours. Serve on buns.

Yield: 8 servings.

Saucy Mandarin Duck

PREP: 30 MIN. + MARINATING
COOK: 4-3/4 HOURS

Taste of Home Test Kitchen

For something a little different, try this savory, sweet duck dish that is flavored with Asian seasonings and mandarin oranges. For a little flair, garnish each serving with toasted sesame seeds.

1 can (14-1/2 ounces) beef broth
1/3 cup tomato paste
2 tablespoons brown sugar
2 tablespoons orange juice concentrate
2 tablespoons soy sauce
2 garlic cloves, minced
1/2 teaspoon salt
1/4 teaspoon pepper
1/8 teaspoon ground allspice
1 domestic duck (4 to 4-1/2 pounds), skinned, deboned and cut into cubes
1/4 pound sliced fresh mushrooms
1/2 cup green pepper strips (1/4-inch thick)
1 tablespoon butter
3 tablespoons cornstarch
1/4 teaspoon ground ginger
1/4 cup 2% milk
1 can (11 ounces) mandarin oranges, drained
Hot cooked rice, optional

1 For marinade, in a small bowl, combine the broth, tomato paste, brown sugar, juice concentrate, soy sauce, garlic, salt, pepper and allspice. Pour 3/4 cup into a large resealable plastic bag; add the duck. Seal bag and turn to coat; refrigerate for 8 hours. Cover and refrigerate remaining marinade.

2 Drain and discard marinade from duck. Transfer duck to a 1-1/2-qt. slow cooker; add reserved marinade. Cover and cook on low for 4-5 hours or until duck is tender.

3 Skim fat from cooking juices. In a small saucepan, saute mushrooms and green pepper in butter. Combine the cornstarch, ginger and milk until smooth. Stir into mushroom mixture; add to slow cooker.

4 Cover and cook on high for 45 minutes or until sauce is thickened. Just before serving, stir in oranges. Serve with rice if desired.

Yield: 3 servings.

Moist & Tender Turkey Breast

PREP: 10 MIN. ■ **COOK:** 4 HOURS

Heidi Vawdrey
Riverton, Utah

There's no need for a special occasion to serve a turkey dinner. This dish will be very popular in your home...your family will love the taste and you will love how quickly it comes together.

1 bone-in turkey breast (6 to 7 pounds)
4 fresh rosemary sprigs
4 garlic cloves, peeled
1 tablespoon brown sugar
1/2 teaspoon coarsely ground pepper
1/4 teaspoon salt

1 Cut turkey breast in half along the bone; place in a greased 6-qt. slow cooker. Place rosemary and garlic around turkey. Combine the brown sugar, pepper and salt; sprinkle over turkey. Cover and cook on low for 4 to 6 hours or until a meat thermometer reads 170°.

Yield: 12 servings.

Sprouting garlic. Sometimes garlic has green sprouts. If you notice these sprouts, cut the garlic clove in half and remove the sprout before you use the clove.

Sausage and Vegetables

PREP: 20 MIN. ■ **COOK:** 5-1/2 HOURS

Ginny Stuby
Altoona, Pennsylvania
This easy and complete meal-in-a-pot is both healthy and delicious. It's wonderful served with a slice of Italian or hot garlic bread. I found the recipe in a magazine and made just a few adjustments to suit my tastes.

1-1/4 pounds sweet or hot Italian turkey sausage links

1 can (28 ounces) diced tomatoes, undrained

2 medium potatoes, cut into 1-inch pieces

4 small zucchini, cut into 1-inch slices

1 medium onion, cut into wedges

1/2 teaspoon garlic powder

1/4 teaspoon crushed red pepper flakes

1/4 teaspoon dried oregano

1/4 teaspoon dried basil

1 tablespoon dry bread crumbs

3/4 cup shredded pepper Jack cheese

1 In a nonstick skillet, cook sausages over medium heat until no longer pink; drain. Place in a 5-qt. slow cooker. Add vegetables and seasonings. Cover and cook on low for 5-1/2 to 6-1/2 hours or until vegetables are tender.

2 Remove sausages and cut into 1-in. pieces; return to slow cooker. Stir in bread crumbs. Serve in bowls; sprinkle with cheese.

Yield: 6 servings.

Curried Chicken With Peaches

PREP: 15 MIN. ■ **COOK:** 3-1/4 HOURS

Heidi Martinez
Colorado Springs, Colorado
I'm always looking for meals I can prepare ahead of time. The chicken chunks bask for hours in snappy spices and seasonings, giving this supper a lot of pizzazz, and the peaches round out the amazing flavors.

1 broiler/fryer chicken (3 pounds), cut up

1/8 teaspoon salt

1/8 teaspoon pepper

1 can (29 ounces) sliced peaches

1/2 cup chicken broth

2 tablespoons butter, melted

1 tablespoon dried minced onion

2 teaspoons curry powder

2 garlic cloves, minced

1/4 teaspoon ground ginger

3 tablespoons cornstarch

3 tablespoons cold water

1/4 cup raisins

Toasted flaked coconut, optional

1 Place chicken in a 5-qt. slow cooker; sprinkle with salt and pepper. Drain peaches, reserving 1/2 cup juice; set peaches aside. In a small bowl, combine the broth, butter, onion, curry, garlic, ginger and reserved juice; pour over chicken. Cover and cook on low for 3-4 hours or until chicken juices run clear.

2 Remove chicken to a serving platter; keep warm. Mix cornstarch and water until smooth; stir into cooking juices. Add raisins. Cover and cook on high for 10-15 minutes or until gravy is thickened. Stir in peaches; heat through. Serve with chicken. Garnish with coconut if desired.

Yield: 4 servings.

Lemonade Chicken

(pictured above)

PREP: 10 MIN. ■ **COOK:** 3-1/4 HOURS

Jenny Cook
Eau Claire, Wisconsin
I don't know where this recipe originally came from, but my mother used to make it for our family when I was little, and now I love to serve it to my family. A sweet and tangy sauce nicely coats chicken that's ready to serve in just a few hours.

6 boneless skinless chicken breast halves (4 ounces each)

3/4 cup thawed lemonade concentrate

3 tablespoons ketchup

2 tablespoons brown sugar

1 tablespoon cider vinegar

2 tablespoons cornstarch

2 tablespoons cold water

1 Place chicken in a 5-qt. slow cooker. In a small bowl, combine the lemonade concentrate, ketchup, brown sugar and vinegar; pour over chicken. Cover and cook on low for 2-1/2 to 3 hours or until chicken is tender.

2 Remove chicken and keep warm. For gravy, combine cornstarch and water until smooth; stir into cooking juices. Cover and cook on high for 30 minutes or until thickened. Return chicken to the slow cooker; heat through.

Yield: 6 servings.

Italian Sausage Sandwiches

PREP: 10 MIN. ■ **COOK:** 4 HOURS

Taste of Home Test Kitchen
Need a different type of sandwich for a party? Try this recipe and every one will be complimenting these great-tasting sandwiches.

2 jars (26 ounces each) meatless spaghetti sauce

2 medium green peppers, cut into strips

2 medium onions, thinly sliced

1/2 teaspoon garlic powder

1/2 teaspoon fennel seed, crushed

2 packages (20 ounces each) Italian turkey sausage links

10 sandwich buns, split

1 In a 3-qt. slow cooker, combine the spaghetti sauce, green peppers, onions, garlic powder and fennel seed. Cover and cook on low for 4 hours or until vegetables are tender.

2 Grill sausages according to package directions. Serve on buns with sauce.

Yield: 10 servings.

Harvest Chicken with Walnut Gremolata

(pictured at left)
PREP: 25 MIN. ■ **COOK:** 5-1/4 HOURS

Patricia Harmon
Baden, Pennsylvania
This recipe is based on a classic veal or lamb dish. It's an elegant, complete dinner.

1 medium butternut squash (about 3 pounds), peeled and cubed

1 can (14-1/2 ounces) diced tomatoes, drained

1 medium onion, chopped

1 celery rib, chopped

1/2 cup reduced-sodium chicken broth

1/4 cup white wine or additional reduced-sodium chicken broth

1 garlic clove, minced

1 teaspoon Italian seasoning

1/4 teaspoon coarsely ground pepper, divided

1/4 cup all-purpose flour

1 teaspoon seasoned salt

6 chicken drumsticks, skin removed

1 cup uncooked orzo pasta

GREMOLATA:

2 tablespoons finely chopped walnuts

2 tablespoons minced fresh parsley

1 garlic clove, minced

1 teaspoon grated lemon peel

1 In a 5-qt. slow cooker, combine the first eight ingredients and 1/8 teaspoon pepper.

2 In a large resealable plastic bag, combine the flour, seasoned salt and remaining pepper. Add chicken, a few pieces at a time, and shake to coat. Place chicken on top of vegetables. Cover and cook on low for 5 hours or until chicken juices run clear. Remove chicken and keep warm.

3 Stir orzo into vegetable mixture; cover and cook 15-20 minutes longer or until orzo is tender. Meanwhile, combine gremolata ingredients.

4 Transfer vegetable mixture to a platter; top with chicken. Sprinkle with gremolata.

Yield: 6 servings.

Coconut Curry Chicken

PREP: 20 MIN. ■ **COOK:** 5 HOURS

Andi Kauffman
Beavercreek, Oregon
My husband and I love this yummy entree! It's a breeze to prepare, and it tastes just like a meal you'd have at your favorite Indian or Thai restaurant.

2 medium potatoes, peeled and cubed

1 small onion, chopped

4 boneless skinless chicken breast halves
(4 ounces each)

1 cup light coconut milk

4 teaspoons curry powder

1 garlic clove, minced

1 teaspoon reduced-sodium chicken bouillon granules

1/4 teaspoon salt

1/4 teaspoon pepper

2 cups hot cooked rice

1/4 cup thinly sliced green onions

Raisins, flaked coconut and chopped unsalted peanuts, optional

1 Place potatoes and onion in a 3- or 4-qt. slow cooker. In a large nonstick skillet coated with cooking spray, brown chicken on both sides. Transfer to slow cooker. In a small bowl, combine the coconut milk, curry, garlic, bouillon, salt and pepper; pour over chicken. Cover and cook on low for 5 hours or until chicken is tender.

2 Serve chicken and sauce with rice; sprinkle with green onions. Garnish with raisins, coconut and peanuts if desired.

Yield: 4 servings.

Citrus Turkey Roast

PREP: 15 MIN. ■ COOK: 5-1/4 HOURS

Kathy Kittell
Lenexa, Kansas
I was skeptical at first about fixing turkey in a slow cooker. But once I tasted this, I was hooked. With a little cornstarch to thicken the juices, the gravy is easy to make.

1 frozen boneless turkey roast, thawed (3 pounds)

1 tablespoon garlic powder

1 tablespoon paprika

1 tablespoon olive oil

2 teaspoons Worcestershire sauce

1/2 teaspoon salt

1/2 teaspoon pepper

8 garlic cloves, peeled

1 cup chicken broth, divided

1/4 cup water

1/4 cup white wine or additional chicken broth

1/4 cup orange juice

1 tablespoon lemon juice

2 tablespoons cornstarch

1 Cut roast in half. Combine the garlic powder, paprika, oil, Worcestershire sauce, salt and pepper; rub over turkey. Place in a 5-qt. slow cooker.

2 Add the garlic, 1/2 cup broth, water, wine, orange juice and lemon juice. Cover and cook on low for 5-6 hours or until a meat thermometer reads 170°.

3 Remove turkey and keep warm. Discard garlic cloves. For gravy, combine cornstarch and remaining broth until smooth; stir into cooking juices. Cover and cook on high for 15 minutes or until thickened. Slice turkey; serve with gravy.

Yield: 12 servings.

Chicken and Red Potatoes

(pictured at left)

PREP: 20 MIN. ■ COOK: 3-1/2 HOURS

Michele Trantham
Waynesville, North Carolina
Try this moist and tender chicken-and-potato dish with its creamy, scrumptious gravy tonight! Just fix it in the morning, then forget about it until dinnertime.

3 tablespoons all-purpose flour

4 boneless skinless chicken breast halves (6 ounces each)

2 tablespoons olive oil

4 medium red potatoes, cut into wedges

2 cups fresh baby carrots, halved lengthwise

1 can (4 ounces) mushroom stems and pieces, drained

4 canned whole green chilies, cut into 1/2-inch slices

1 can (10-3/4 ounces) condensed cream of onion soup, undiluted

1/4 cup 2% milk

1/2 teaspoon chicken seasoning

1/4 teaspoon salt

1/4 teaspoon dried rosemary, crushed

1/4 teaspoon pepper

1 Place flour in a large resealable plastic bag. Add chicken, one piece at a time; shake to coat. In a large skillet, brown chicken in oil on both sides.

2 Meanwhile, place the potatoes, carrots, mushrooms and chilies in a greased 5-qt. slow cooker. In a small bowl, combine the remaining ingredients. Pour half of soup mixture over vegetables.

3 Transfer chicken to slow cooker; top with remaining soup mixture. Cover and cook on low for 3-1/2 to 4 hours or until chicken is tender.

Yield: 4 servings.

Editor's Note: This recipe was tested with McCormick's Montreal Chicken Seasoning. Look for it in the spice aisle.

Satisfying Chicken And Veggies

PREP: 20 MIN. ■ **COOK:** 4 HOURS

Kat Sadi
San Luis Obispo, California
I'm happy to share the recipe for this tasty meal-in-one supper with chicken and vegetables seasoned with herbs. The nice thing about this delicious entree is that cleanup is a breeze.

2 medium potatoes, peeled and cut into 1-inch pieces (about 1-1/2 cups)

1 cup thickly sliced onion

1/2 cup sliced celery

1 medium carrot, cut into 1-inch pieces

1 medium sweet yellow pepper, cut into 1-inch pieces

1 broiler/fryer chicken (3 to 4 pounds), cut up and skin removed

1 jar (26 ounces) meatless spaghetti sauce

1 cup water

1-1/2 teaspoons minced garlic

1/4 teaspoon salt

1/4 teaspoon dried oregano

1/4 teaspoon dried basil

1/4 teaspoon pepper

1 Place the vegetables in a 5-qt. slow cooker. Top with chicken. Combine the remaining ingredients; pour over chicken. Cover and cook on low for 4 to 4-1/2 hours or until chicken juices run clear and vegetables are tender.

Yield: 6 servings.

Herbed Slow Cooker Chicken

(pictured above)

PREP: 5 MIN. ■ **COOK:** 4 HOURS

Sundra Hauck
Bogalusa, Louisiana
These well-seasoned chicken breasts cook up juicy and flavorful. My daughter, who has two young sons to keep up with, shared this great recipe with me several years ago.

1 tablespoon olive oil

1 teaspoon paprika

1/2 teaspoon garlic powder

1/2 teaspoon seasoned salt

1/2 teaspoon dried thyme

1/2 teaspoon dried basil

1/2 teaspoon pepper

1/2 teaspoon browning sauce, optional

4 bone-in chicken breast halves (6 ounces each)

1/2 cup chicken broth

1 In a small bowl, combine the oil, seasonings and browning sauce if desired; rub over chicken. Place in a 5-qt. slow cooker; add broth. Cover and cook on low for 4-5 hours or until chicken is tender.

Yield: 4 servings.

Herbed Chicken And Shrimp

PREP: 15 MIN. ■ **COOK:** 4-1/2 HOURS

Diana Knight
Reno, Nevada

Tender chicken and shrimp make a flavorful combination that's easy to prepare, yet elegant enough to serve at a dinner party. This meal practically cooks itself while I'm busy cleaning the house. I serve it over hot cooked rice with crusty bread and a green salad.

1 teaspoon salt

1 teaspoon pepper

1 broiler/fryer chicken (3 to 4 pounds), cut up and skin removed

1/4 cup butter

1 large onion, chopped

1 can (8 ounces) tomato sauce

1/2 cup white wine or chicken broth

1 garlic clove, minced

1 teaspoon dried basil

1 pound uncooked medium shrimp, peeled and deveined

1 Combine salt and pepper; rub over the chicken pieces. In a large skillet, brown chicken on all sides in butter. Transfer to an ungreased 5-qt. slow cooker.

2 In a large bowl, combine onion, tomato sauce, wine, garlic and basil; pour over chicken. Cover and cook on low for 4-5 hours or until chicken juices run clear.

3 Stir in the shrimp. Cover and cook on high for 20-30 minutes or until shrimp turn pink.

Yield: 4 servings.

Shrimp count. *Shrimp are classified and sold by size. Shrimp count indicates the number of shrimp of a certain size that are in a pound. The terms used to describe the counts are not consistent from store to store, which is why the count is the best indication of size. Medium shrimp have a count of 31 to 40 per pound.*

Slow 'n' Easy Barbecued Chicken

(pictured above)

PREP: 20 MIN. ■ **COOK:** 3-1/4 HOURS

Dreama Hughes
London, Kentucky

I rely on this yummy recipe often during the summer and fall when I know I'm going to be working in the yard all day. I just pair it with a side vegetable. The sauce is also delicious with pork or beef.

1/4 cup water

3 tablespoons brown sugar

3 tablespoons white vinegar

3 tablespoons ketchup

2 tablespoons butter

2 tablespoons Worcestershire sauce

1 tablespoon lemon juice

1 teaspoon salt

1 teaspoon paprika

1 teaspoon ground mustard

1/2 teaspoon cayenne pepper

1 broiler/fryer chicken (2-1/2 to 3 pounds), cut up and skin removed

4 teaspoons cornstarch

1 tablespoon cold water

1 In a small saucepan, combine the water, brown sugar, vinegar, ketchup, butter, Worcestershire sauce, lemon juice and seasonings. Bring to a boil. Reduce heat; simmer, uncovered, for 5 minutes. Remove from the heat.

2 Place the chicken in a 3-qt. slow cooker. Top with sauce. Cover and cook on low for 3-4 hours or until chicken juices run clear.

3 Remove chicken to a serving platter; keep warm. Skim fat from cooking juices; transfer to a small saucepan. Bring liquid to a boil. Combine cornstarch and water until smooth. Gradually stir into the pan. Bring to a boil; cook and stir for 2 minutes or until thickened. Spoon some of the sauce over chicken and serve the remaining sauce on the side.

Yield: 4 servings.

Apple Chicken Stew

PREP: 10 MIN. ■ **COOK:** 4 HOURS

Carol Mathias
Lincoln, Nebraska
We have many local apple orchards. In the fall, we always make sure to pick up some cider. It is the perfect flavor complement to this stew.

- 4 medium potatoes, cubed
- 4 medium carrots, cut into 1/4-inch slices
- 1 medium red onion, halved and sliced
- 1 celery rib, thinly sliced
- 1-1/2 teaspoons salt
- 3/4 teaspoon dried thyme
- 1/2 teaspoon pepper
- 1/4 to 1/2 teaspoon caraway seeds
- 2 pounds boneless skinless chicken breasts, cubed
- 2 tablespoons olive oil
- 1 large tart apple, peeled and cubed
- 1-1/4 cups apple cider or juice
- 1 tablespoon cider vinegar
- 1 bay leaf
- Minced fresh parsley

1 Layer the potatoes, carrots, onion and celery in a 5-qt. slow cooker. Combine the salt, thyme, pepper and caraway; sprinkle half over vegetables.

2 In a large skillet, saute chicken in oil until browned; transfer to slow cooker. Top with apple. In a small bowl, combine apple cider and vinegar; pour over chicken and apple. Sprinkle with remaining salt mixture. Top with bay leaf.

3 Cover and cook on high for 4-5 hours or until chicken and vegetables are tender. Discard bay leaf. Stir before serving. Sprinkle with parsley.

Yield: 6-8 servings.

Orange Chicken With Sweet Potatoes

(pictured above)
PREP: 25 MIN. ■ **COOK:** 3-1/2 HOURS

Vicki Smith
Okeechobee, Florida
Orange peel and pineapple juice lend a fruity taste to this super chicken and sweet potato dish. Served over rice, this appealing entree is bound to win you compliments.

- 3 medium sweet potatoes, peeled and sliced
- 2/3 cup plus 3 tablespoons all-purpose flour, divided
- 1 teaspoon salt
- 1 teaspoon onion powder
- 1 teaspoon ground nutmeg
- 1 teaspoon ground cinnamon
- 1 teaspoon pepper
- 4 boneless skinless chicken breast halves (5 ounces each)
- 2 tablespoons butter
- 1 can (10-3/4 ounces) condensed cream of chicken soup, undiluted
- 3/4 cup unsweetened pineapple juice
- 2 teaspoons brown sugar
- 1 teaspoon grated orange peel
- 1/2 pound sliced fresh mushrooms
- Hot cooked rice

1 Layer sweet potatoes in a 3-qt. slow cooker. In a large resealable plastic bag, combine 2/3 cup flour and seasonings; add chicken, one piece at a time, and shake to coat. In a large skillet over medium heat, cook chicken in butter for 3 minutes on each side or until lightly browned. Arrange chicken over sweet potatoes.

2 Place remaining flour in a small bowl. Stir in the soup, pineapple juice, brown sugar and orange peel until blended. Add mushrooms; pour over chicken. Cover and cook on low for 3-1/2 to 4 hours or until chicken and potatoes are tender. Serve with rice.

Yield: 4 servings.

Lime Chicken Tacos

PREP: 10 MIN. ■ **COOK:** 5-1/2 HOURS

Tracy Gunter
Boise, Idaho
Lime adds zest to this easy filling for tortillas, and leftovers would be a refreshing topping to any taco salad as well.

1-1/2 pounds boneless skinless chicken breasts

3 tablespoons lime juice

1 tablespoon chili powder

1 cup frozen corn

1 cup chunky salsa

12 flour tortillas (6 inches), warmed

Sour cream, shredded cheddar cheese and shredded lettuce, optional

1 Place the chicken in a 3-qt. slow cooker. Combine the lime juice and chili powder; pour over the chicken. Cover and cook on low for 5-6 hours or until the chicken is tender.

2 Remove chicken; cool slightly. Shred meat with two forks and return to the slow cooker. Stir in corn and salsa. Cover and cook on low for 30 minutes or until heated through. Serve in tortillas with sour cream, cheese and lettuce if desired.

Yield: 12 tacos.

> **How much juice in a lime?** The average lime will yield about 2 tablespoons of juice. You'll need two limes for Lime Chicken Tacos. Any leftover juice can be frozen in an airtight container for future use.

Chicken Stew With Gnocchi

PREP: 25 MIN ■ **COOK:** 6-1/2 HOURS

Marge Drake
Juniata, Nebraska
My chicken stew makes the house smell wonderful as it gently bubbles in the slow cooker. One whiff and my family heads to the kitchen to see if it's ready.

3 medium parsnips, peeled and cut into 1/2-inch pieces

2 large carrots, cut into 1/2-inch slices

2 celery ribs, chopped

1 large sweet potato, peeled and cut into 1-inch cubes

4 green onions, chopped

3 pounds bone-in chicken thighs, skin removed

1/2 teaspoon dried sage leaves

1/4 teaspoon salt

1/4 teaspoon pepper

4 cups chicken broth

1 cup water

3 tablespoons cornstarch

1/4 cup cold water

1 package (16 ounces) potato gnocchi

Hot pepper sauce, optional

1 Place the parsnips, carrots, celery, sweet potato and onions in a 5-qt. slow cooker. Top with chicken; sprinkle with the sage, salt and pepper. Add broth and water. Cover and cook on low for 6 hours or until chicken is tender.

2 Remove chicken; when cool enough to handle, remove meat from bones and discard bones. Cut meat into bite-size pieces and return to the slow cooker.

3 Mix cornstarch and cold water until smooth; stir into stew. Add gnocchi. Cover and cook on high for 30 minutes or until thickened. Season with hot pepper sauce if desired.

Yield: 8 servings (3 quarts).

Southwest Turkey Stew

(pictured above)
PREP: 15 MIN. ■ **COOK:** 5 HOURS

Stephanie Hutchinson
Helix, Oregon
I prefer main dishes that enable me to stay on my diet but still eat what the rest of the family eats. This stew is a hit with my husband and our young children.

1-1/2 pounds turkey breast tenderloins, cubed

2 teaspoons canola oil

1 can (15 ounces) turkey chili with beans, undrained

1 can (14-1/2 ounces) diced tomatoes

1 medium sweet red pepper, cut into 3/4-inch pieces

1 medium green pepper, cut into 3/4-inch pieces

3/4 cup chopped onion

3/4 cup salsa

3 garlic cloves, minced

1-1/2 teaspoons chili powder

1/2 teaspoon salt

1/2 teaspoon ground cumin

1 tablespoon minced fresh cilantro, optional

1 In a nonstick skillet, brown turkey in oil; transfer to a 3-qt. slow cooker. Stir in the chili, tomatoes, peppers, onion, salsa, garlic, chili powder, salt and cumin. Cover and cook on low for 5-6 hours or until turkey is tender. Garnish with cilantro if desired.

Yield: 6 servings.

Greek Chicken Dinner

PREP: 20 MIN. ■ COOK: 5-1/4 HOURS

Terri Christensen
Montague, Michigan
I got this dish from my sister, and my family really likes it a lot. The amount of garlic might seem high, but it's just right. You get every bit of the flavor without it overpowering the chicken.

---

6 medium Yukon Gold potatoes, quartered

1 broiler/fryer chicken (3-1/2 pounds), cut up and skin removed

2 large onions, quartered

1 whole garlic bulb, separated and peeled

3 teaspoons dried oregano

1 teaspoon salt

3/4 teaspoon pepper

1/2 cup plus 1 tablespoon water, divided

1 tablespoon olive oil

4 teaspoons cornstarch

1 Place potatoes in a 5-qt. slow cooker. Add the chicken, onions and garlic. Combine the oregano, salt, pepper and 1/2 cup water; pour over chicken and vegetables. Drizzle with oil. Cover and cook on low for 5-6 hours or until chicken juices run clear and vegetables are tender.

2 Remove chicken and vegetables to a serving platter; keep warm. Strain cooking juices and skim fat; transfer to a small saucepan. Bring liquid to a boil. Combine cornstarch and remaining water until smooth. Gradually stir into the pan. Bring to a boil; cook and stir for 2 minutes or until thickened. Serve with chicken and vegetables.

Yield: 6 servings.

Prosciutto Chicken Cacciatore

(pictured above)

PREP: 30 MIN. ■ COOK: 4 HOURS

Sandra Putnam
Corvallis, Montana
I tailored my mother's recipe for this hearty entree to slow cooker convenience. It's great for busy weeknights.

---

2 pounds boneless skinless chicken thighs

1-1/2 pounds boneless skinless chicken breast halves

1/2 cup all-purpose flour

1 teaspoon salt

1/4 teaspoon pepper

3 tablespoons olive oil

1 can (14-1/2 ounces) chicken broth

1 can (14-1/2 ounces) diced tomatoes, undrained

1 cup sliced fresh mushrooms

1 medium onion, chopped

1 package (3 ounces) thinly sliced prosciutto or deli ham, coarsely chopped

1 tablespoon diced pimientos

2 garlic cloves, minced

1/2 teaspoon Italian seasoning

Hot cooked linguine

Grated Parmesan cheese

1 Cut chicken into serving-size pieces. In a large resealable plastic bag, combine the flour, salt and pepper. Add chicken, a few pieces at a time, and shake to coat. In a large skillet, brown chicken in oil in batches. Transfer to a 5-qt. slow cooker.

2 Stir in the broth, tomatoes, mushrooms, onion, prosciutto, pimientos, garlic and Italian seasoning. Cover and cook on low for 4 to 4-1/2 hours or until chicken juices run clear. Serve with a slotted spoon over linguine; sprinkle with cheese.

Yield: 6-8 servings.

Turkey with Mushroom Sauce

PREP: 10 MIN. ■ **COOK:** 7-1/4 HOURS

Myra Innes
Auburn, Kansas
When we were first married, I didn't have an oven, so I made this tender turkey in the slow cooker. These days, I rely on this recipe because it frees up the oven to make other dishes for large get-togethers.

---

1 boneless turkey breast (3 pounds), cut in half

2 tablespoons butter, melted

2 tablespoons dried parsley flakes

1/2 teaspoon salt

1/2 teaspoon dried tarragon

1/8 teaspoon pepper

1 jar (4-1/2 ounces) sliced mushrooms, drained
or 1 cup sliced fresh mushrooms

1/2 cup white wine or chicken broth

2 tablespoons cornstarch

1/4 cup cold water

1 Place the turkey skin side up in a 5-qt. slow cooker. Brush with butter. Sprinkle with the parsley, salt, tarragon and pepper. Top with the mushrooms. Pour wine over all. Cover and cook on low for 7-8 hours or until a meat thermometer reads 170°.

2 Remove turkey to a serving platter; keep warm. Skim fat from cooking juices; transfer to a small saucepan. Bring liquid to a boil. Combine cornstarch and cold water until smooth. Gradually stir into the pan. Bring to a boil; cook and stir for 2 minutes or until thickened. Serve with turkey.

Yield: 8 servings.

> **Thawing a turkey breast.** The turkey breast should be completely thawed before it is cooked. Allow at least 24 hours to thaw the turkey breast in the refrigerator. To thaw in cold water, place the turkey breast in a waterproof bag. Submerge in cold water for 30 minutes. Repeat with fresh cold water every 30 minutes until the meat is thawed.

Chicken and Peppers

PREP: 20 MIN. ■ **COOK:** 4 HOURS

Brenda Nolen
Simpsonville, South Carolina

I put this recipe together one day when I had leftover peppers and wanted something easy with tomatoes. To my delight, the taste reminds me of pizza...something I love but can no longer eat! It's great with steamed broccoli.

**6 boneless skinless chicken breast halves
(4 ounces each)**

1 jar (26 ounces) garden-style spaghetti sauce

1 medium onion, sliced

1/2 each small green, sweet yellow and red peppers, julienned

1/4 cup grated Parmesan cheese

2 garlic cloves, minced

1 teaspoon dried oregano

1 teaspoon dried basil

1/2 teaspoon salt

1/4 teaspoon pepper

4-1/2 cups uncooked spiral pasta

Shaved Parmesan cheese, optional

1 Place chicken in a 3-qt. slow cooker. In a large bowl, combine the spaghetti sauce, onion, peppers, cheese, garlic, oregano, basil, salt and pepper. Pour over chicken. Cover and cook on low for 4-5 hours or until chicken is tender.

2 Meanwhile, cook pasta according to package directions; drain. Serve chicken with pasta and sauce. Top with shaved Parmesan cheese if desired.

Yield: 6 servings.

Sweet and Saucy Chicken

PREP: 30 MIN. ■ **COOK:** 6 HOURS

Patricia Weir
Chilliwack, British Columbia
I can't remember where this dish came from, but I've been making it for several years. Everyone who tries it enjoys it. When the chicken is done cooking, it's so tender it falls off the bone.

- 1 broiler/fryer chicken (4 pounds),
  cut up and skin removed
- 3/4 cup packed brown sugar
- 1/4 cup all-purpose flour
- 2/3 cup water
- 1/3 cup white vinegar
- 1/3 cup reduced-sodium soy sauce
- 2 tablespoons ketchup
- 1 tablespoon dried minced onion
- 1 teaspoon prepared mustard
- 1/4 teaspoon garlic powder
- 1/4 teaspoon salt
- 1/4 teaspoon pepper
- Hot cooked rice or egg noodles, optional

1 Place chicken in a 3-qt. slow cooker. In a small saucepan, combine brown sugar and flour. Stir in the water, vinegar and soy sauce. Add the ketchup, onion, mustard, garlic powder, salt and pepper. Bring to a boil; cook and stir for 1-2 minutes or until thickened.

2 Pour sauce over chicken. Cover and cook on low for 6-8 hours or until the chicken juices run clear. Serve with rice or noodles if desired.

Yield: 6 servings.

Fruited Chicken

(pictured above)

PREP: 10 MIN. ■ **COOK:** 4 HOURS

Mirien Church
Aurora, Colorado
I've worked full-time for more than 30 years, and this super entree has been a lifesaver. It smells heavenly while it is simmering.

- 1 large onion, sliced
- 6 boneless skinless chicken
  breast halves (6 ounces each)
- 1/3 cup orange juice
- 2 tablespoons soy sauce
- 2 tablespoons Worcestershire
  sauce
- 2 tablespoons Dijon mustard
- 1 tablespoon grated
  orange peel
- 2 garlic cloves, minced
- 1/2 cup chopped dried
  apricots
- 1/2 cup dried cranberries
- Hot cooked rice

1 Place onion and chicken in a 5-qt. slow cooker. In a small bowl, combine the orange juice, soy sauce, Worcestershire sauce, mustard, orange peel and garlic; pour over chicken. Sprinkle with apricots and cranberries. Cover and cook on low for 4-5 hours or until chicken is tender. Serve with rice.

Yield: 6 servings.

Honey Pineapple Chicken

PREP: 15 MIN. ■ **COOK:** 3 HOURS

Carol Gillespie
Chambersburg, Pennsylvania
Sweet pineapple and salty soy sauce season this flavorful chicken entree. I adapted the idea from a stovetop recipe.

> **3 pounds boneless skinless chicken breast halves**
>
> **2 tablespoons canola oil**
>
> **1 can (8 ounces) unsweetened crushed pineapple, undrained**
>
> **1 cup packed brown sugar**
>
> **1/2 cup honey**
>
> **1/3 cup lemon juice**
>
> **1/4 cup butter, melted**
>
> **2 tablespoons prepared mustard**
>
> **2 teaspoons soy sauce**

1 In a large skillet, brown chicken in oil in batches on both sides; transfer to a 5-qt. slow cooker. Combine the remaining ingredients; pour over chicken. Cover and cook on low for 3-4 hours or until chicken is tender.

2 Strain pan juices, reserving pineapple. Serve pineapple with the chicken.

Yield: 12 servings.

Moist Drumsticks

(pictured above)
PREP: 10 MIN. ■ **COOK:** 5-1/4 HOURS

Lianne Felton
Riverside, California
I found this in my mom's recipe box years ago. It's very quick to prepare and gives the house a wonderful aroma while it's cooking. My daughter, Molly, just loves it!

> **3 pounds chicken drumsticks, skin removed**
>
> **1 can (8 ounces) tomato sauce**
>
> **1/2 cup soy sauce**
>
> **1/4 cup packed brown sugar**
>
> **1 teaspoon minced garlic**
>
> **3 tablespoons cornstarch**
>
> **1/4 cup cold water**

1 Place drumsticks in a 5-qt. slow cooker. In a small bowl, combine the tomato sauce, soy sauce, brown sugar and garlic; pour over chicken. Cover and cook on low for 5-6 hours or until chicken juices run clear.

2 Remove chicken and vegetables to a serving platter; keep warm. Skim fat from cooking juices; transfer to a small saucepan. Bring liquid to a boil. Combine cornstarch and water until smooth. Gradually stir into the pan. Bring to a boil; cook and stir for 2 minutes or until thickened. Serve with chicken.

Yield: 6 servings.

> ***Removing chicken skin.*** *It can be hard to get a secure grip on uncooked chicken skin. One of the easiest ways to remove the skin from drumsticks is to grip the skin at the wide end of the drumstick with a paper towel. Then pull it back over the drumstick to the narrow end, pulling it completely off the meat.*

Soft Chicken Tacos

PREP: 30 MIN. ■ **COOK:** 5-1/4 HOURS

Cheryl Newendorp
Pella, Iowa
My family loves these tacos. The chicken also makes a great topping for salad.

1 broiler/fryer chicken (3-1/2 pounds), cut up and skin removed
1 can (8 ounces) tomato sauce
1 can (4 ounces) chopped green chilies
1/3 cup chopped onion
2 tablespoons chili powder
2 tablespoons Worcestershire sauce
1/4 teaspoon garlic powder
10 flour tortillas (8 inches), warmed
1-1/4 cups shredded cheddar cheese
1-1/4 cups salsa
1-1/4 cups shredded lettuce
1 large tomato, chopped
3/4 cup sour cream, optional

1 Place the chicken in a 3-qt. slow cooker. In a small bowl, combine the tomato sauce, chilies, onion, chili powder, Worcestershire sauce and garlic powder; pour over the chicken. Cover and cook on low for 5-6 hours or until the chicken juices run clear.

2 Remove chicken; cool slightly. Shred with two forks and return to the slow cooker; heat through. Spoon 1/2 cup chicken mixture down the center of each tortilla. Top with cheese, salsa, lettuce, tomato and sour cream if desired; roll up.

Yield: 5 servings.

Indonesian Peanut Chicken

(pictured above)

PREP: 15 MIN. ■ **COOK:** 4-1/4 HOURS

Sarah Newman
Brooklyn Center, Minnesota
Here's a great make-ahead dinner! I cut up fresh chicken, put it in a bag with the remaining slow-cooker ingredients and freeze. To cook, simply remove the bag a day ahead to thaw in the fridge, then pour all the contents into a slow cooker.

1-1/2 pounds boneless skinless chicken breasts, cut into 1-inch cubes
1/3 cup chopped onion
1/3 cup water
1/4 cup reduced-fat creamy peanut butter
3 tablespoons chili sauce
1/4 teaspoon salt
1/4 teaspoon cayenne pepper
1/4 teaspoon pepper
3 cups cooked brown rice
6 tablespoons chopped salted peanuts
6 tablespoons chopped sweet red pepper

1 Place chicken in a 4-qt. slow cooker. In a small bowl, combine the onion, water peanut butter, chili sauce, salt, cayenne and pepper; pour over chicken. Cover and cook on low for 4-6 hours or until chicken is no longer pink.

2 Remove chicken; cool slightly. Shred meat with two forks and return to slow cooker; heat through. Serve with rice. Sprinkle with peanuts and red pepper.

Yield: 6 servings.

Turkey in Cream Sauce

PREP: 20 MIN. ■ **COOK:** 7-1/4 HOURS

Kathy-Jo Winterbottom
Pottstown, Pennsylvania
I've been relying on this recipe for tender turkey since I first moved out on my own years ago. I serve it whenever I invite new guests to the house, and I'm constantly writing out the recipe.

1-1/4 cups white wine or chicken broth
1 medium onion, chopped
2 garlic cloves, minced
2 bay leaves
2 teaspoons dried rosemary, crushed
1/2 teaspoon pepper
3 turkey breast tenderloins (3/4 pound each)
3 tablespoons cornstarch
1/2 cup half-and-half cream or whole milk
1/2 teaspoon salt

1 In a 3-qt. slow cooker, combine the wine, onion, garlic and bay leaves. Combine rosemary and pepper; rub over turkey. Place in slow cooker. Cover and cook on low for 7-8 hours or until turkey is tender.

2 Remove turkey to a serving platter; keep warm. Strain and skim fat from cooking juices; transfer to a small saucepan. Bring liquid to a boil. Combine the cornstarch, cream and salt until smooth. Gradually stir into the pan. Bring to a boil; cook and stir for 2 minutes or until thickened. Slice turkey; serve with cream sauce.

Yield: 9 servings.

Sweet Pepper Chicken

(pictured above)
PREP: 10 MIN. ■ **COOK:** 4 HOURS

Ann Johnson
Dunn, North Carolina
Sweet red and green pepper strips add attractive color to this delicious chicken. The creamy sauce is great.

6 bone-in chicken breast halves, skin removed
1 tablespoon canola oil
2 cups sliced fresh mushrooms
1 medium onion, halved and sliced
1 medium green pepper, julienned
1 medium sweet red pepper, julienned
1 can (10-3/4 ounces) condensed cream of chicken soup, undiluted
1 can (10-3/4 ounces) condensed cream of mushroom soup, undiluted
Hot cooked rice

1 In a large skillet, brown chicken in oil on both sides. Transfer to a 5-qt. slow cooker. Top with mushrooms, onion and peppers. Combine the soups; pour over vegetables. Cover and cook on low for 4-5 hours or until chicken is tender. Serve with rice.

Yield: 6 servings.

Cornish Hens With Potatoes

PREP: 20 MIN. ■ **COOK:** 6-8 HOURS

Deborah Randall
Abbeville, Louisiana
For a wonderful holiday meal with only a fraction of the work, consider this special and sensational dinner. I serve it with green beans and French bread.

- **4 Cornish game hens (20 ounces each)**
- **2 tablespoons canola oil**
- **4 large red potatoes, cut into 1/8-inch slices**
- **4 bacon strips, cut into 1-inch pieces**
- **Lemon-pepper seasoning and garlic powder to taste**
- **Minced fresh parsley**

1 In a large skillet, brown hens in oil. Place the potatoes in a 5-qt. slow cooker. Top with the hens and bacon. Sprinkle with lemon-pepper and garlic powder.

2 Cover and cook on low for 6-8 hours or until a meat thermometer reads 180° and potatoes are tender. Thicken the cooking juices if desired. Sprinkle the hens with parsley.

Yield: 4 servings.

About Cornish game hens. Cornish game hens are actually chickens that are 4 to 6 weeks old and a hybrid of White Rock and Cornish chickens. These individual serving-size chickens make an elegant presentation. If you wish to have two servings from each hen, then it is best to split the hen in half before cooking.

Slow-Cooked Southwest Chicken

(pictured above)

PREP: 15 MIN. ■ **COOK:** 6-1/4 HOURS

Brandi Castillo
Santa Maria, California
With just 15 minutes of prep, you'll be out of the kitchen in no time. This delectable, low-fat dish gets even better served with reduced-fat sour cream and chopped cilantro.

- **2 cans (15 ounces each) black beans, rinsed and drained**
- **1 can (14-1/2 ounces) reduced-sodium chicken broth**
- **1 can (14-1/2 ounces) diced tomatoes with mild green chilies, undrained**
- **1/2 pound boneless skinless chicken breast**
- **1 jar (8 ounces) chunky salsa**
- **1 cup frozen corn**
- **1 tablespoon dried parsley flakes**
- **1 teaspoon ground cumin**
- **1/4 teaspoon pepper**
- **3 cups hot cooked rice**

1 In a 3-qt. slow cooker, combine the beans, broth, tomatoes, chicken, salsa, corn and seasonings. Cover and cook on low for 6-8 hours or until chicken is tender.

2 Remove chicken; cool slightly. Shred with two forks and return to the slow cooker; heat through. Serve with rice.

Yield: 6 servings.

Herbed Turkey Breasts

PREP: 15 MIN. + MARINATING
COOK: 3-1/2 HOURS

Laurie Mace
Los Ososo, California
Tender, moist turkey breasts are enhanced with fresh sage, thyme and marjoram in this comforting entree.

2 cans (14-1/2 ounces each) chicken broth

1 cup lemon juice

1/2 cup packed brown sugar

1/2 cup fresh sage

1/2 cup minced fresh thyme

1/2 cup lime juice

1/2 cup cider vinegar

1/2 cup olive oil

2 envelopes onion soup mix

1/4 cup Dijon mustard

2 tablespoons minced fresh marjoram

3 teaspoons paprika

2 teaspoons garlic powder

2 teaspoons pepper

1 teaspoon salt

2 boneless turkey breasts (2 pounds each)

1 In a bowl, combine first 15 ingredients. Process mixture in batches in a blender until blended. Pour 3-1/2 cups marinade into a large resealable plastic bag; add the turkey. Seal bag and turn to coat; refrigerate for 8 hours or overnight. Cover and refrigerate remaining marinade.

2 Drain and discard marinade from turkey. Place turkey in a 5-qt. slow cooker; add reserved marinade. Cover and cook on high for 3-1/2 to 4-1/2 hours or until a meat thermometer reads 170°.

Yield: 14-16 servings.

Slow-Cooked Orange Chicken

(pictured above)

PREP: 10 MIN. ■ **COOK:** 4-1/2 HOURS

Nancy Wit
Fremont, Nebraska
I created this recipe in an effort to prepare a dish lower in calories and fat. Everyone likes the taste, including my grandchildren. A hint of orange gives the chicken a citrus flavor. It travels well, and I often take it to potluck suppers.

1 broiler/fryer chicken (3 pounds), cut up and skin removed

3 cups orange juice

1 cup chopped celery

1 cup chopped green pepper

1 can (4 ounces) mushroom stems and pieces, drained

4 teaspoons dried minced onion

1 tablespoon minced fresh parsley or 1 teaspoon dried parsley flakes

1/2 teaspoon salt, optional

1/4 teaspoon pepper

3 tablespoons cornstarch

3 tablespoons cold water

Hot cooked rice, optional

Additional minced fresh parsley, optional

1 Combine the chicken, orange juice, vegetables, parsley, salt if desired and pepper in a 3-qt. slow cooker. Cover and cook on low for 4-5 hours or until chicken juices run clear.

2 Combine cornstarch and water until smooth; stir into cooking liquid. Cover and cook on high for 30-45 minutes or until thickened. Serve with rice and sprinkle with parsley if desired.

Yield: 4 servings.

Chicken, Bean And Rice Nachos

PREP: 20 MIN. ■ **COOK:** 5-1/4 HOURS

Barbara Schweitzer
Chesapeake, Virginia
You can't go wrong with this sure-fire dinnertime hit. When you're craving nachos but need more than a snack, this makes one zesty meal.

1-1/2 pounds boneless skinless chicken breasts
1 jar (16 ounces) salsa
1 can (15 ounces) black beans, rinsed and drained
1 can (7 ounces) Mexicorn, drained
1 package (8 ounces) cream cheese, cubed
3 cups cooked rice
3/4 cup shredded Mexican cheese blend
Tortilla chips

1 Place the chicken in a 3-qt. slow cooker. In a small bowl, combine the salsa, beans and corn; pour over chicken. Cover and cook on low for 5-6 hours or until the chicken is tender.

2 Remove chicken; cool slightly. Shred with two forks and return to slow cooker. Stir in cream cheese; heat through. To serve, place the rice in serving bowls; top with chicken mixture and cheese blend. Serve with tortilla chips.

Yield: 6 servings.

Why rinse beans? The liquid that surrounds canned beans is salty, thick and murky. Rinsing the beans in a colander under cold running water will remove the liquid and excess salt. If you don't rinse the beans, the dish can be too salty and have an undesirable flavor or texture.

Turkey Thigh Supper

(pictured above)

PREP: 10 MIN. ■ **COOK:** 7 HOURS

Betty Gingrich
Oxford, Arkansas
This family-pleasing meal-in-one has it all...delicious, fall-off-the-bone turkey thighs, tasty vegetables and a homemade sauce. You can substitute chicken breasts for the turkey or honey-flavored barbecue sauce for the soup mixture.

3 medium red potatoes, cut into chunks
1/2 pound fresh baby carrots
2 medium onions, cut into chunks
4 turkey thighs, skin removed
1 can (10-3/4 ounces) condensed tomato soup, undiluted
1/3 cup water
1 teaspoon minced garlic
1 teaspoon Italian seasoning
1/2 to 1 teaspoon salt

1 In a 5-qt. slow cooker, layer the potatoes, carrots and onions. Top with turkey. Combine the soup, water, garlic, Italian seasoning and salt; pour over turkey. Cover and cook on high for 7-8 hours or until the turkey juices run clear and vegetables are tender.

Yield: 4 servings.

Turkey Leg Pot Roast

PREP: 15 MIN. ■ **COOK:** 5 HOURS

Rick and Vegas Pearson
Cadillac, Michigan
Well-seasoned turkey legs and tender veggies make this meal ideal for a crisp fall day. Moist and satisfying, this recipe couldn't be more comforting!

- 3 medium potatoes, peeled and quartered
- 2 cups fresh baby carrots
- 2 celery ribs, cut into 2-1/2-inch pieces
- 1 medium onion, peeled and quartered
- 3 garlic cloves, peeled and quartered
- 1/2 cup chicken broth

- 3 turkey drumsticks (8 ounces each), skin removed
- 2 teaspoons seasoned salt
- 1 teaspoon dried thyme
- 1 teaspoon dried parsley flakes
- 1/4 teaspoon pepper

1 In a greased 5-qt. slow cooker, combine the potatoes, carrots, celery, onion, garlic and broth. Place drumsticks over vegetables. Sprinkle with the seasoned salt, thyme, parsley and pepper. Cover; cook on low for 5 to 5-1/2 hours or until turkey juices run clear.

Yield: 3 servings.

Stuffed Chicken Rolls

PREP: 25 MIN. + CHILLING
COOK: 4 HOURS

Jean Sherwood
Kenneth City, Florida
The wonderful aroma of this moist, delicious chicken cooking sparks our appetites. The ham and cheese rolled inside is a tasty surprise. They're especially nice served over rice or pasta.

6 boneless skinless chicken breast halves
(8 ounces each)

6 slices fully cooked ham

6 slices Swiss cheese

1/4 cup all-purpose flour

1/4 cup grated Parmesan cheese

1/2 teaspoon rubbed sage

1/4 teaspoon paprika

1/4 teaspoon pepper

1/4 cup canola oil

1 can (10-3/4 ounces) condensed cream of
chicken soup, undiluted

1/2 cup chicken broth

Chopped fresh parsley, optional

1 Flatten chicken to 1/8-in. thickness. Place ham and cheese on each breast. Roll up and tuck in ends; secure with a toothpick.

2 In a large shallow bowl, combine the flour, cheese, sage, paprika and pepper; coat chicken on all sides. Cover and refrigerate for 1 hour.

3 In a large skillet, brown chicken in oil over medium-high heat. Transfer to a 5-qt. slow cooker. Combine soup and broth; pour over chicken. Cover and cook on low for 4-5 hours or until chicken is no longer pink. Remove toothpicks. Garnish with parsley if desired.

Yield: 6 servings.

Saucy Chicken Thighs

(pictured above)

PREP: 20 MIN. ■ **COOK:** 4 HOURS

Kim Puckett
Reagan, Tennessee
Everyone raves about how sweet the sauce is for these chicken thighs. They're such a breeze because as they simmer away, you are free to do other things.

9 bone-in chicken thighs
(about 3-1/4 pounds)

1/2 teaspoon salt

1/4 teaspoon pepper

1-1/2 cups barbecue sauce

1/2 cup honey

2 teaspoons prepared mustard

2 teaspoons Worcestershire
sauce

1/8 to 1/2 teaspoon hot
pepper sauce

1 Sprinkle chicken with salt and pepper. Place on a broiler pan. Broil 4-5 in. from the heat for 3-4 minutes on each side or until lightly browned. Transfer to a 5-qt. slow cooker.

2 In a small bowl, combine the barbecue sauce, honey, mustard, Worcestershire sauce and pepper sauce. Pour over chicken; stir to coat. Cover and cook on low for 4-5 hours or until chicken juices run clear.

Yield: 9 servings.

Squash 'n' Chicken Stew

PREP: 15 MIN. ■ **COOK:** 6 HOURS

Taste of Home Test Kitchen
This home-style stew is colorful and full-flavored. Chicken thighs are gently cooked with stewed tomatoes, butternut squash, green peppers and onion for meal-in-one convenience.

> 2 pounds boneless skinless chicken thighs, cut into 1/2-inch pieces
> 1 can (28 ounces) stewed tomatoes, cut up
> 3 cups cubed butternut squash
> 2 medium green peppers, cut into 1/2-inch pieces
> 1 small onion, sliced and separated into rings
> 1 cup water
> 1 teaspoon salt
> 1 teaspoon ground cumin
> 1/2 teaspoon ground coriander
> 1/2 teaspoon pepper
> 2 tablespoons minced fresh parsley
> Hot cooked couscous, optional

1 In a 5-qt. slow cooker, combine the chicken, vegetables, water, salt, cumin, coriander and pepper. Cover and cook on low for 6-7 hours or until chicken juices run clear. Sprinkle with parsley. Serve with couscous if desired.

Yield: 5 servings.

> ***Storing dried seasonings.*** *Dried herbs and seasonings lose their flavor over time. For best flavor, use them within 6 months. Buy infrequently used herbs and seasonings in the smallest container available. If you have had them for longer than 6 months, they may still be used, but the flavor will not be as strong.*

Italian Turkey Sandwiches

(pictured above)
PREP: 10 MIN. ■ **COOK:** 5 HOURS

Carol Riley
Ossian, Indiana
I hope you enjoy these meaty turkey sandwiches as much as my group does. The recipe makes plenty, so it's great for potlucks. Leftovers are just as good reheated the next day.

> 1 bone-in turkey breast (6 pounds), skin removed
> 1 medium onion, chopped
> 1 small green pepper, chopped
> 1/4 cup chili sauce
> 3 tablespoons white vinegar
> 2 tablespoons dried oregano or Italian seasoning
> 4 teaspoons beef bouillon granules
> 12 kaiser or hard rolls, split

1 Cut turkey breast in half along the bone; place in a greased 5-qt. slow cooker. Add onion and green pepper.

2 In a small bowl, combine the chili sauce, vinegar, oregano and bouillon; pour over turkey and vegetables. Cover and cook on low for 5-6 hours or until a meat thermometer reads 170°.

3 Remove turkey; cool slightly. Shred with two forks and return to the slow cooker; heat through. Spoon 1/2 cup onto each roll.

Yield: 12 servings.

Teriyaki Chicken

PREP: 15 MIN. ■ **COOK:** 4-1/4 HOURS

Gigi Miller
Stoughton, Wisconsin
Chicken, rice and a sweet-salty sauce create an entree that's packed with Asian flavor. Your family will love this flavorful, savory meal.

12 boneless skinless chicken thighs (about 3 pounds)
3/4 cup sugar
3/4 cup soy sauce
6 tablespoons cider vinegar
3/4 teaspoon ground ginger
3/4 teaspoon minced garlic
1/4 teaspoon pepper

4-1/2 teaspoons cornstarch
4-1/2 teaspoons cold water
Hot cooked rice, optional

1 Place chicken in a 4-qt. slow cooker. In a large bowl, combine the sugar, soy sauce, vinegar, ginger, garlic and pepper. Pour over chicken. Cover and cook on low for 4-5 hours or until chicken is tender.

2 Remove chicken to a serving platter; keep warm. Skim fat from cooking juices; transfer to a small saucepan. Bring liquid to a boil. Combine cornstarch and water until smooth. Gradually stir into the pan. Bring to a boil; cook and stir for 2 minutes or until thickened. Serve with chicken and rice if desired.

Yield: 6 servings.

Rosemary Chicken with White Beans

(pictured at left)

PREP: 15 MIN. ■ **COOK:** 3 HOURS

Sharon Johannes
Ashley, Illinois

With a full-time job and an active child, I use my slow cookers at least twice a week...sometimes having two or three going at once with different dishes. I've made this recipe for years, tweaking it along the way, and now it's a just perfect!

> **6 boneless skinless chicken breast halves (6 ounces each)**
>
> **1 tablespoon canola oil**
>
> **2 cans (15-1/2 ounces each) great northern beans, rinsed and drained**
>
> **1 cup sliced fresh carrots**
>
> **1/2 cup sliced celery**
>
> **2/3 cup Italian salad dressing**
>
> **2 teaspoons dried rosemary, crushed**
>
> **1/2 teaspoon salt**
>
> **1 teaspoon pepper**

1 In a large skillet, brown chicken in oil in batches on both sides. Place the beans, carrots and celery in a 5-qt. slow cooker; top with chicken.

2 In a small bowl, combine the salad dressing, rosemary, salt and pepper; pour over chicken. Cover and cook on low for 3-4 hours or until chicken is tender.

Yield: 6 servings.

Zesty Mexican Chicken

PREP: 15 MIN. ■ **COOK:** 3-1/2 HOURS

Michelle Sheldon
Middletown, Delaware

A hint of lime juice helps tame the heat in this zesty, tender chicken with crunchy vegetables.

> **6 boneless skinless chicken breast halves (4 ounces each)**
>
> **1 can (14-1/2 ounces) diced tomatoes**
>
> **1 large onion, chopped**
>
> **1 medium green pepper, chopped**
>
> **3 garlic cloves, minced**
>
> **2 tablespoons lime juice**
>
> **1 tablespoon hot pepper sauce**
>
> **1/4 teaspoon salt**
>
> **1/4 teaspoon pepper**
>
> **3 cups hot cooked rice**

1 Place chicken in a 3- or 4-qt. slow cooker coated with cooking spray. In a large bowl, combine the tomatoes, onion, green pepper, garlic, lime juice, pepper sauce, salt and pepper. Pour over chicken. Cover and cook on low for 3-1/2 to 4 hours or until chicken is tender. Serve with rice.

Yield: 6 servings.

> *About rosemary.* Rosemary is native to the Mediterranean but is now grown in many home gardens. It has a pronounced flavor that hints of pine and lemon. A little rosemary will go a long way in flavoring a dish.

Chicken with Mushroom Gravy

PREP: 10 MIN. ■ **COOK:** 4-1/4 HOURS

Darolyn Jones
Fishers, Indiana
This deliciously moist chicken is a longtime favorite with family and friends. It's so easy, comforting and rich. A friend shared the recipe years ago, and I adapted it by adding a few new ingredients. I like to serve it over mashed potatoes.

4 boneless skinless chicken breast halves
(6 ounces each)
1 can (12 ounces) mushroom gravy
1 cup 2% milk

1 can (8 ounces) mushroom stems and pieces, drained
1 can (4 ounces) chopped green chilies
1 envelope Italian salad dressing mix
1 package (8 ounces) cream cheese, cubed

1 In a 3-qt. slow cooker, combine the chicken, gravy, milk, mushrooms, chilies and dressing mix. Cover and cook on low for 4 to 4-1/2 hours or until the chicken is tender.

2 Stir in cream cheese; cover and cook 15 minutes longer or until cheese is melted.

Yield: 4 servings.

Sweet 'n' Tangy Chicken

PREP: 15 MIN. ■ **COOK:** 4-3/4 HOURS

Joan Airey
Rivers, Manitoba
My slow cooker comes in handy during the haying and
harvesting seasons. We're so busy that if supper isn't prepared
before I serve lunch, it won't get done on time. This recipe
is hearty, delicious and fuss-free.

1 medium onion, chopped

1-1/2 teaspoons minced garlic

1 broiler/fryer chicken (3 pounds), cut up
and skin removed

2/3 cup ketchup

1/3 cup packed brown sugar

1 tablespoon chili powder

1 tablespoon lemon juice

1 teaspoon dried basil

1/2 teaspoon salt

1/4 teaspoon pepper

1/8 teaspoon hot pepper sauce

2 tablespoons cornstarch

3 tablespoons cold water

1 In a 3-qt. slow cooker, combine onion and garlic;
top with chicken. In a small bowl, combine the
ketchup, brown sugar, chili powder, lemon juice,
basil, salt, pepper and pepper sauce; pour over
chicken. Cover and cook on low for 4-1/2 to
5 hours or until chicken juices run clear.

2 Remove chicken to a serving platter; keep warm.
Transfer cooking juices to a saucepan. Skim fat
from cooking juices; transfer to a small saucepan.
Bring liquid to a boil. Combine cornstarch and water
until smooth. Gradually stir into the pan. Bring to a
boil; cook and stir for 2 minutes or until thickened.
Serve with chicken.

Yield: 4 servings.

Sage Turkey Thighs

PREP: 10 MIN. ■ **COOK:** 6-1/4 HOURS

Natalie Swanson
Baltimore, Maryland
I created this for my boys, who love dark meat. It's more convenient than cooking a whole turkey. It reminds me of our traditional Thanksgiving turkey and stuffing.

4 medium carrots, halved

1 medium onion, chopped

1/2 cup water

2 garlic cloves, minced

1-1/2 teaspoons rubbed sage, divided

2 turkey thighs or turkey drumsticks
(2 pounds total), skin removed

1 teaspoon browning sauce, optional

1/4 teaspoon salt

1/8 teaspoon pepper

1 tablespoon cornstarch

1/4 cup cold water

1 In a 3-qt. slow cooker, combine the carrots, onion, water, garlic and 1 teaspoon sage. Top with turkey. Sprinkle with remaining sage. Cover and cook on low for 6-8 hours or until turkey juices run clear.

2 Remove turkey to a serving platter; keep warm. Strain broth, reserving vegetables. Skim fat from cooking juices; transfer to a small saucepan. Stir in browning sauce, if desired, salt and pepper.

3 Place vegetables in a food processor; cover and process until smooth. Add to cooking juices. Bring to a boil. Combine cornstarch and water until smooth. Gradually stir into the pan. Bring to a boil; cook and stir for 2 minutes or until thickened. Serve with turkey.

Yield: 4 servings.

Turkey Enchiladas

(pictured above)

PREP: 10 MIN. ■ **COOK:** 6-1/4 HOURS

Stella Schams
Tempe, Arizona
Here's a different way to serve an economical cut of meat. I simmer turkey thighs with tomato sauce, green chiles and seasonings until they're fork-tender and flavorful. Then I shred the meat and serve it in tortillas with other fresh fixings.

2 pounds turkey thighs
or drumsticks

1 can (8 ounces) tomato sauce

1 can (4 ounces) chopped
green chilies

1/3 cup chopped onion

2 tablespoons Worcestershire
sauce

1 to 2 tablespoons chili powder

1/4 teaspoon garlic powder

8 flour tortillas (6 inches),
warmed

Optional toppings: chopped
green onions, sliced ripe
olives, chopped tomatoes,
shredded cheddar cheese,
sour cream and/or shredded
lettuce

1 Remove skin from turkey. Place in a 5-qt. slow cooker. In a small bowl, combine the tomato sauce, chilies, onion, Worcestershire sauce, chili powder and garlic powder; pour over turkey. Cover and cook on low for 6-8 hours or until turkey is tender.

2 Remove turkey; cool slightly. Shred with two forks and return to the slow cooker; heat through.

3 Spoon about 1/2 cup of turkey mixture down the center of each tortilla. Fold bottom of tortilla over filling and roll up. Add toppings of your choice.

Yield: 4 servings.

Chicken Stew Over Biscuits

PREP: 5 MIN. ■ **COOK:** 8 HOURS

Kathy Garrett
Browns Mills, New Jersey
A pleasant sauce coats this chicken and veggie dinner that's slow-cooked to perfection, then served over biscuits.

    2 envelopes chicken gravy mix
    2 cups water
    3/4 cup white wine
    1 tablespoon minced fresh parsley
    1 to 2 teaspoons chicken bouillon granules
    1 teaspoon minced garlic
    1/2 teaspoon pepper
    5 medium carrots, cut into 1-inch chunks
    1 large onion, cut into eight wedges
    1 broiler/fryer chicken (3 to 4 pounds),
    cut up, skin removed
    3 tablespoons all-purpose flour
    1/3 cup cold water
    1 tube (7-1/2 ounces) refrigerated
    buttermilk biscuits

1 In a 5-qt. slow cooker, combine the gravy mix, water, wine, parsley, bouillon, garlic and pepper until blended. Add the carrots, onion and chicken. Cover and cook on low for 7-8 hours.

2 In a small bowl, combine the flour and cold water until smooth; gradually stir into slow cooker. Cover and cook on high for 1 hour or until thickened.

3 Meanwhile, bake biscuits according to package directions. Place biscuits in soup bowls; top with stew.

Yield: 5 servings.

Chicken Athena

(pictured above)

PREP: 15 MIN. ■ **COOK:** 4 HOURS

Radelle Knappenberger
Oviedo, Florida
Greek flavors abound in this tasty and tender chicken dish. Olives, sun-dried tomatoes, lemon juice and balsamic vinegar combine with chicken for a special treat any night of the week.

    6 boneless skinless chicken
    breast halves (6 ounces each)
    2 medium onions, chopped
    1/3 cup sun-dried tomatoes
    (not packed in oil), chopped
    1/3 cup pitted Greek olives,
    chopped
    2 tablespoons lemon juice
    1 tablespoon balsamic vinegar
    3 garlic cloves, minced
    1/2 teaspoon salt

1 Place chicken in a 3-qt. slow cooker. Add all the remaining ingredients. Cover and cook on low for 4 hours or until chicken is tender.

Yield: 6 servings.

Chipotle-Marmalade Chicken

PREP: 15 MIN. ■ **COOK:** 4-1/4 HOURS

Cittie
Taste of Home Online Community
Big on flavor and easy on the cook's time,
is what makes this recipe so appealing. The
sweet-hot sauce gets its heat from the chipotle
pepper. I serve this dish with a side of rice to
use up every delectable drop of the sauce.

> 4 boneless skinless chicken breast halves
> (6 ounces each)
> 1/4 teaspoon salt
> Dash pepper
> 1/2 cup chicken broth
> 1/3 cup orange marmalade
> 1 tablespoon canola oil
> 1 tablespoon balsamic vinegar
> 1 tablespoon minced chipotle pepper
> in adobo sauce
> 1 tablespoon honey
> 1 teaspoon chili powder
> 1/4 teaspoon garlic powder
> 4 teaspoons cornstarch
> 2 tablespoons cold water

1 Sprinkle chicken with salt and pepper.
Transfer to a 4- or 5-qt. slow cooker.
In a small bowl, combine the broth,
marmalade, oil, vinegar, chipotle pepper,
honey, chili powder and garlic powder;
pour over chicken. Cover and cook on low
for 4-5 hours or until chicken is tender.

2 Remove the chicken to a serving platter;
keep warm. Skim fat from cooking juices;
transfer to a small saucepan. Bring liquid
to a boil. Combine cornstarch and water
until smooth. Gradually stir into the
pan. Bring to a boil; cook and stir for
2 minutes or until thickened. Serve
with the chicken.

Yield: 4 servings.

Editor's Note: Freeze leftover chipotle pepper in adobo
sauce in 1- or 2-pepper portions for use in other recipes.

Slow-Cooked Turkey Sandwiches

(pictured above)
PREP: 15 MIN. ■ **COOK:** 3 HOURS

Diane Twait Nelsen
Ringsted, Iowa
These sandwiches have been such a hit at office potlucks that I keep
copies of the recipe in my desk to hand out.

> 6 cups cubed cooked turkey
> 2 cups cubed process cheese
> (Velveeta)
> 1 can (10-3/4 ounces)
> condensed cream of chicken
> soup, undiluted
>
> 1 can (10-3/4 ounces)
> condensed cream of
> mushroom soup, undiluted
> 1/2 cup finely chopped onion
> 1/2 cup chopped celery
> 22 wheat sandwich buns, split

1 In a 3-qt. slow cooker, combine the turkey, cheese, soups,
onion and celery. Cover and cook on low for 3-4 hours or until
onion and celery are tender and cheese is melted. Stir before
spooning onto buns.

Yield: 22 servings.

Greek Garlic Chicken

PREP: 20 MIN. ■ **COOK:** 3-1/2 HOURS

Margee Berry
Trout Lake, Washington
Lively flavors of the Greek Isles come through in this mouthwatering chicken entree. I created this recipe so my husband and I could have an awesome dinner after a busy day out and about.

1/2 cup chopped onion

1 tablespoon plus 1 teaspoon olive oil, divided

3 tablespoons minced garlic

2-1/2 cups chicken broth, divided

1/4 cup pitted Greek olives, chopped

3 tablespoons chopped sun-dried tomatoes (not packed in oil)

1 tablespoon quick-cooking tapioca

2 teaspoons grated lemon peel

1 teaspoon dried oregano

6 boneless skinless chicken breast halves (6 ounces each)

1-3/4 cups uncooked couscous

1/2 cup crumbled feta cheese

1 In a small skillet, saute onion in 1 tablespoon oil until crisp-tender. Add garlic; cook 1 minute longer. Transfer to a 5-qt. slow cooker.

2 Stir in 3/4 cup broth, olives, tomatoes, tapioca, lemon peel and oregano. Add chicken. Cover and cook on low for 3-1/2 to 4 hours or until chicken is tender.

3 In a large saucepan, bring remaining oil and broth to a boil. Stir in couscous. Cover and remove from the heat; let stand for 5 minutes or until broth is absorbed. Serve with chicken; sprinkle with feta cheese.

Yield: 6 servings.

Sweet-and-Sour Chicken Wings

(pictured above)
PREP: 15 MIN. ■ **COOK:** 3-1/4 HOURS

June Eberhardt
Marysville, California
These wings are perfect for holiday gatherings. Because they come with plenty of sauce, I sometimes serve them over rice as a main dish. Any way you do it, this sweet and tangy medley will be a hit!

1 cup sugar

1 cup cider vinegar

1/2 cup ketchup

2 tablespoons reduced-sodium soy sauce

1 teaspoon chicken bouillon granules

16 chicken wings

6 tablespoons cornstarch

1/2 cup cold water

1 In a small saucepan, combine the sugar, vinegar, ketchup, soy sauce and bouillon. Bring to a boil; cook and stir until sugar is dissolved. Place chicken wings in a 3-qt. slow cooker; add vinegar mixture. Cover and cook on low for 3 to 3-1/2 hours or until chicken juices run clear.

2 Transfer wings to a serving dish and keep warm. Skim fat from cooking juices; transfer to a small saucepan. Bring liquid to a boil. Combine cornstarch and water until smooth. Gradually stir into the pan. Bring to a boil; cook and stir for 2 minutes or until thickened. Spoon over chicken. Serve with a slotted spoon.

Yield: 4 servings.

Barbecue Chicken Sandwiches

PREP: 20 MIN. ■ **COOK:** 5 HOURS

Lynn Ireland
Lebanon, Wisconsin
I love to use my slow cooker. In fact, I have three of them in various sizes! These saucy chicken sandwiches are real crowd-pleasers.

3 pounds boneless skinless chicken thighs

1 cup ketchup

1 small onion, chopped

1/4 cup water

1/4 cup cider vinegar

2 tablespoons Worcestershire sauce

1 tablespoon brown sugar

1 garlic clove, minced

1 bay leaf

2 teaspoons paprika

1 teaspoon dried oregano

1 teaspoon chili powder

1/2 teaspoon salt

1/2 teaspoon pepper

10 kaiser rolls, split

1 Place chicken in a 5-qt. slow cooker. In a small bowl, combine the ketchup, onion, water, vinegar, Worcestershire sauce, brown sugar, garlic, bay leaf and seasonings. Pour over chicken. Cover and cook on low for 5 hours or until chicken is tender.

2 Discard bay leaf. Remove chicken; cool slightly. Shred chicken with two forks and return to slow cooker; heat through. Serve on rolls.

Yield: 10 servings.

Mushroom Meat Loaf

(pictured above)

PREP: 30 MIN. ■ **COOK:** 3-1/4 HOURS

Tyler Sherman
Williamsburg, Virginia
Although I don't consider myself much of a cook, my meat loaf is delicious. The mushrooms and ground turkey are a flavorful combination, and the sauce has a nice zip to it.

2 eggs, lightly beaten

1-1/3 cups soft bread crumbs

8 ounces large portobello mushrooms, stems removed and finely chopped

1 small onion, finely chopped

2 garlic cloves, minced

3/4 teaspoon salt

1/2 teaspoon dried thyme

1/4 teaspoon pepper

1 pound lean ground turkey

1/4 cup chili sauce

2 teaspoons stone-ground mustard

1/8 teaspoon cayenne pepper

1 Cut three 20-in. x 3-in. strips of heavy-duty foil; crisscross so they resemble spokes of a wheel. Place strips on the bottom and up the sides of a 3-qt. slow cooker coated with cooking spray. Coat strips with cooking spray.

2 In a large bowl, combine the eggs, bread crumbs, mushrooms, onion, garlic, salt, thyme and pepper. Crumble turkey over mixture and mix well. Shape into a 7-1/2-in. x 4-in. loaf. Place meat loaf in the center of the strips.

3 Cover and cook on low for 3-4 hours or until no pink remains and a meat thermometer reads 160°.

4 In a small bowl, combine the chili sauce, mustard and cayenne; pour over meat. Cover and cook for 15 minutes longer or until heated through and meat thermometer reads 165°. Using foil strips as handles, remove the meat loaf to a platter.

Yield: 6 servings.

Chicken with Beans and Potatoes

(pictured at left)

PREP: 20 MIN. ■ COOK: 4 HOURS

Taste of Home Test Kitchen
This all-in-one entree is great to make when your afternoon is going to be busy. The onion soup mix adds lots of flavor to the broth.

> 2 pounds boneless skinless chicken breasts, cut into 1-inch cubes
>
> 1/2 teaspoon lemon-pepper seasoning
>
> 1 tablespoon canola oil
>
> 1 pound fresh green beans, trimmed
>
> 1 pound small red potatoes, quartered
>
> 1/2 pound medium fresh mushrooms, halved
>
> 1/2 cup thinly sliced sweet onion
>
> 2 cans (14-1/2 ounces each) chicken broth
>
> 2 tablespoons onion soup mix
>
> 2 teaspoons Worcestershire sauce
>
> 1 teaspoon grated lemon peel
>
> 1/2 teaspoon salt
>
> 1/2 teaspoon pepper
>
> 1/4 teaspoon garlic powder

1 Sprinkle chicken with lemon-pepper. In a large skillet, cook chicken in oil over medium heat for 4-5 minutes or until lightly browned.

2 In a 5 or 6-qt. slow cooker, layer the green beans, potatoes, mushrooms and onion. In a small bowl, combine the remaining ingredients; pour over vegetables. Top with chicken.

3 Cover and cook on low for 4-5 hours or until vegetables are tender. Serve with a slotted spoon.

Yield: 10 servings.

Citrus Chicken

PREP: 15 MIN. ■ COOK: 4 HOURS

Barbara Easton
North Vancouver, British Columbia
Bold-flavored ingredients are tempered by the taste of oranges, creating a mouthwatering dish that's guaranteed to impress.

> 2 medium oranges, cut into wedges
>
> 1 medium green pepper, chopped
>
> 1 broiler/fryer chicken (3 to 4 pounds), cut up and skin removed
>
> 1 cup orange juice
>
> 1/2 cup chili sauce
>
> 2 tablespoons soy sauce
>
> 1 tablespoon molasses
>
> 1 teaspoon ground mustard
>
> 1 teaspoon minced garlic
>
> 1/4 teaspoon pepper
>
> Hot cooked rice

1 Place oranges and green pepper in a 5-qt. slow cooker coated with cooking spray. Top with chicken. Combine the juice, chili sauce, soy sauce, molasses, mustard, garlic and pepper; pour over chicken. Cover and cook on low for 4-5 hours or until chicken juices run clear. Serve with rice.

Yield: 4 servings.

Slow-Cooked Asian Chicken

PREP: 20 MIN. ■ **COOK:** 5 HOURS

Ruth Seitz
Columbus Junction, Iowa
Extremely tender chicken is smothered in a dark, rich sauce in this easy and elegant supper. It's so nice to find another tantalizing way to serve chicken. Sprinkled with almonds, this is a dish I proudly serve to family or guests.

> 1 broiler/fryer chicken (3-1/2 to 4 pounds), cut up
> 2 tablespoons canola oil
> 1/3 cup soy sauce
> 2 tablespoons brown sugar

2 tablespoons water
1 garlic clove, minced
1 teaspoon ground ginger
1/4 cup slivered almonds

1 In a large skillet over medium heat, brown chicken in oil on both sides. Transfer to a 5-qt. slow cooker.

2 In a small bowl, combine the soy sauce, brown sugar, water, garlic and ginger; pour over chicken. Cover and cook on low for 5-6 hours or until chicken juices run clear. Remove chicken to a serving platter and sprinkle with almonds.

Yield: 4-6 servings.

pasta & more

Chunky Pasta Sauce

(pictured at left)

PREP: 15 MIN. ■ COOK: 6 HOURS

Christy Hinrichs
Parkville, Missouri
Your kitchen will smell heavenly when it's time to dish up this hearty meal. With beef, pork and lots of veggies over pasta, this entree has it all. Add the extra 1/2 cup water if you want your sauce a bit thinner.

1 pound ground beef

1/2 pound ground pork

2 cans (28 ounces each) diced tomatoes

1/2 to 1 cup water

1 can (6 ounces) tomato paste

1 medium onion, cut into wedges

1 medium sweet red pepper, cut into 1-inch pieces

1 cup chopped carrots

2 tablespoons sugar

2 teaspoons minced garlic

1 teaspoon salt

1 teaspoon dried basil

1 teaspoon dried oregano

1 teaspoon pepper

6 cups cooked bow tie pasta

1 In a large skillet, cook beef and pork over medium heat until no longer pink; drain. Transfer to a 3-qt. slow cooker.

2 Stir in the tomatoes, water, tomato paste, vegetables, sugar, garlic and seasonings. Cover and cook on low for 6-7 hours or until vegetables are tender. Serve with pasta.

Yield: 8 servings.

Zippy Bean Stew

(pictured at right)

PREP: 10 MIN. ■ COOK: 4 HOURS

Debbie Matthews
Bluefield, West Virginia
This bean stew is a staple for my coworkers and me once the weather turns cool. Although this is a low-fat entree, it definitely doesn't taste like one!

1 can (14-1/2 ounces) vegetable broth or reduced-sodium chicken broth

1 can (16 ounces) kidney beans, rinsed and drained

1 can (15 ounces) pinto beans, rinsed and drained

1 can (14-1/2 ounces) diced tomatoes and green chilies

1 can (4 ounces) chopped green chilies, undrained

2 cups frozen corn, thawed

3 cups water

1 large onion, chopped

2 medium carrots, sliced

2 garlic cloves, minced

2 teaspoons chili powder

1 Combine all ingredients in a 3-qt. slow cooker. Cover and cook on high for 4-5 hours or until heated through and flavors are blended.

Yield: 6 servings.

Burgundy Lamb Shanks

(pictured above)

PREP: 10 MIN. ■ **COOK:** 8-1/4 HOURS

Mrs. F. W. Creutz
Southold, New York
For those who love fall-from-the-bone lamb, this recipe fills the bill.
Burgundy wine adds a special touch to the sauce.

4 lamb shanks (about 20 ounces each)	1/2 cup chopped onion
Salt and pepper to taste	1 medium carrot, chopped
2 tablespoons dried parsley flakes	1 teaspoon olive oil
2 teaspoons minced garlic	1 cup Burgundy wine or beef broth
1/2 teaspoon dried oregano	1 teaspoon beef bouillon granules
1/2 teaspoon grated lemon peel	

1 Sprinkle lamb with salt and pepper. Place in a 5-qt. slow cooker. Sprinkle with the parsley, garlic, oregano and lemon peel.

2 In a small saucepan, saute onion and carrot in oil for 3-4 minutes or until tender. Stir in wine and bouillon. Bring to a boil, stirring occasionally. Pour over lamb. Cover and cook on low for 8 hours or until meat is tender.

3 Remove lamb and keep warm. Strain cooking juices and skim fat. In a small saucepan, bring juices to a boil; cook until liquid is reduced by half. Serve with lamb.

Yield: 4 servings.

Vegetarian Tortilla Lasagna

PREP: 20 MIN. ■ **COOK:** 3 HOURS

Connie McDowell
Greenwood, Delaware
You won't miss the meat in this savory delight. The layered main course is as tasty as it is impressive. Serve warm wedges alongside tortilla chips or a green salad.

1 can (14-1/2 ounces) diced tomatoes with basil, oregano and garlic
1 cup chunky salsa
1 can (6 ounces) tomato paste
1/2 teaspoon ground cumin
2 cans (15-1/2 ounces each) hominy, rinsed and drained
1 can (15 ounces) black beans, rinsed and drained
3 flour tortillas (10 inches)
2 cups (8 ounces) shredded Monterey Jack cheese
1/4 cup sliced ripe olives

1 Cut three 25-in. x 3-in. strips of heavy-duty foil; crisscross so they resemble spokes of a wheel. Place strips on the bottom and up the sides of a round 5-qt. slow cooker. Coat strips with cooking spray.

2 In a large bowl, combine the tomatoes, salsa, tomato paste and cumin. Stir in hominy and beans. Place one tortilla on the bottom of slow cooker. Top with a third of the hominy mixture and cheese. Repeat layers twice. Sprinkle with olives. Cover and cook on low for 3 to 3-1/2 hours or until heated through.

3 Using foil strips as handles, remove the lasagna to a platter. Let stand for 5 minutes before cutting into wedges.

Yield: 8 servings.

Hearty Cheese Tortellini

PREP: 30 MIN. ■ **COOK:** 6-1/4 HOURS

Christine Eilerts
Tulsa, Oklahoma
This is a wonderful recipe that is simple enough for an everyday meal but good enough for company. It makes a large amount, so it feeds plenty of people. I serve it with steamed broccoli covered in a cheese sauce and fresh bread.

1/2 pound bulk Italian sausage

1/2 pound lean ground beef (90% lean)

1 jar (24 ounces) marinara sauce

1 can (14-1/2 ounces) Italian diced tomatoes

1 cup sliced fresh mushrooms

1 package (9 ounces) refrigerated cheese tortellini

1 cup (4 ounces) shredded part-skim mozzarella cheese

1 In a small skillet, cook sausage and beef over medium heat until no longer pink; drain. Transfer to a 3-qt. slow cooker.

2 Stir in marinara sauce, tomatoes and mushrooms. Cover and cook on low for 6-7 hours or until heated through.

3 Prepare tortellini according to package directions; stir into meat mixture. Sprinkle with cheese. Cover and cook for 15 minutes or until cheese is melted.

Yield: 6 servings.

Thai Shrimp and Rice

PREP: 30 MIN. ■ **COOK:** 3 HOURS 20 MIN.

Paula Marchesi
Lenhartsville, Pennsylvania
Raisins and coconut milk add a lovely hint of
sweetness to this Thai dish. Your kitchen will be
filled with the delightful scent of freshly grated
lime peel and minced gingerroot as this cooks.

 2 cans (14-1/2 ounces each) chicken broth
 2 cups uncooked converted rice
 1 large carrot, shredded
 1 medium onion, chopped
 1/2 cup each chopped sweet red
 and green pepper
 1/2 cup water
 1/2 cup coconut milk
 1/3 cup lime juice
 1/4 cup flaked coconut
 1/4 cup each raisins and golden raisins
 8 garlic cloves, minced
 1 tablespoon grated lime peel
 1 tablespoon minced fresh gingerroot
 1 teaspoon salt
 1 teaspoon each ground coriander
 and cumin
 1/2 teaspoon cayenne pepper
 1 pound cooked medium shrimp, peeled
 and deveined
 1/2 cup fresh snow peas, cut into thin strips

1 In a 5-qt. slow cooker, combine the broth,
rice, vegetables, water, milk, lime juice,
coconut, raisins, garlic, lime peel and
seasonings. Cover and cook on low for
3 hours or until rice is tender.

2 Stir in the shrimp and peas. Cover and
cook 20 minutes longer or until mixture
is heated through.

Yield: 8 servings.

Sweet Potato Lentil Stew

(pictured above)
PREP: 5 MIN. ■ **COOK:** 5 HOURS

Heather Gray
Little Rock, Arkansas
Years ago, I fell in love with the spicy flavor and wonderful aroma of this
hearty, meatless stew. If you like, you can serve it as a topper for meat
or poultry. It's great either way!

 4 cups vegetable broth
 3 cups sweet potatoes,
 peeled and cubed (about
 1-1/4 pounds)
 3 medium carrots, cut
 into chunks
 1 medium onion, chopped

 1-1/2 cups dried lentils, rinsed
 4 garlic cloves, minced
 1/2 teaspoon ground cumin
 1/4 teaspoon ground ginger
 1/4 teaspoon cayenne pepper
 1/4 cup minced fresh cilantro
 1/4 teaspoon salt

1 In a 3-qt. slow cooker, combine the broth, vegetables, lentils,
garlic, cumin, ginger and cayenne. Cover and cook on low for
5-6 hours or until vegetables are tender. Stir in cilantro and salt.

Yield: 6 servings.

Vegetarian Stuffed Peppers

(pictured at right)

PREP: 30 MIN. ■ **COOK:** 3-1/2 HOURS

Melissa McCabe
Long Beach, California
These filling and flavorful peppers are an updated version of my mom's stuffed peppers, which were a favorite when I was growing up in upstate New York. Whenever I make them, I'm reminded of home.

- **6 large sweet peppers**
- **2 cups cooked brown rice**
- **3 small tomatoes, chopped**
- **1 cup frozen corn, thawed**
- **1 small sweet onion, chopped**
- **1/3 cup canned red beans, rinsed and drained**
- **1/3 cup canned black beans, rinsed and drained**
- **3/4 cup cubed Monterey Jack cheese**
- **1 can (4-1/4 ounces) chopped ripe olives**
- **4 fresh basil leaves, thinly sliced**
- **3 garlic cloves, minced**
- **1 teaspoon salt**
- **1/2 teaspoon pepper**
- **3/4 cup meatless spaghetti sauce**
- **1/2 cup water**
- **4 tablespoons grated Parmesan cheese, divided**

1 Cut tops off peppers and remove seeds; set aside. In a large bowl, combine the rice, tomatoes, corn, onion and beans. Stir in the Monterey Jack cheese, olives, basil, garlic, salt and pepper. Spoon into the peppers.

2 Combine spaghetti sauce and water; pour half into an oval 5-qt. slow cooker. Add stuffed peppers. Top with remaining sauce. Sprinkle with 2 tablespoons Parmesan cheese. Cover and cook on low for 3-1/2 to 4 hours or until peppers are tender and filling is heated through. Sprinkle with remaining Parmesan cheese.

Yield: 6 servings.

Egg Noodle Lasagna

PREP: 15 MIN. ■ **COOK:** 4 HOURS

Mary Oberlin
Selinsgrove, Pennsylvania
I was lucky enough to receive this recipe from one of my friends. The perfect take-along for charity events and church potlucks, the comforting crowd-pleaser satisfies everyone who tries it.

- **6-1/2 cups uncooked wide egg noodles**
- **3 tablespoons butter**
- **1-1/2 pounds ground beef**
- **2-1/4 cups spaghetti sauce**
- **6 ounces process cheese (Velveeta), cubed**
- **3 cups (12 ounces) shredded mozzarella cheese**

1 Cook noodles according to package directions; drain. Add butter; toss to coat.

2 In a large skillet, cook beef over medium heat until no longer pink; drain.

3 Spread a fourth of the spaghetti sauce into an ungreased 5-qt. slow cooker. Layer with a third of the noodles, a third of the beef, a third of the remaining sauce and a third of the cheeses. Repeat layers twice. Cover and cook on low for 4 hours or until cheese is melted and lasagna is heated through.

Yield: 12-16 servings.

Pizza in a Pot

PREP: 15 MIN. ■ **COOK:** 3 HOURS

Dianna Cline
Phillippi, West Virginia
With warm breadsticks or garlic toast on the side, this is one dinner I know my family will always eagerly eat.

1-1/2 pounds ground beef

1 medium green pepper, chopped

1 medium onion, chopped

1 can (15 ounces) tomato sauce

1 jar (14 ounces) pizza sauce

2 tablespoons tomato paste

3 cups spiral pasta, cooked and drained

2 packages (3-1/2 ounces each) sliced pepperoni

2 cups (8 ounces) shredded part-skim mozzarella cheese

1 In a large skillet, cook the beef, green pepper and onion over medium heat until meat is no longer pink; drain. Stir in the tomato sauce, pizza sauce and tomato paste.

2 In a 5-qt. slow cooker, layer the pasta, beef mixture, pepperoni and cheese. Cover and cook on low for 3-4 hours or until heated through.

Yield: 8 servings.

Editor's Note: If you'd like, substitute 1/2 pound bulk Italian sausage for the pepperoni in Pizza in a Pot. Cook it along with the ground beef, green pepper and onion.

Lamb with Orzo

PREP: 30 MIN. ■ **COOK:** 8-1/4 HOURS

Dan Kelmenson
West Bloomfield, Michigan
Looking to switch up your slow cooker staples?
Consider this lamb entree. A terrific meal-in-one,
it certainly adds flair to dinnertime doldrums.
A splash of lemon juice and zesty lemon peel
complement the flavors of fresh spinach and
feta cheese.

1 boneless lamb shoulder roast (3 pounds)

3 tablespoons lemon juice

3 garlic cloves, minced

2 teaspoons dried oregano

2 teaspoons grated lemon peel

1/4 teaspoon salt

1 package (16 ounces) orzo pasta

2 packages (9 ounces each) fresh spinach, torn, divided

1 cup (4 ounces) crumbled feta cheese, divided

1 Cut roast in half. Place in a 5-qt. slow cooker. Drizzle with lemon juice. Sprinkle with the garlic, oregano, lemon peel and salt. Cover and cook on low for 8-10 hours or until meat is tender.

2 Cook orzo according to package directions. Remove lamb from slow cooker. Shred meat with two forks; set aside and keep warm.

3 Skim fat from cooking juices if necessary; return 1 cup cooking juices to slow cooker. Add one package of spinach. Cook on high for 5-10 minutes or until spinach is wilted. Drain orzo; add to spinach mixture. Stir in reserved meat and 1/2 cup feta cheese.

4 To serve, arrange remaining fresh spinach on nine individual plates. Top with lamb mixture. Sprinkle each with remaining feta cheese.

Yield: 9 servings.

Hunter's Delight

(pictured above)
PREP: 15 MIN. ■ **COOK:** 6 HOURS

Terry Paull
Eagle River, Wisconsin
We live in the north woods so we usually have an ample supply of
venison. This is a favorite recipe our mom made often.

1/2 pound sliced bacon, diced

2-1/2 pounds red potatoes, thinly sliced

2 medium onions, sliced

1-1/2 pounds boneless venison steak, cubed

2 cans (14-3/4 ounces each) cream-style corn

3 tablespoons Worcestershire sauce

1 teaspoon sugar

1/2 to 1 teaspoon seasoned salt

1 In a large skillet, cook bacon over medium heat until crisp; drain. Place potatoes and onions in a 5-qt. slow cooker. Top with venison and bacon.

2 In a large bowl, combine the corn, Worcestershire sauce, sugar and seasoned salt; pour over the top. Cover and cook on low for 6-8 hours or until meat and potatoes are tender.

Yield: 8 servings.

Meat Sauce for Spaghetti

(pictured above)

PREP: 30 MIN. ■ COOK: 8 HOURS

Mary Tallman
Arbor Vitae, Wisconsin
Here's a thick, hearty sauce that transforms ordinary spaghetti and garlic bread into a filling feast.

1 pound ground beef	1 can (8 ounces) tomato sauce
1 pound bulk Italian sausage	1 can (6 ounces) tomato paste
1 can (28 ounces) crushed tomatoes, undrained	1 tablespoon brown sugar
	1 tablespoon Italian seasoning
1 medium green pepper, chopped	2 garlic cloves, minced
	1/2 teaspoon salt
1 medium onion, chopped	1/4 teaspoon pepper
1 cup finely chopped carrots	Hot cooked spaghetti
1 cup water	

1 In a large skillet, cook beef and sausage over medium heat until no longer pink; drain. Transfer to a 5-qt. slow cooker.

2 Stir in the tomatoes, green pepper, onion, carrots, water, tomato sauce, tomato paste, brown sugar, Italian seasoning, garlic, salt and pepper. Cover and cook on low for 8-10 hours or until bubbly. Serve with spaghetti.

Yield: 9 servings.

Slow-Cooked Lamb Chops

PREP: 10 MIN. ■ COOK: 5-1/2 HOURS

Sandra McKenzie
Braham, Minnesota
This is my favorite recipe for lamb chops. It's great for people who are trying lamb for the first time since the meat turns out extra tender and tasty. I wrap the chops in bacon because that's how I prepare venison, and I think it really enhances the flavor.

4 bacon strips

4 lamb shoulder blade chops, trimmed

2-1/4 cups thinly sliced peeled potatoes

1 cup thinly sliced carrots

1/2 teaspoon dried rosemary, crushed

1/4 teaspoon garlic powder

1/4 teaspoon salt

1/4 teaspoon pepper

1/4 cup chopped onion

2 garlic cloves, minced

1 can (10-3/4 ounces) condensed cream of mushroom soup, undiluted

1/3 cup 2% milk

1 jar (4-1/2 ounces) sliced mushrooms, drained

1 Wrap bacon around lamb chops; secure with toothpicks. Place in a 3-qt. slow cooker. Cover and cook on high for 1-1/2 hours.

2 Remove chops; discard toothpicks and bacon. Drain liquid from slow cooker. Add potatoes and carrots; top with lamb chops. Sprinkle with rosemary, garlic powder, salt, pepper, onion and garlic.

3 In a small bowl, combine soup and milk. Add mushrooms. Pour over the chops. Cover and cook on low for 4-6 hours or until meat and vegetables are tender.

Yield: 4 servings.

Italian Shrimp 'n' Pasta

PREP: 10 MIN. ■ COOK: 7-1/2 HOURS

Karen Scaglione
Nanuet, New York
This dish is always a hit! The shrimp, orzo, tomatoes and cayenne pepper remind me of a Creole favorite, but the Italian seasoning adds a different twist. The strips of chicken thighs stay nice and moist during cooking.

1 pound boneless skinless chicken thighs, cut into 2-inch x 1-inch strips

2 tablespoons canola oil

1 can (28 ounces) crushed tomatoes

2 celery ribs, chopped

1 medium green pepper, cut into 1-inch pieces

1 medium onion, coarsely chopped

2 garlic cloves, minced

1 tablespoon sugar

1/2 teaspoon salt

1/2 teaspoon Italian seasoning

1/8 to 1/4 teaspoon cayenne pepper

1 bay leaf

1/2 cup uncooked orzo pasta or other small pasta

1 pound cooked medium shrimp, peeled and deveined

1 In a large skillet, brown chicken in oil; transfer to a 3-qt. slow cooker. Stir in the next 10 ingredients. Cover and cook on low for 7-8 hours or until chicken is no longer pink.

2 Discard the bay leaf. Stir in the pasta; cover and cook on high for 15 minutes or until the pasta is tender. Stir in the shrimp; cover and cook for 5 minutes longer or until heated through.

Yield: 6-8 servings.

Tangy Venison Stroganoff

(pictured above)

PREP: 10 MIN. ■ COOK: 3-1/4 HOURS

Ellen Spes
Caro, Michigan
Here, chunks of venison and chopped onion are slowly simmered for hours. Sour cream is stirred in at the end to create a silky, delicious sauce.

1-1/2 pounds boneless venison steak, cubed

1 medium onion, sliced

1 can (10-1/2 ounces) condensed beef broth, undiluted

1 tablespoon Worcestershire sauce

1 tablespoon ketchup

1 teaspoon curry powder

1/2 teaspoon ground ginger

1/2 teaspoon salt

1/4 teaspoon pepper

4-1/2 teaspoons cornstarch

1/2 cup sour cream

2 tablespoons prepared horseradish

Hot cooked noodles or pasta

1 Place venison and onion in a 3-qt. slow cooker. Combine the broth, Worcestershire sauce, ketchup and seasonings; pour over venison. Cover and cook on high for 3 to 3-1/2 hours or until meat is tender.

2 In a small bowl, combine the cornstarch, sour cream and horseradish. Gradually stir into venison mixture. Cover and cook 15 minutes longer or until sauce is thickened. Serve with noodles or pasta.

Yield: 4 servings.

Corn Bread-Topped Frijoles

(pictured at left)

PREP: 20 MIN. ■ **COOK:** 3 HOURS

Suzanne Caldwell
Artesia, New Mexico
This budget-friendly dish is loaded with fresh Southwestern flavors.

---

    1 medium onion, chopped
    1 medium green pepper, chopped
    1 tablespoon canola oil
    2 garlic cloves, minced
    1 can (16 ounces) kidney beans, rinsed
      and drained
    1 can (15 ounces) pinto beans, rinsed
      and drained
    1 can (14-1/2 ounces) diced tomatoes,
      undrained
    1 can (8 ounces) tomato sauce
    1 teaspoon chili powder
    1/2 teaspoon pepper
    1/8 teaspoon hot pepper sauce
 CORN BREAD TOPPING:
    1 cup all-purpose flour
    1 cup yellow cornmeal
    1 tablespoon sugar
    1-1/2 teaspoons baking powder
    1/2 teaspoon salt
    2 eggs, lightly beaten
    1-1/4 cups fat-free milk
    1 can (8-3/4 ounces) cream-style corn
    3 tablespoons canola oil

1 In a skillet, saute onion and green pepper
   in oil. Add garlic; cook for 1 minute.
   Transfer to a greased 5-qt. slow cooker.
   Stir in the beans, tomatoes, tomato
   sauce, chili powder, pepper and hot
   pepper sauce. Cover and cook on
   high for 1 hour.

2 In a bowl, combine flour, cornmeal, sugar,
   baking powder and salt. Combine eggs,
   milk, corn and oil; add to dry ingredients
   and mix well. Spoon over bean mixture.
   Cover and cook on high for 2 hours or
   until a toothpick inserted near the center
   of corn bread comes out clean.

Yield: 8 servings.

Meatball Tortellini

PREP: 10 MIN. ■ **COOK:** 3 HOURS

Tracie Bergeron
Chauvin, Louisiana
I combined some favorite staples from our freezer and pantry to come up with this easy dinner. It takes only a few minutes to toss together.

---

    1 package (16 ounces) frozen
    California-blend vegetables,
    thawed
    1 package frozen fully cooked
    Italian meatballs (12 ounces),
    thawed
    2 cups uncooked dried cheese
    tortellini

    2 cans (10-3/4 ounces
    each) condensed cream of
    mushroom soup, undiluted
    2-1/4 cups water
    1 teaspoon Creole seasoning

1 In a 3-qt. slow cooker, combine the vegetables, meatballs and
   tortellini. In a large bowl, whisk the soup, water and Creole
   seasoning. Pour over vegetable-meatball mixture; stir well.
   Cover and cook on low for 3-4 hours or until the tortellini
   and vegetables are tender.

Yield: 6-8 servings.

Editor's Note: The following spices may be substituted for 1 teaspoon Creole seasoning:
1/4 teaspoon each salt, garlic powder and paprika; and a pinch each of dried thyme,
ground cumin and cayenne pepper.

Hearty Jambalaya

(pictured at right)

PREP: 15 MIN. ■ **COOK:** 6-1/4 HOURS

Jennifer Fulk
Moreno Valley, California
I love anything with Cajun spices, so I came up with this jambalaya that's just as good as any served in a restaurant. If you can't find Andouille sausage, hot links, smoked sausage or chorizo will also work. I like to serve it with warm cornbread.

1 can (28 ounces) diced tomatoes, undrained

1 pound fully cooked andouille sausage links, cubed

1/2 pound boneless skinless chicken breasts, cut into 1-inch cubes

1 can (8 ounces) tomato sauce

1 cup diced onion

1 small sweet red pepper, diced

1 small green pepper, diced

1 cup chicken broth

1 celery rib with leaves, chopped

2 tablespoons tomato paste

2 teaspoons dried oregano

2 teaspoons Cajun seasoning

1-1/2 teaspoons minced garlic

2 bay leaves

1 teaspoon Louisiana-style hot sauce

1/2 teaspoon dried thyme

1 pound cooked medium shrimp, peeled and deveined

Hot cooked rice

1 In a 5-qt. slow cooker, combine the first 16 ingredients. Cover and cook on low for 6-7 hours or until the chicken is no longer pink.

2 Stir in shrimp. Cover and cook 15 minutes longer or until heated through. Discard bay leaves. Serve with rice.

Yield: 8 servings.

Veggie Lasagna

PREP: 25 MIN. ■ **COOK:** 3-1/2 HOURS

Laura Davister
Little Suamico, Wisconsin
This "veggie-licious" alternative to traditional lasagna makes use of slow cooker convenience. I like it best with chunky spaghetti sauce.

3/4 cup meatless spaghetti sauce

1/2 cup sliced zucchini

1/2 cup shredded part-skim mozzarella cheese

3 tablespoons 1% cottage cheese

2 tablespoons grated Parmesan cheese

2 tablespoons beaten egg

1/2 teaspoon Italian seasoning

1/8 teaspoon garlic powder

2 no-cook lasagna noodles

4 cups fresh baby spinach

1/2 cup sliced fresh mushrooms

1 Spread 1 tablespoon spaghetti sauce in a 1-1/2-qt. slow cooker coated with cooking spray. Top with half of the zucchini. Combine the cheeses, egg, Italian seasoning and garlic powder; spoon a third over zucchini.

2 Break noodles into 1-in. pieces; sprinkle half over cheese mixture. Spread 1 tablespoon sauce over noodles. Top with half of the spinach and mushrooms. Repeat layers. Top with remaining cheese mixture and spaghetti sauce. Cover and cook on low for 3-1/2 to 4 hours or until noodles are tender.

Yield: 2 servings.

Spicy Meatballs With Sauce

(pictured at left)

PREP: 30 MIN. ■ **COOK:** 5 HOURS

Rosanne Bergman
Alta Loma, California

I rely on Italian sausage to make my meatballs. Not only do they taste great, but they also cook to perfection along with a sensational homemade sauce.

> 1 egg, lightly beaten
> 3/4 cup crushed seasoned salad croutons
> 1/2 cup finely chopped onion
> 1/4 cup finely chopped green pepper
> 1 teaspoon garlic powder
> 1 teaspoon ground cumin
> 1 teaspoon dried oregano
> 1 teaspoon pepper
> 1 pound ground turkey
> 1 pound bulk Italian sausage

SAUCE:

> 3 tablespoons cornstarch
> 1 tablespoon sugar
> 3/4 cup beef broth
> 2 cans (28 ounces each) crushed tomatoes
> 3 medium carrots, diced
> 1 can (6 ounces) tomato paste
> 1 envelope onion soup mix
> 3 garlic cloves, minced
> 1 teaspoon dried basil
> 1/2 teaspoon crushed red pepper flakes
> Hot cooked pasta

1 In a large bowl, combine the egg, croutons, onion, green pepper, garlic powder, cumin, oregano and pepper. Crumble turkey and sausage over mixture and mix well. Shape into 1-in. balls. Place in a 5-qt. slow cooker.

2 In a large bowl, combine the cornstarch, sugar and broth until smooth; stir in the tomatoes, carrots, tomato paste, soup mix, garlic, basil and pepper flakes. Pour over meatballs. Cover and cook on low for 5-6 hours or until meat is no longer pink. Serve with pasta.

Yield: 8 servings (1 cup sauce with 5 meatballs).

Slow Cooker Salmon Loaf

PREP: 10 MIN. ■ **COOK:** 4 HOURS

Kelly Ritter
Douglasville, Georgia

As a stay-at-home mom, I'm always looking for quick, easy recipes that can be prepared ahead of time. I also don't like to heat up my oven during our hot Georgia summers. I adapted this recipe from one I found in an old slow cooker book of my grandma's. I like to serve it with macaroni and cheese and pinto beans.

> 2 eggs, lightly beaten
> 2 cups seasoned stuffing croutons
> 1 cup chicken broth
> 1 cup grated Parmesan cheese
> 1/4 teaspoon ground mustard
> 1 can (14-3/4 ounces) salmon, drained, bones and skin removed

1 Cut three 20-in. x 3-in. strips of heavy duty foil; crisscross so they resemble spokes of a wheel. Place the strips on the bottom and up the sides of a 3-qt. slow cooker. Coat strips with cooking spray.

2 In a large bowl, combine the eggs, croutons, broth, cheese and mustard. Add salmon and mix well. Gently shape mixture into a round loaf. Place in the center of the strips. Cover and cook on low for 4-6 hours or until a meat thermometer reads 160°. Using foil strips as handles, remove the loaf to a platter.

Yield: 6 servings.

Spicy Seafood Stew

PREP: 30 MIN. ■ **COOK:** 4-3/4 HOURS

Bonnie Marlow
Ottoville, Ohio

This zippy stew is very quick to prepare. The hardest part is peeling and dicing the potatoes, and even that can be done the night before. Just place the potatoes in water and store them in the refrigerator overnight to speed up assembly the next day.

2 pounds potatoes, peeled and diced

1 pound carrots, sliced

2 jars (6 ounces each) sliced mushrooms, drained

1 jar (26 ounces) spaghetti sauce

1-1/2 teaspoons ground turmeric

1-1/2 teaspoons minced garlic

1 teaspoon cayenne pepper

3/4 teaspoon salt

1-1/2 cups water

1 pound sea scallops

1 pound uncooked medium shrimp, peeled and deveined

1 In a 5-qt. slow cooker, combine the vegetables, spaghetti sauce and seasonings. Cover and cook on low for 4-1/2 to 5 hours or until potatoes are tender.

2 Stir in the water, scallops and shrimp. Cover and cook for 15-20 minutes or until scallops are opaque and shrimp turn pink.

Yield: 9 servings.

Creamy Chicken Fettuccine

PREP: 15 MIN. ■ **COOK:** 3 HOURS

Melissa Cowser
Greenville, Texas
Convenient canned soup and process American cheese hurry
along the prep for this creamy sauce loaded with delicious
chunks of chicken.

**1-1/2 pounds boneless skinless chicken breasts,
cut into cubes**

1/2 teaspoon onion powder

1/2 teaspoon garlic powder

1/8 teaspoon pepper

**1 can (10-3/4 ounces) condensed cream of chicken
soup, undiluted**

**1 can (10-3/4 ounces) condensed cream of celery
soup, undiluted**

4 ounces process American cheese, cubed

1 can (2-1/4 ounces) sliced ripe olives, drained

1 jar (2 ounces) diced pimientos, drained, optional

1 package (16 ounces) fettuccine or spaghetti

Thin breadsticks, optional

1 Place the chicken in a 3-qt. slow cooker; sprinkle
with onion powder, garlic powder and pepper. Top
with soups. Cover and cook on high for 3-4 hours
or until chicken is no longer pink.

2 Stir in the cheese, olives and pimientos if desired.
Cover and cook until cheese is melted. Meanwhile,
cook fettuccine according to package directions;
drain. Serve with chicken and breadsticks if desired.

3 **Yield: 6 servings.**

Venison Meatballs

PREP: 30 MIN. ■ **COOK:** 4-1/4 HOURS

Geraldine Mennear
Mastic, New York

These meatballs are a savory blend of ground venison and pork sausage, with water chestnuts for crunch. This is my husband's favorite venison recipe. Even my coworkers, who normally don't like game meat, enjoy it.

1 egg, lightly beaten

1 cup soft bread crumbs

1 can (8 ounces) water chestnuts, drained and finely chopped

1/4 cup soy sauce

2 teaspoons ground ginger

1 garlic clove, minced

1 pound ground venison

1 pound bulk pork sausage

3 to 4 teaspoons canola oil, divided

1/2 pound fresh mushrooms, sliced

1 can (14-1/2 ounces) chicken broth

1-1/4 cups cold water, divided

3 tablespoons cornstarch

Hot cooked noodles

1 In a bowl, combine the egg, bread crumbs, water chestnuts, soy sauce, ginger and garlic. Crumble the venison and sausage over the mixture and mix well. Shape into 1-in. balls. In a skillet over medium heat, brown meatballs in batches in 2 teaspoons oil, adding 1 teaspoon oil if needed. Transfer meatballs to a 3-qt. slow cooker.

2 In the same skillet, saute mushrooms in 1 teaspoon oil until tender. Stir in the broth and 1 cup cold water. Pour over the meatballs. Cover and cook on low for 4-5 hours or until a meat thermometer reads 160°.

3 Remove meatballs and mushrooms with a slotted spoon; keep warm. Strain cooking juices into a saucepan. Combine cornstarch and remaining water until smooth; add to saucepan. Bring to a boil; cook and stir for 2 minutes or until thickened. Serve over the meatballs, mushrooms and noodles.

Yield: 8-10 servings.

Ham Tetrazzini

(pictured above)

PREP: 15 MIN. ■ **COOK:** 4 HOURS

Susan Blair
Sterling, Michigan

I've served this at parties, family dinners and potlucks. Everyone is pleasantly surprised to find they're eating a lighter version of this classic dish.

1 can (10-3/4 ounces) reduced-sodium condensed cream of mushroom soup, undiluted

1 cup sliced fresh mushrooms

1 cup cubed fully cooked ham

1/2 cup fat-free evaporated milk

2 tablespoons white wine or water

1 teaspoon prepared horseradish

1 package (7 ounces) spaghetti

1/2 cup shredded Parmesan cheese

1 In a 3-qt. slow cooker, combine the soup, mushrooms, ham, milk, wine and horseradish. Cover and cook on low for 4 hours. Cook spaghetti according to package directions; drain. Add the spaghetti and cheese to slow cooker; toss to coat.

Yield: 5 servings.

Southern Barbecue Spaghetti Sauce

PREP: 10 MIN. ■ COOK: 4 HOURS

Rhonda Melanson
Sarnia, Ontario
I revamped our favorite sloppy joe recipe into this thick spaghetti sauce that simmers in the slow cooker. The flavor is jazzy enough to be interesting to adults, yet mild enough to be enjoyed by children.

1 pound lean ground turkey

2 medium onions, chopped

1-1/2 cups sliced fresh mushrooms

1 medium green pepper, chopped

2 garlic cloves, minced

1 can (14-1/2 ounces) diced tomatoes, undrained

1 can (12 ounces) tomato paste

1 can (8 ounces) tomato sauce

1 cup ketchup

1/2 cup beef broth

2 tablespoons Worcestershire sauce

2 tablespoons brown sugar

1 tablespoon ground cumin

2 teaspoons chili powder

12 cups hot cooked spaghetti

1 In a large nonstick skillet, cook the turkey, onions, mushrooms, green pepper and garlic over medium heat until meat is no longer pink; drain. Transfer to a 3-qt. slow cooker.

2 Stir in the tomatoes, tomato paste, tomato sauce, ketchup, broth, Worcestershire sauce, brown sugar, cumin and chili powder. Cover and cook on low for 4-5 hours. Serve sauce with the spaghetti.

Yield: 12 servings.

Two-Bean Chili

(pictured at left)
PREP: 40 MIN. ■ COOK: 8 HOURS

Ronald Johnson
Elmhurst, Illinois
The first time I had this chili, I was at a party. I was on my second bowl before I realized it had no meat!

1/2 pound sliced fresh mushrooms

1 large green pepper, chopped

1 large sweet red pepper, chopped

2 celery ribs, chopped

1 medium onion, chopped

1 jalapeno pepper, seeded and chopped

1 tablespoon olive oil

4 garlic cloves, minced

2 teaspoons ground cumin

1 teaspoon dried oregano

1 can (28 ounces) diced tomatoes, undrained

1 can (16 ounces) red beans, rinsed and drained

1 can (15 ounces) black beans, rinsed and drained

1 large carrot, chopped

1/2 cup water

1/2 cup barbecue sauce

1/4 cup chili powder

1 teaspoon Liquid Smoke, optional

Optional toppings: sour cream, hot pepper sauce, shredded cheddar cheese, onion and/or tortilla chips

1 In a large skillet over medium heat, cook vegetables in oil until onion is tender. Add the garlic, cumin and oregano; cook and stir 1 minute longer. Transfer to a 5-qt. slow cooker.

2 Stir in the remaining ingredients except toppings. Cover and cook on low for 8 hours or until vegetables are tender. Serve with toppings if desired.

Yield: 6 servings (2 quarts).

Editor's Note: When cutting hot peppers, disposable gloves are recommended. Avoid touching your face.

Red Clam Sauce

PREP: 25 MIN. ■ **COOK:** 3 HOURS

JoAnn Brown
LaTrobe, Pennsylvania
This dish tastes like it's been slaved over all day. Instead,
it cooks while you do other things.

1 medium onion, chopped

1 tablespoon canola oil

2 garlic cloves, minced

2 cans (6-1/2 ounces each) chopped clams, undrained

1 can (14-1/2 ounces) diced tomatoes, undrained

1 can (6 ounces) tomato paste

1/4 cup minced fresh parsley

1 bay leaf

1 teaspoon sugar

1 teaspoon dried basil

1/2 teaspoon dried thyme

6 ounces linguine, cooked and drained

1 In a small skillet, saute onion in oil until tender.
Add garlic; cook 1 minute longer. Transfer to a
1-1/2- or 2-qt. slow cooker.

2 Stir in the clams, tomatoes, tomato paste, parsley,
bay leaf, sugar, basil and thyme. Cover and cook
on low for 3-4 hours or until heated through.
Discard bay leaf. Serve with linguine.

Yield: 4 servings.

Mincing parsley. Parsley can be messy to mince.
Here's a tip to keep things clean. Simply place
parsley in a small glass container and snip sprigs
with kitchen shears until minced.

soup & chili

Turkey Chili

(pictured at left)

PREP: 20 MIN. ■ **COOK:** 6-1/2 HOURS

Celesta Zanger
Bloomfield Hills, Michigan

I've taken my mother's milder recipe for chili and made it thicker and more robust. It's a favorite at my house, especially in fall and winter.

- 1 pound lean ground turkey
- 3/4 cup each chopped onion, celery and green pepper
- 1 can (28 ounces) diced tomatoes, undrained
- 1 jar (26 ounces) meatless spaghetti sauce
- 1 can (16 ounces) hot chili beans, undrained
- 1-1/2 cups water
- 1/2 cup frozen corn
- 2 tablespoons chili powder
- 1 teaspoon ground cumin
- 1/4 teaspoon pepper
- 1/8 to 1/4 teaspoon cayenne pepper
- 1 can (16 ounces) kidney beans, rinsed and drained
- 1 can (15 ounces) pinto beans, rinsed and drained
- Sour cream, optional

1 In a large nonstick skillet, cook the turkey, onion, celery and green pepper over medium heat until meat is no longer pink and vegetables are tender; drain. Transfer to a 5-qt. slow cooker.

2 Add the tomatoes spaghetti sauce, chili beans, water, corn and seasonings. Cover and cook on high for 1 hour. Reduce heat to low; cook for 5-6 hours.

3 Add kidney and pinto beans; cook 30 minutes longer. Garnish with sour cream if desired.

Yield: 13 servings (3-1/4 quarts).

No-Fuss Potato Soup

(pictured at right)

PREP: 15 MIN. ■ **COOK:** 7-1/2 HOURS

Dotty Egge
Pelican Rapids, Minnesota

For a busy-day supper, my family loves to have big steaming, delicious bowls of this soup, along with fresh bread from our bread machine.

- 6 cups cubed peeled potatoes
- 2 cups chopped onion
- 1/2 cup chopped celery
- 1/2 cup thinly sliced carrots
- 5 cups water
- 1/4 cup butter, cubed
- 4 teaspoons chicken bouillon granules or 2 vegetable bouillon cubes
- 2 teaspoons salt
- 1/4 teaspoon pepper
- 1 can (12 ounces) evaporated milk
- 3 tablespoons minced fresh parsley
- Minced chives, optional

1 In a 5-qt. slow cooker, combine the vegetables, water, butter, bouillon, salt and pepper. Cover and cook on high for 7-8 hours or until the vegetables are tender.

2 Add milk and parsley. Cover and cook 30-60 minutes longer or until heated through. Garnish with chives if desired.

Yield: 8-10 servings (about 3 quarts).

Parmesan Potato Soup

PREP: 20 MIN. ■ **COOK:** 5-1/2 HOURS

Mary Shivers
Ada, Oklahoma

I decided to add some character to a basic potato chowder by adding roasted red peppers. The extra flavor gives a deliciously unique twist to an otherwise ordinary dish.

8 medium potatoes, peeled and cut into 1/2-inch cubes

1 large onion, chopped

1 jar (7 ounces) roasted sweet red peppers, drained and chopped

1 small celery rib, chopped

6 cups chicken broth

1/2 teaspoon garlic powder

1/2 teaspoon seasoned salt

1/2 teaspoon pepper

1/8 teaspoon rubbed sage

1/3 cup all-purpose flour

2 cups heavy whipping cream, divided

1 cup grated Parmesan cheese, divided

8 bacon strips, cooked and crumbled

2 tablespoons minced fresh cilantro

1 In a 5- or 6-qt. slow cooker, combine the vegetables, broth and seasonings. Cover and cook on low for 5-6 hours or until vegetables are tender.

2 In a small bowl, combine flour and 1/2 cup cream until smooth; add to slow cooker. Stir in 3/4 cup cheese, bacon, cilantro and remaining cream. Cover and cook for 30 minutes or until slightly thickened. Ladle into bowls; sprinkle with remaining cheese.

Yield: 12 servings (3 quarts).

Beef Barley Soup

(pictured above)

PREP: 15 MIN. ■ **COOK:** 9 HOURS

Ginny Perkins
Columbiana, Ohio

My hubby doesn't usually consider a bowl of soup dinner, but this hearty, comforting soup, served with corn bread on the side, got a thumbs up...even from him!

1-1/2 pounds beef stew meat

1 tablespoon canola oil

1 can (14-1/2 ounces) diced tomatoes

1 cup chopped onion

1 cup diced celery

1 cup sliced fresh carrots

1/2 cup chopped green pepper

4 cups beef broth

2 cups water

1 cup spaghetti sauce

2/3 cup medium pearl barley

1 tablespoon dried parsley flakes

2 teaspoons salt

1-1/2 teaspoons dried basil

3/4 teaspoon pepper

1 In a large skillet, brown meat in oil over medium heat; drain. Meanwhile, in a 5-qt. slow cooker, combine the vegetables, broth, water, spaghetti sauce, barley and seasonings. Stir in beef. Cover and cook on low for 9-10 hours or until meat is tender. Skim fat from cooking juices.

Yield: 8 servings (2-1/2 quarts).

White Bean Chicken Chili

PREP: 35 MIN. ■ **COOK:** 3 HOURS

Kristine Bowles
Albuquerque, New Mexico
My sister shared this chili recipe with me. I usually double it and add one extra can of beans. I like to serve it with cheddar biscuits or warmed tortillas.

3/4 **pound boneless skinless chicken breasts, cubed**

1/2 **teaspoon salt**

1/4 **teaspoon pepper**

1 **medium onion, chopped**

1 **jalapeno pepper, seeded and chopped**

2 **teaspoons dried oregano**

1 **teaspoon ground cumin**

2 **tablespoons olive oil**

4 **garlic cloves, minced**

2 **cans (15 ounces each) white kidney or cannellini beans, rinsed and drained, divided**

3 **cups chicken broth, divided**

1-1/2 **cups (6 ounces) shredded cheddar cheese**

Sour cream and minced fresh cilantro, optional

1 Sprinkle chicken with salt and pepper. In a large skillet over medium heat, cook the chicken, onion, jalapeno, oregano and cumin in oil for 3-4 minutes or until chicken is browned and vegetables are crisp-tender. Add garlic; cook 1 minute longer. Transfer to a 3-qt. slow cooker.

2 In a small bowl, mash 1 cup of beans. Add 1/2 cup broth; stir until blended. Add to the slow cooker with the remaining beans and broth. Cover and cook on low for 3 to 3-1/2 hours or until chicken is tender.

3 Stir before serving. Sprinkle with cheese. Garnish with sour cream and cilantro if desired.

Yield: 6 servings.

Editor's Note: When cutting hot peppers, disposable gloves are recommended. Avoid touching your face.

Halibut Chowder

PREP: 20 MIN. ■ **COOK:** 5-1/2 HOURS

Donna Goutermont
Juneau, Alaska
Try this simple way to mix up dinner standbys. Mashed potato flakes thicken this easy chowder, and you can adjust the chili powder and cayenne to suit your taste.

2 cups water

2 cups 2% milk

2 medium potatoes, cubed

1 large onion, chopped

1 cup mashed potato flakes

1 can (8 ounces) tomato sauce

2 garlic cloves, minced

1 teaspoon celery salt

1 teaspoon dried parsley flakes

1/2 teaspoon ground mustard

1/4 teaspoon chili powder

1/4 teaspoon cayenne pepper

1 pound halibut fillets, cut into chunks

1 tablespoon butter

1 In a 3-qt. slow cooker, combine water, milk, potatoes, onion, potato flakes, tomato sauce, garlic and seasonings. Cover and cook on low for 5 hours or until potatoes are tender.

2 Add halibut and butter. Cover and cook 30-45 minutes longer or until fish flakes easily with a fork.

Yield: 6 servings.

Heartier soup. For a more substantial Vegetable Barley Soup add some meat. To keep the soup on the lighter side, in a large skillet, cook about 1-1/2 pounds of lean ground turkey over medium heat until no longer pink. Drain grease and add meat to the slow cooker along with the vegetables. Or, if you're not keeping track of your calories, add about a pound of small meatballs...either homemade or purchased frozen meatballs (thaw them before using).

Vegetable Barley Soup

(pictured above)
PREP: 25 MIN. ■ **COOK:** 8-1/4 HOURS

Mary Tallman
Arbor Vitae, Wisconsin
You'll love this delicious vegetarian soup brimming with veggies and barley, and the great news is it's good for you, too!

1 large sweet potato, peeled and cubed

1-1/2 cups fresh baby carrots, halved

1-1/2 cups frozen cut green beans

1-1/2 cups frozen corn

3 celery ribs, thinly sliced

1 small onion, chopped

1/2 cup chopped green pepper

2 garlic cloves, minced

6 cups water

2 cans (14-1/2 ounces each) vegetable broth

1 cup medium pearl barley

1 bay leaf

1-3/4 teaspoons salt

1/2 teaspoon fennel seed, crushed

1/4 teaspoon pepper

1 can (14-1/2 ounces) Italian diced tomatoes, undrained

1 In a 5-qt. slow cooker, combine the vegetables and garlic. Stir in the water, broth, barley, bay leaf and seasonings. Cover and cook on low for 8-9 hours or until the barley and vegetables are tender.

2 Stir in tomatoes; cover and cook on high for 10-20 minutes or until heated through. Discard bay leaf before serving.

Yield: 12 servings (about 3-1/2 quarts).

All-Day Soup

PREP: 25 MIN. ■ **COOK:** 8 HOURS

Cathy Logan
Sparks, Nevada

I start this soup in the morning, and by evening, dinner's ready to go! My family loves all of the hearty vegetable and steak pieces, all smothered in a zesty tomato broth.

1 beef flank steak (1-1/2 pounds), cut into 1/2-inch cubes

1 medium onion, chopped

1 tablespoon olive oil

5 medium carrots, thinly sliced

4 cups shredded cabbage

4 medium red potatoes, diced

2 celery ribs, diced

2 cans (14-1/2 ounces each) diced tomatoes, undrained

2 cans (14-1/2 ounces each) beef broth

1 can (10-3/4 ounces) condensed tomato soup, undiluted

1 tablespoon sugar

2 teaspoons Italian seasoning

1 teaspoon dried parsley flakes

1 In a skillet, brown steak and onion in oil; drain. Transfer to a 5-qt. slow cooker.

2 Stir in all the remaining ingredients. Cover and cook on low for 8-10 hours or until meat is tender.

Yield: 8 servings (about 3 quarts).

Cutting steak into cubes. *It is easier to slice and cube uncooked steak when it is partially frozen. If the steak is thawing in the refrigerator, using a sharp knife, cut it into cubes before it is completely defrosted. If it is fresh steak, then place it in the freezer for 30-60 minutes before cubing.*

Chicken Chili

(pictured above)

PREP: 10 MIN. ■ **COOK:** 5 HOURS

Taste of Home Test Kitchen

A spicy chicken chili is a nice change of pace from the typical beef chili. Assemble this midday and supper will be ready and waiting for you.

1-1/2 pounds boneless skinless chicken breasts, cut into 1/2-inch cubes

1 cup chopped onion

3 tablespoons canola oil

1 can (15 ounces) white kidney or cannellini beans, rinsed and drained

1 can (14-1/2 ounces) diced tomatoes, undrained

1 can (14-1/2 ounces) diced tomatoes with mild green chilies, undrained

1 cup frozen corn

1 teaspoon salt

1 teaspoon ground cumin

1 teaspoon minced garlic

1/2 teaspoon celery salt

1/2 teaspoon ground coriander

1/2 teaspoon pepper

Sour cream and shredded cheddar cheese, optional

1 In a large skillet, saute chicken and onion in oil for 5 minutes or until chicken is browned. Transfer to a 5-qt. slow cooker.

2 Stir in the beans, tomatoes, corn and seasonings. Cover and cook on low for 5 hours or until chicken is no longer pink. Garnish with sour cream and cheese if desired.

Yield: 6 servings.

Mexican Chicken Soup

PREP: 10 MIN. ■ COOK: 3 HOURS

Marlene Kane
Lainesburg, Michigan

This zesty dish is loaded with chicken, corn and black beans in a mildly spicy red broth. As a busy mom, I'm always looking for dinner recipes that can be prepared in the morning. The kids love the taco-like taste of this easy soup.

1-1/2 pounds boneless skinless chicken breasts, cubed

2 teaspoons canola oil

1/2 cup water

1 envelope reduced-sodium taco seasoning

1 can (32 ounces) V8 juice

1 jar (16 ounces) salsa

1 can (15 ounces) black beans, rinsed and drained

1 package (10 ounces) frozen corn, thawed

6 tablespoons reduced-fat cheddar cheese

6 tablespoons reduced-fat sour cream

2 tablespoons minced fresh cilantro

1 In a large nonstick skillet, saute chicken in oil until no longer pink. Add water and taco seasoning; simmer, uncovered, until chicken is well coated. Transfer to a 5-qt. slow cooker.

2 Stir in the V8 juice, salsa, beans and corn. Cover and cook on low for 3-4 hours or until heated through. Serve with cheese, sour cream and cilantro.

Yield: 6 servings.

Lime Navy Bean Chili

PREP: 15 MIN. + SOAKING
COOK: 5 HOURS

Connie Thomas
Jensen, Utah

A lip-smacking touch of lime flavors a filling family favorite. I love relying on my slow cooker. It is a comfort knowing that a warm meal is waiting for you.

1-1/4 cups dried navy beans

3 cups water

2 bone-in chicken breast halves
(7 ounces each), skin removed

1 cup frozen corn

1 medium onion, chopped

1 can (4 ounces) chopped green chilies

4 garlic cloves, minced

1 tablespoon chicken bouillon granules

1 teaspoon ground cumin

1/2 teaspoon chili powder

2 tablespoons lime juice

1 Sort beans and rinse with cold water. Place beans in a large saucepan; add water to cover by 2 in. Bring to a boil; boil for 2 minutes. Remove from the heat; cover and let soak for 1 to 4 hours or until beans are softened. Drain and rinse beans, discarding liquid.

2 In a 3-qt. slow cooker, combine the beans, water, chicken, corn, onion, chilies, garlic, bouillon, cumin and chili powder. Cover and cook on low for 5-6 hours or until chicken and beans are tender.

3 Remove chicken breasts; set aside until cool enough to handle. Remove meat from bones; discard bones and cut chicken into bite-size pieces. Return chicken to pan. Stir in lime juice just before serving.

Yield: 6 servings.

Sauerkraut Sausage Soup

(pictured above)

PREP: 20 MIN. ■ **COOK:** 5 HOURS

Yvonne Kett
Appleton, Wisconsin

My husband and I make our own sauerkraut and grow many of the vegetables in this simple soup. It makes a great weeknight supper.

4 cups chicken broth

1 pound smoked Polish sausage, cut into 1/2-inch slices

1 can (16 ounces) sauerkraut, rinsed and well drained

2 cups sliced fresh mushrooms

1-1/2 cups cubed peeled potatoes

1 can (10-3/4 ounces) condensed cream of mushroom soup, undiluted

1-1/4 cups chopped onions

2 large carrots, sliced

2 celery ribs, chopped

2 tablespoons white vinegar

2 teaspoons dill weed

1 teaspoon sugar

1/4 teaspoon pepper

1 In a 5-qt. slow cooker, combine all the ingredients. Cover and cook on low for 5-6 hours or until vegetables are tender.

Yield: 10 servings (2-1/2 quarts).

Vegetable Bean Soup

PREP: 30 MIN. ■ **COOK:** 6 HOURS

Belinda Moran
Woodbury, Tennessee

Kitchen staples and canned goods help me get this heartwarming soup on the table with very little preparation. Feel free to change the ingredients according to your tastes by adding a few of your favorite vegetables, or swap out some of the beans with the variety you like best.

2 cans (14-1/2 ounces each) petite diced tomatoes

1 can (16 ounces) kidney beans, rinsed and drained

1 can (15-1/4 ounces) whole kernel corn, drained

1 can (15 ounces) garbanzo beans or chickpeas, rinsed and drained

1 can (15 ounces) black beans, rinsed and drained

1 can (10 ounces) diced tomatoes and green chilies

1 can (8 ounces) tomato sauce

1 cup chopped green pepper

1 cup chopped zucchini

3/4 cup water

1/2 cup chopped onion

1/2 cup chopped celery

2 tablespoons chili powder

4 teaspoons dried oregano

2 garlic cloves, minced

1 teaspoon ground cumin

1 teaspoon pepper

1/2 teaspoon salt

2 bay leaves

1 In a 5-qt. slow cooker, combine all the ingredients. Cover and cook on low for 6-8 hours or until vegetables are tender. Discard bay leaves before serving.

Yield: 7 servings.

Slow-Cooked Corn Chowder

(pictured above)

PREP: 10 MIN. ■ **COOK:** 6 HOURS

Mary Hogue
Rochester, Pennsylvania

I combine and refrigerate the ingredients for this easy chowder the night before. It makes it so easy to just start the meal and go on about my day.

2-1/2 cups 2% milk

1 can (14-3/4 ounces) cream-style corn

1 can (10-3/4 ounces) condensed cream of mushroom soup, undiluted

1-3/4 cups frozen corn

1 cup frozen shredded hash brown potatoes

1 cup cubed fully cooked ham

1 large onion, chopped

2 teaspoons dried parsley flakes

2 tablespoons butter

Salt and pepper to taste

1 In a 3-qt. slow cooker, combine all the ingredients. Cover and cook on low for 6 hours.

Yield: 8 servings (2 quarts).

Italian Chili

PREP: 20 MIN. ■ **COOK:** 6-1/2 HOURS

Taste of Home Test Kitchen
By adding Italian seasoning and fresh veggies, an Italian spin was added to this traditional Southwestern-style chili.

1 pound ground beef

1/2 pound bulk Italian sausage

1 can (28 ounces) diced tomatoes

1 can (8 ounces) tomato sauce

1 cup chopped onion

1 cup chopped sweet red pepper

1 cup water

1/2 cup chopped celery

1/4 cup beef broth

1 tablespoon chili powder

1 tablespoon Italian seasoning

1 teaspoon sugar

1 teaspoon minced garlic

1/2 teaspoon salt

1 can (16 ounces) kidney beans, rinsed and drained

1 cup sliced fresh mushrooms

1 cup diced zucchini

3 tablespoons minced fresh parsley

Shredded part-skim mozzarella cheese, optional

1 In a large skillet, cook beef and sausage over medium heat until no longer pink. Meanwhile, in a 3-qt. slow cooker, combine the tomatoes, tomato sauce, onion, red pepper, water, celery, broth, chili powder, Italian seasoning, sugar, garlic and salt.

2 Drain beef mixture; add to the slow cooker. Cover and cook on low for 6 hours or until vegetables are tender.

3 Add the beans, mushrooms, zucchini and parsley. Cover and cook on high for 30 minutes or until vegetables are tender. Sprinkle with cheese if desired.

Yield: 6 servings.

Zesty Italian Soup

(pictured above)

PREP: 15 MIN. ■ **COOK:** 7 HOURS

Myrna Sippel
Thompson, Illinois
While visiting my sister-in-law, we had a delicious Italian soup at a local restaurant. We decided to duplicate it at home and came up with this recipe. Vary the seasonings and types of tomatoes to suit your tastes.

1 pound bulk Italian sausage

3 cans (14-1/2 ounces each) reduced-sodium chicken broth

1 can (15 ounces) black beans, rinsed and drained

1 can (15 ounces) pinto beans, rinsed and drained

1 can (14-1/2 ounces) diced tomatoes and green chilies, undrained

1 can (14-1/2 ounces) Italian diced tomatoes

1 large carrot, chopped

1 jalapeno pepper, seeded and chopped

1-1/2 teaspoons Italian seasoning

1 teaspoon dried minced garlic

1-1/2 cups cooked elbow macaroni

1 In a large skillet, cook sausage over medium heat until no longer pink; drain. Transfer to a 5-qt. slow cooker.

2 Stir in the broth, beans, tomatoes, carrot, jalapeno, Italian seasoning and garlic. Cover and cook on low for 7-8 hours or until heated through. Just before serving, stir in macaroni.

Yield: 10 servings (3-1/2 quarts).

Editor's Note: When cutting hot peppers, disposable gloves are recommended. Avoid touching your face.

Hearty Taco Chili

PREP: 30 MIN. ■ **COOK:** 6 HOURS

Julie Neuhalfen
Glenwood, Iowa
Ranch dressing mix and taco seasoning give this hearty mixture extra special flavor. Folks will come back for seconds.

> 2 pounds ground beef
> 1 can (16 ounces) kidney beans, rinsed and drained
> 1 can (15 ounces) pinto beans, rinsed and drained
> 1 can (15 ounces) black beans, rinsed and drained
> 1 can (14 ounces) hominy, rinsed and drained
> 1 can (10 ounces) diced tomatoes and green chilies, undrained
> 1 can (8 ounces) tomato sauce
> 1 small onion, chopped
> 1 envelope ranch salad dressing mix
> 1 envelope taco seasoning
> 1/2 teaspoon pepper
> 2 cans (14-1/2 ounces each) diced tomatoes, undrained
> 1 can (4 ounces) chopped green chilies
> Corn chips, sour cream and shredded cheddar cheese, optional

1 In a large skillet, cook beef over medium heat until no longer pink; drain. Transfer to a 5-qt. slow cooker.

2 Add the beans, hominy, tomatoes, tomato sauce, onion, salad dressing mix, taco seasoning and pepper. In a blender, combine diced tomatoes and green chilies; cover and process until smooth. Add to the slow cooker. Cover and cook on low for 6 hours.

3 Serve with corn chips, sour cream and cheese if desired.

Yield: 11 servings (2-3/4 quarts).

Forgotten Minestrone

(pictured above)

PREP: 15 MIN. ■ **COOK:** 7-1/2 HOURS

Marsha Ransom
South Haven, Michigan
This soup gets its name because the broth simmers for hours, allowing me to work on my freelance writing. But after one taste, you and your family will agree this full-flavored soup is truly unforgettable!

> 1 pound beef stew meat, cut into 1/2-inch cubes
> 1 can (28 ounces) diced tomatoes, undrained
> 1 medium onion, chopped
> 2 tablespoons minced dried parsley
> 2-1/2 teaspoons salt, optional
> 1-1/2 teaspoons ground thyme
> 1 beef bouillon cube
> 1/2 teaspoon pepper
> 6 cups water
> 1 medium zucchini, halved and thinly sliced
> 2 cups chopped cabbage
> 1 can (15 ounces) garbanzo beans or chickpeas, rinsed and drained
> 1 cup uncooked elbow macaroni
> 1/4 cup grated Parmesan cheese, optional

1 In a 5-qt. slow cooker, combine the meat, tomatoes, onion, parsley, salt if desired, thyme, bouillon, pepper and water. Cover and cook on low for 7-9 hours or until meat is tender.

2 Add the zucchini, cabbage, beans and macaroni; cover and cook on high for 30-45 minutes or until vegetables are tender. Sprinkle each serving with cheese if desired.

Yield: 8 servings (2 quarts).

Savory Winter Soup

PREP: 20 MIN. ■ **COOK:** 8 HOURS

Dana Simmons
Lancaster, Ohio
Even my father, who doesn't particularly like soup, enjoys my tasty version of traditional vegetable soup. He asked me to share the recipe with Mom, and I gladly obliged!

2 pounds ground beef

3 medium onions, chopped

1 garlic clove, minced

3 cans (10-1/2 ounces each) condensed beef broth, undiluted

1 can (28 ounces) diced tomatoes, undrained

3 cups water

1 cup each diced carrots and celery

1 cup fresh or frozen cut green beans

1 cup cubed peeled potatoes

2 tablespoons minced fresh parsley or 2 teaspoons dried parsley flakes

1 teaspoon dried basil

1/2 teaspoon dried thyme

Salt and pepper to taste

1 In a large skillet, cook the beef and onions over medium heat until the meat is no longer pink. Add the garlic and cook 1 minute longer. Drain. Transfer to a 5-qt. slow cooker.

2 Stir in all the remaining ingredients. Cover and cook on high for 8 hours or until heated through.

Yield: 14 servings (3-1/2 quarts).

Editor's Note: To save chopping time, use frozen sliced carrots and thawed cubed hash brown potatoes in Savory Winter Soup.

Broccoli Potato Soup

(pictured above)

PREP: 25 MIN. ■ **COOK:** 4-1/2 HOURS

Crystal Kelso
Sandy, Oregon
For a very comforting soup with a nice, creamy texture, try this one with nutritious broccoli and chunks of potato. The red pepper flakes add a hint of spice, and the fresh herbs make this a truly delicious soup.

1 pound small red potatoes, cubed

1 large onion, chopped

1 large carrot, coarsely chopped

7 garlic cloves, minced

3 cups water

1 can (14-1/2 ounces) condensed cream of broccoli soup, undiluted

1 teaspoon each minced fresh thyme, basil and parsley

1 teaspoon garlic powder

1/2 teaspoon salt

1/2 teaspoon crushed red pepper flakes

1/4 teaspoon pepper

2 cups frozen chopped broccoli, thawed and drained

1 cup (4 ounces) shredded Havarti cheese

1 Place the potatoes, onion, carrot and garlic in a 4- or 5-qt. slow cooker. Add the water, soup and seasonings. Cover and cook on low for 4-5 hours or until heated through.

2 Stir in broccoli and cheese. Cover and cook for 30 minutes or until broccoli is tender.

Yield: 8 cups (2 quarts).

Italian Chicken Chili

PREP: 20 MIN. ■ COOK: 6-3/4 HOURS

Genise Krause
Sturgeon Bay, Wisconsin
Though the list of ingredients may seem long, this recipe takes just 20 minutes of prep before it simmers into a heartwarming main course. Each bite brings variety in taste and texture, not to mention loads of Italian flavor.

1/2 pound bulk Italian sausage

1 teaspoon olive oil

1 pound boneless skinless chicken breasts, cut into 1-inch cubes

1 can (28 ounces) crushed tomatoes

1 can (28 ounces) diced tomatoes, undrained

1 can (15 ounces) white kidney or cannellini beans, rinsed and drained

2 celery ribs, chopped

1 cup chopped onion

1 small sweet red pepper, chopped

1/2 cup dry red wine or chicken broth

2 tablespoons chili powder

2 teaspoons dried oregano

2 teaspoons minced garlic

1 teaspoon dried thyme

1 medium zucchini, diced

1 cup sliced fresh mushrooms

1/4 cup minced fresh parsley

Shredded Italian cheese blend, optional

1 In a large skillet, cook sausage in oil over medium heat until no longer pink; drain. Transfer to a 5-qt. slow cooker.

2 Stir in the chicken, tomatoes, beans, celery, onion, red pepper, wine, chili powder, oregano, garlic and thyme. Cover and cook on low for 6 hours or until chicken is no longer pink.

3 Stir in the zucchini and mushrooms. Cover and cook on high for 45 minutes or until vegetables are tender. Sprinkle with parsley. Serve with cheese if desired.

Yield: 8 servings (2-3/4 quarts).

Baked Potato Soup

(pictured above)

PREP: 35 MIN. ■ COOK: 6-1/4 HOURS

Barbara Bleigh
Colonial Heights, Virginia
The only thing that beats the comforting flavor of this thick and hearty potato soup is possibly the idea that it simmers on its own all day.

2 large onions, chopped

3 tablespoons butter

2 tablespoons all-purpose flour

2 cups water, divided

4 cups chicken broth

2 medium potatoes, peeled and diced

1-1/2 cups mashed potato flakes

1/2 pound sliced bacon, cooked and crumbled

3/4 teaspoon pepper

1/2 teaspoon salt

1/2 teaspoon dried basil

1/8 teaspoon dried thyme

1 cup half-and-half cream

1/2 cup shredded cheddar cheese

2 green onions, sliced

1 In a large skillet, saute onions in butter until tender. Stir in flour. Gradually stir in 1 cup water. Bring to a boil; cook and stir for 2 minutes or until thickened. Transfer to a 5-qt. slow cooker.

2 Add the broth, potatoes, potato flakes, bacon, pepper, salt, basil, thyme and remaining water. Cover and cook on low for 6-8 hours or until potatoes are tender. Stir in cream; heat through. Garnish with cheese and green onions.

Yield: 10 servings (2-1/2 quarts).

French Onion Soup

PREP: 15 MIN. ■ **COOK:** 8 HOURS

Kris Ritter
Pittsburgh, Pennsylvania
Topped with a slice of French bread and provolone cheese, individual servings of this fabulous soup are sure to be enjoyed by everyone at your dinner table.

1 large sweet onion, thinly sliced (about 4 cups)

1/4 cup butter, cubed

2 cans (14-1/2 ounces each) beef broth

2 tablespoons sherry or additional beef broth

1/2 teaspoon pepper

4 slices French bread (1/2 inch thick), toasted

4 slices provolone cheese

1 Place onion and butter in a 1-1/2-qt. slow cooker coated with cooking spray. Cover and cook on low for 6 hours or until onion is tender.

2 Stir in the broth, sherry and pepper. Cover and cook 2-3 hours longer or until heated through.

3 Ladle soup into ovenproof bowls. Top each with a slice of toast and the cheese. Broil 4-6 in. from the heat for 2-3 minutes or until the cheese is melted. Serve the soup immediately.

Yield: 4 servings.

Other great cheeses. Provolone cheese is wonderful on the French Onion Soup featured here, but feel free to experiment with other delightful cheeses, such as Swiss, mozzarella, Brie, shredded Parmesan, shredded Romano or Monterey Jack.

Spinach Bean Soup

PREP: 20 MIN. ■ **COOK:** 6-1/4 HOURS

Brenda Jeffers
Ottumwa, Iowa
This meatless soup is great for a busy weeknight supper after I get home from my job as a college nursing professor. The soup provides plenty of nutrients to keep me healthy.

3 cans (14-1/2 ounces each) vegetable broth

1 can (15-1/2 ounces) great northern beans, rinsed and drained

1 can (15 ounces) tomato puree

1/2 cup finely chopped onion

1/2 cup uncooked converted long grain rice

2 garlic cloves, minced

1 teaspoon dried basil

1/2 teaspoon salt

1/4 teaspoon pepper

1 package (6 ounces) fresh baby spinach, coarsely chopped

1/4 cup shredded Parmesan cheese

1 In a 4-qt. slow cooker, combine the broth, beans, tomato puree, onion, rice, garlic and seasonings. Cover and cook on low for 6-7 hours or until heated through.

2 Stir in spinach. Cover and cook for 15 minutes or until spinach is wilted. Sprinkle with cheese.

Colony Mountain Chili

PREP: 25 MIN. ■ **COOK:** 6 HOURS

Marjorie O'Dell
Bow, Washington
My husband created this chili for a local cooking contest, and it won the People's Choice award. It's loaded with beef, Italian sausage, tomatoes and beans and seasoned with chili powder, cumin and red pepper flakes for zip.

1 pound beef top sirloin steak, cut into 3/4-inch cubes

4 Italian sausage links, casings removed and cut into 3/4-inch slices

2 tablespoons olive oil, divided

1 medium onion, chopped

2 green onions, thinly sliced

3 garlic cloves, minced

2 teaspoons beef bouillon granules

1 cup boiling water

1 can (6 ounces) tomato paste

3 tablespoons chili powder

2 tablespoons brown sugar

2 tablespoons Worcestershire sauce

2 teaspoons ground cumin

1 to 2 teaspoons crushed red pepper flakes

1 teaspoon salt

1/2 teaspoon pepper

3 cans (14-1/2 ounces each) stewed tomatoes, cut up

2 cans (15 ounces each) pinto beans, rinsed and drained

Shredded cheddar cheese

1 In a large skillet, brown the beef and sausage in 1 tablespoon oil; drain. Transfer meat to a 5-qt. slow cooker.

2 In the same skillet, saute onion and green onions in remaining oil until tender. Add; garlic; cook 1 minute longer. Transfer to slow cooker.

3 In a small bowl, dissolve bouillon in water. Stir in the tomato paste, chili powder, brown sugar, Worcestershire sauce and seasonings until blended; add to slow cooker. Stir in tomatoes and beans.

4 Cover and cook on high for 6-8 hours or until the meat is tender. Serve with cheese if desired.

Yield: 10 servings (2-1/2 quarts).

Home-Style Chicken Soup

(pictured above)

PREP: 15 MIN. ■ **COOK:** 6-1/4 HOURS

Kathy Rairigh
Milford, Indiana
I've relied on this easily prepared broth on many occasions. My mom gave me the recipe, and we love it.

1 can (14-1/2 ounces) chicken broth

1 can (14-1/2 ounces) diced tomatoes, undrained

1 cup cubed cooked chicken

1 can (8 ounces) mushroom stems and pieces, drained

1/4 cup sliced fresh carrot

1/4 cup sliced celery

1 bay leaf

1/8 teaspoon dried thyme

3/4 cup cooked egg noodles

1 In a 1-1/2-qt. slow cooker, combine the broth, tomatoes, chicken, mushrooms, carrot, celery, bay leaf and thyme. Cover and cook on low for 6 hours.

2 Stir in noodles; cover and cook on high for 10 minutes. Discard bay leaf.

Yield: 4 servings.

Make it your own. This chicken soup is a fabulous recipe that lends itself to being easily customized for individual tastes. Add 1/4 to 1/2 cup of your favorite frozen vegetables, such as peas, corn, green beans, broccoli or cauliflower. Add a twist by using cooked rotini for the uncooked egg noodles.

Chunky Chicken Soup

PREP: 15 MIN. ■ **COOK:** 4-1/2 HOURS

Nancy Clow
Mallorytown, Ontario
I am a stay-at-home mom who relies on my slow cooker for fast, nutritious meals with minimal cleanup and prep time. I knew this recipe was a hit when I didn't have any leftovers and my husband asked me to make it again.

1-1/2 pounds boneless skinless chicken breasts, cut into 2-inch strips

2 teaspoons canola oil

2/3 cup finely chopped onion

2 medium carrots, chopped

2 celery ribs, chopped

1 cup frozen corn

2 cans (10-3/4 ounces each) condensed cream of potato soup, undiluted

1-1/2 cups chicken broth

1 teaspoon dill weed

1 cup frozen peas

1/2 cup half-and-half cream

1 In a large skillet over medium-high heat, brown chicken in oil or until no longer pink. With a slotted spoon, transfer to a 5-qt. slow cooker.

2 Add the onion, carrots, celery and corn. In a large bowl, whisk the soup, broth and dill until blended; stir into slow cooker. Cover and cook on low for 4 hours or until vegetables are tender.

3 Stir in the peas and cream. Cover and cook 30 minutes longer or until soup is heated through.

Yield: 7 servings.

Zippy Spanish Rice Soup

(pictured above)
PREP: 25 MIN. ■ **COOK:** 4 HOURS

Marilyn Schetz
Cuyahoga Falls, Ohio
I created this recipe after ruining a dinner of Spanish rice. I tried to salvage the dish by adding more water, cilantro and green chiles. It was a hit with the whole family. It's hearty enough to be a main meal with the addition of a garden salad and some corn bread.

1 pound lean ground beef (90% lean)

1 medium onion, chopped

3 cups water

1 jar (16 ounces) salsa

1 can (14-1/2 ounces) diced tomatoes, undrained

1 jar (7 ounces) roasted sweet red peppers, drained and chopped

1 can (4 ounces) chopped green chilies

1 envelope taco seasoning

1 tablespoon dried cilantro flakes

1/2 cup uncooked converted rice

1 In a large skillet, cook the beef and onion over medium heat until meat is no longer pink; drain. Transfer beef mixture to a 4- or 5-qt. slow cooker.

2 Add the water, salsa, tomatoes, red peppers, chilies, taco seasoning and cilantro. Stir in rice. Cover and cook on low for 4-5 hours or until rice is tender.

Yield: 8 servings (about 2 quarts).

Great Northern Bean Chili

PREP: 20 MIN. ■ **COOK:** 4 HOURS

mamesmom
Taste of Home Online Community
Seven ingredients make this mild version of a Southwestern chicken chili. I like to add a dash of hot sauce and some sour cream on top, and serve it with tortilla chips.

**2 pounds boneless skinless chicken breasts,
cut into 1-inch cubes**

1 tablespoon canola oil

**1 jar (48 ounces) great northern beans, rinsed
and drained**

1 jar (16 ounces) salsa

1 can (14-1/2 ounces) chicken broth

1 teaspoon ground cumin, optional

2 cups (8 ounces) shredded Monterey Jack cheese

1 In a large skillet, brown chicken in oil; drain. In a 4- or 5-qt. slow cooker, combine the beans, salsa, broth, cumin if desired and chicken. Cover and cook on low for 4-6 hours or until chicken is tender. Serve with cheese.

Yield: 8 servings (2-1/2 quarts).

Great toppings. The toppings for chili make it a fun dish to eat. Set out bowls of toppings and let your group mix-and-match to create their own unique bowl of chili. Here's a few suggestions for the toppings: jalapeno pepper rings, crushed tortillas, sliced ripe olives, sliced green onions, shredded cheese, chopped red pepper, sour cream, minced fresh cilantro or chopped tomatoes.

Smoked Sausage Gumbo

(pictured above)

PREP: 20 MIN. ■ **COOK:** 4 HOURS

Sharon Delaney-Chronis
South Milwaukee, Wisconsin

Serve up the flavors of the bayou! You'll leave the table satisfied, as it's chock-full of veggies, seasonings and sausage. Add in even more Cajun flavor with andouille sausage.

2 celery ribs, chopped	1 pound smoked kielbasa or Polish sausage, cut into 1/2-inch pieces
1 medium onion, chopped	
1 medium green pepper, chopped	
	1 can (14-1/2 ounces) diced tomatoes, undrained
1 medium carrot, chopped	2 teaspoons dried oregano
2 tablespoons olive oil	2 teaspoons dried thyme
1/4 cup all-purpose flour	1/8 teaspoon cayenne pepper
1 cup chicken broth	Hot cooked rice

1 In a large skillet, saute the celery, onion, green pepper and carrot in oil until tender. Stir in flour until blended; gradually add broth. Bring to a boil. Cook and stir for 2 minutes or until thickened. Transfer to a 3-qt. slow cooker.

2 Stir in the sausage, tomatoes, oregano, thyme and cayenne. Cover and cook on low for 4-5 hours or until heated through. Serve with rice.

Yield: 5 servings.

Beef and Three-Bean Chili

PREP: 20 MIN. ■ **COOK:** 5-1/2 HOURS

Nancy Whitford
Edwards, New York

This is one of my favorite recipes; it makes my kitchen smell so good! We love eating it with homemade bread or cornbread.

1-1/2 pounds beef stew meat, cut into 1-inch pieces

2 teaspoons chili powder

1-1/3 cups chopped onion

2 tablespoons canola oil

1 can (16 ounces) kidney beans, rinsed and drained

1 can (15 ounces) white kidney or cannellini beans, rinsed and drained

1 can (15 ounces) black beans, rinsed and drained

2 cans (14-1/2 ounces each) diced tomatoes, undrained

1 cup beef broth

1 can (6 ounces) tomato paste

2 jalapeno peppers, seeded and chopped

1 tablespoon brown sugar

2 teaspoons minced garlic

1/2 teaspoon salt

1/2 teaspoon pepper

1/4 teaspoon ground cumin

Sour cream, optional

1 Place beef in a large resealable plastic bag; add chili powder and toss to coat. In a large skillet over medium heat, brown beef and onion in oil.

2 Meanwhile, in a 5-qt. slow cooker coated with cooking spray, combine the beans, tomatoes, broth, tomato paste, jalapenos, brown sugar, garlic, salt, pepper and cumin. Stir in beef, onion and drippings.

3 Cover and cook on low for 5-1/2 to 6-1/2 hours or until meat is tender. Serve with sour cream if desired.

Yield: 9 servings (2-1/4 quarts).

Editor's Note: When cutting hot peppers, disposable gloves are recommended. Avoid touching your face.

Chicken Soup With Beans

PREP: 10 MIN. ■ **COOK:** 6 HOURS

Penny Peronia
West Memphis, Arkansas
I put lime-flavored tortilla chips at the bottom of individual bowls before ladling in this Southwestern soup. Loaded with chicken, beans, corn, tomatoes and green chilies, it's fulfilling and fuss-free.

- 1 large onion, chopped
- 1 tablespoon canola oil
- 2 garlic cloves, minced
- 1-1/4 pounds boneless skinless chicken breasts, cooked and cubed
- 2 cans (15-1/2 ounces each) great northern beans, rinsed and drained
- 2 cans (11 ounces each) white or shoepeg corn, drained
- 1 can (10 ounces) diced tomatoes and green chilies, undrained
- 3 cups water
- 1 can (4 ounces) chopped green chilies
- 2 tablespoons lime juice
- 1 teaspoon lemon-pepper seasoning
- 1 teaspoon ground cumin
- 1/4 teaspoon salt
- 1/4 teaspoon pepper

1 In a small skillet, saute onion in oil until tender. Add garlic; cook 1 minute longer. Transfer to a 5-qt. slow cooker.

2 Stir in all the remaining ingredients. Cover and cook on low for 6-7 hours or until heated through.

Yield: 12 servings (3 quarts).

Spice it up. Add a bit of zip to the Vegetable Minestrone by substituting V8 or spicy hot V8 juice for the tomato juice.

Vegetable Minestrone

(pictured above)

PREP: 15 MIN. ■ **COOK:** 6-1/2 HOURS

Alice Peacock
Grandview, Missouri
My husband and I created this recipe to replicate the minestrone soup at our favorite Italian restaurant. It's nice to have this ready to eat for our evening meal on days when we have a really busy schedule. To make the soup vegetarian, use vegetable broth instead of beef broth.

- 2 cans (14-1/2 ounces each) beef broth
- 1 can (16 ounces) kidney beans, rinsed and drained
- 1 can (15 ounces) great northern beans, rinsed and drained
- 1 can (14-1/2 ounces) Italian-style stewed tomatoes
- 1 large onion, chopped
- 1 medium zucchini, thinly sliced
- 1 medium carrot, shredded
- 3/4 cup tomato juice
- 1 teaspoon dried basil
- 3/4 teaspoon dried oregano
- 1/4 teaspoon garlic powder
- 1 cup frozen cut green beans, thawed
- 1/2 cup frozen chopped spinach, thawed
- 1/2 cup small shell pasta
- 1/2 cup shredded Parmesan cheese

1 In a 4- or 5-qt. slow cooker, combine the broth, beans, tomatoes, onion, zucchini, carrot, tomato juice and seasonings. Cover and cook on low for 6-7 hours or until vegetables are tender.

2 Stir in the green beans, spinach and pasta. Cover and cook for 30 minutes or until heated through. Sprinkle with cheese.

Yield: 8 servings (2-1/2 quarts).

Cincinnati Chili

(pictured above)

PREP: 25 MIN. ■ **COOK:** 5-1/2 HOURS

Joyce Alm
Thorp, Washington

The chocolate in this recipe threw me off at first, but now it's the only way I make chili. You'll find layers of delicious flavor in this heartwarming dish. It's well-worth the time it takes.

3 pounds ground beef	1 ounce unsweetened chocolate, coarsely chopped
1-1/2 cups chopped onions	1-1/2 teaspoons ground cinnamon
1-1/2 teaspoons minced garlic	
2 cans (16 ounces each) kidney beans, rinsed and drained	1-1/2 teaspoons ground cumin
	1 teaspoon salt
2 cans (15 ounces each) tomato sauce	1 teaspoon dried oregano
	1/2 teaspoon pepper
2 cups beef broth	1/8 teaspoon ground cloves
1/4 cup chili powder	Hot cooked spaghetti
1/4 cup red wine vinegar	Shredded cheddar cheese and sliced green onions, optional
1/4 cup Worcestershire sauce	

1 In a Dutch oven, cook the beef and onions over medium heat until meat is no longer pink. Add garlic; cook 1 minute longer. Drain.

2 In a 5-qt. slow cooker, combine the beans, tomato sauce, broth, chili powder, vinegar, Worcestershire sauce, chocolate, cinnamon, cumin, salt, oregano, pepper and cloves. Stir in beef mixture. Cover and cook on low for 5-1/2 to 6 hours or until heated through.

3 Serve with the spaghetti. Garnish with cheese and green onions if desired.

Yield: 10 servings (2-1/2 quarts).

Veggie-Sausage Cheese Soup

PREP: 55 MIN. ■ **COOK:** 7 HOURS

Richard Grant
Hudson, New Hampshire

I took this soup to a potluck at work, where it was well received...and was the only dish prepared by a guy! The great combination of textures and flavors had everyone asking for the recipe.

2 medium onions, finely chopped

1 each medium green and sweet red pepper, chopped

2 celery ribs, chopped

1 tablespoon olive oil

4 garlic cloves, minced

1 pound smoked kielbasa or Polish sausage, cut into 1/4-inch slices

2 medium potatoes, diced

1 can (14-3/4 ounces) cream-style corn

1 can (14-1/2 ounces) chicken broth

1 can (10-3/4 ounces) condensed cream of mushroom soup, undiluted

2 medium carrots, sliced

1 cup whole kernel corn

1 cup sliced fresh mushrooms

1 tablespoon Worcestershire sauce

1 tablespoon Dijon mustard

1 tablespoon dried basil

1 tablespoon dried parsley flakes

1/2 teaspoon pepper

2 cups (8 ounces) shredded sharp cheddar cheese

1 can (12 ounces) evaporated milk

1 In a large skillet, saute the onions, peppers and celery in oil until tender. Add garlic; cook 1 minute longer. Transfer to a 5-qt. slow cooker.

2 Stir in the sausage, potatoes, cream-style corn, broth, soup, carrots, corn, mushrooms, Worcestershire sauce, Dijon mustard and seasonings. Cover and cook on low for 6-1/2 to 7-1/2 hours or until vegetables are tender.

3 Stir in cheese and milk. Cook on low 30 minutes longer or until cheese is melted. Stir until blended.

Yield: 16 servings (4 quarts).

Cream of Cauliflower Soup

PREP: 30 MIN. ■ **COOK:** 3-1/2 HOURS

Ruth Worden
Mossena, New York
When a chill is in the air, I like to make soups for the family. Cheese adds flavor and heartiness to this one, which is my own recipe.

1 large head cauliflower, broken into florets

2 cups chicken broth

2 tablespoons reduced-sodium chicken bouillon granules

2 cups half-and-half cream

2 cups 2% milk

1 medium carrot, shredded

2 bay leaves

1/4 teaspoon garlic powder

1/2 cup mashed potato flakes

2 cups (8 ounces) shredded cheddar cheese

Paprika

1 In a large saucepan, combine the cauliflower, broth and bouillon. Bring to a boil. Reduce heat; cover and cook for 20 minutes or until tender. Mash cauliflower. Transfer to a 3-qt. slow cooker.

2 Stir in the cream, milk, carrot, bay leaves and garlic powder. Cover and cook on low for 3 hours.

3 Stir in potato flakes. Cook 30 minutes longer or until thickened. Discard bay leaves. Cool slightly.

4 In a blender, process soup in batches until smooth. Return to the slow cooker; stir in cheese. Cook until soup is heated through and cheese is melted. Garnish with paprika.

Yield: 8 servings (2 quarts).

Beef & Vegetable Soup

(pictured above)
PREP: 20 MIN. ■ **COOK:** 8 HOURS

Tammy Landry
Saucier, Mississippi
I've been making this for a lot of years. The beer makes people stop and wonder what the unique flavor in the soup is. Try it; I know you'll love it!

1 pound lean ground beef (90% lean)

1/2 cup chopped sweet onion

1 bottle (12 ounces) beer or nonalcoholic beer

1 can (10-1/2 ounces) condensed beef broth, undiluted

1-1/2 cups sliced fresh carrots

1-1/4 cups water

1 cup chopped peeled turnip

1/2 cup sliced celery

1 can (4 ounces) mushroom stems and pieces, drained

1 teaspoon salt

1 teaspoon pepper

1 bay leaf

1/8 teaspoon ground allspice

1 In a large skillet, cook beef and onion over medium heat until meat is no longer pink; drain. Transfer to a 5-qt. slow cooker.

2 Stir in all the remaining ingredients. Cover and cook on low for 8-10 hours or until heated through. Discard bay leaf.

Yield: 6 servings.

Veggie Potato Soup

PREP: 20 MIN. ■ **COOK:** 5-1/2 HOURS

Hannah Thompson
Scotts Valley, California
Chock-full of potatoes, this vegetarian soup is as filling as it is flavorful. Serve on cold winter nights with crusty bread or take some to work...with this in store, you'll really look forward to lunch.

---

6 medium potatoes, cubed

1 medium carrot, thinly sliced

1 large leek (white portion only), chopped

3 cans (14-1/2 ounces each) vegetable broth

1/4 cup butter, cubed

1 garlic clove, minced

1 teaspoon dried thyme

3/4 teaspoon salt

1/4 teaspoon dried marjoram

1/4 teaspoon pepper

1/4 cup all-purpose flour

1-1/2 cups half-and-half cream

1 cup frozen peas, thawed

1 In a 5-qt. slow cooker, combine the vegetables, broth, butter, garlic and seasonings. Cover and cook on low for 5-6 hours or until vegetables are tender.

2 In a small bowl, combine flour and cream until smooth; add to slow cooker. Stir in peas. Cover and cook on high for 30 minutes or until the soup is slightly thickened.

Yield: 11 servings (2-3/4 quarts).

Spicy Two-Bean Chili

PREP: 20 MIN. ■ **COOK:** 8 HOURS

Lesley Pew
Lynn, Massachusetts
Chili fans will get a kick out of this untraditional recipe. Tomatoes with green chilies, lime juice and kidney and black beans give it an original twist. It's wonderful ladled over rice.

2 pounds ground beef

3 large onions, chopped

6 garlic cloves, minced

2 cans (16 ounces each) kidney beans, rinsed and drained

2 cans (15 ounces each) black beans, rinsed and drained

2 cans (10 ounces each) diced tomatoes and green chilies, undrained

1 can (14-1/2 ounces) chicken broth

1/2 cup lime juice

6 tablespoons cornmeal

1/4 cup chili powder

4 teaspoons dried oregano

3 teaspoons ground cumin

2 teaspoons salt

2 teaspoons rubbed sage

1/2 teaspoon white pepper

1/2 teaspoon paprika

1/2 teaspoon pepper

Hot cooked rice

Shredded cheddar cheese

1 In a Dutch oven, cook beef and onions over medium heat until meat is no longer pink. Add garlic; cook 1 minute longer; drain. Transfer to a 5-qt. slow cooker.

2 Stir in the beans, tomatoes, broth, lime juice, cornmeal and seasonings. Cover and cook on low for 8 hours or until heated through. Serve with rice; sprinkle with cheese.

Yield: 11 servings (2-3/4 quarts).

Zippy Steak Chili

(pictured above)

PREP: 15 MIN. ■ **COOK:** 6 HOURS

Denise Habib
Poolesville, Maryland
Looking for a thick, chunky chili with an extra-special kick? Try this recipe. It was given to me by a coworker originally from Texas. I've made it on numerous occasions and the gang always enjoys it.

1 pound beef top sirloin steak, cut into 1/2-inch cubes

1/2 cup chopped onion

2 tablespoons canola oil

2 tablespoons chili powder

1 teaspoon garlic powder

1 teaspoon ground cumin

1 teaspoon dried oregano

1 teaspoon pepper

2 cans (10 ounces each) diced tomatoes and green chilies, undrained

1 can (15-1/2 ounces) chili starter

Shredded cheddar cheese, chopped onion and sour cream, optional

1 In a large skillet, cook steak and onion in oil over medium heat until meat is no longer pink. Sprinkle with seasonings.

2 In a 5-qt. slow cooker, combine the tomatoes and chili starter. Stir in the beef mixture. Cover and cook on low for 6-8 hours or until the meat is tender. Serve with cheese, onion and sour cream if desired.

Yield: 5 servings.

Editor's Note: This recipe was tested with Bush's Traditional Chili Starter.

Hearty Sausage-Chicken Chili

PREP: 20 MIN. ■ **COOK:** 4 HOURS

Carolyn Etzler
Thurmont, Maryland
The company I work for has an annual Chili Cook-Off, and this unusual entry of mine was a winner. It combines two other recipes and includes a touch or two of my own.

> 1 pound Italian turkey sausage links, casings removed
> 3/4 pound boneless skinless chicken thighs, cut into 3/4-inch pieces
> 1 medium onion, chopped
> 2 cans (14-1/2 ounces each) diced tomatoes with mild green chilies, undrained
> 2 cans (8 ounces each) tomato sauce
> 1 can (16 ounces) kidney beans, rinsed and drained
> 1 can (15 ounces) white kidney or cannellini beans, rinsed and drained
> 1 can (15 ounces) pinto beans, rinsed and drained
> 1 can (15 ounces) black beans, rinsed and drained
> 1 teaspoon chili powder
> 1/2 teaspoon garlic powder
> 1/8 teaspoon pepper

1 Crumble sausage into a large nonstick skillet coated with cooking spray. Add chicken and onion; cook and stir over medium heat until meat is no longer pink. Drain. Transfer to a 5-qt. slow cooker.

2 Stir in the remaining ingredients. Cover and cook on low for 4 hours.

Yield: 11 servings (2-3/4 quarts).

Split Pea Soup

(pictured above)

PREP: 25 MIN. ■ **COOK:** 4-1/4 HOURS

Heidi Schmidgall
Hancock, Minnesota
In less than half an hour, I can have the ingredients for my satisfying pea soup simmering away. What a great treat to enjoy on a chilly night.

> 1 package (16 ounces) dried green split peas
> 2 smoked ham hocks
> 2 quarts water
> 2 medium carrots, halved lengthwise and thinly sliced
> 1 medium onion, chopped
> 1 celery rib, thinly sliced
> 1 garlic clove, minced
>
> 1 bay leaf
> 1 teaspoon chicken bouillon granules
> 1 teaspoon dried thyme
> 3/4 teaspoon salt
> 1/2 teaspoon garlic salt
> 1/2 teaspoon dried basil
> 1/2 teaspoon dried marjoram
> 1/2 teaspoon pepper

1 In a 5-qt. slow cooker, combine all the ingredients. Cover and cook on high for 4-5 hours or until peas are tender. Skim fat; discard bay leaf.

2 Remove ham hock from the slow cooker. When cool enough to handle, remove meat from bones; discard bones and cut ham into small pieces. Return meat to slow cooker; heat through.

Yield: 8 servings (2 quarts).

Veggie Meatball Soup

PREP: 20 MIN. ■ **COOK:** 6 HOURS

Penny Fagan
Mobile, Alabama

Loaded with veggies, meatballs and spices, this meal-in-one soup is hearty enough to warm up any blustery day. It's a dish you'll make again and again!

1 package (12 ounces) frozen fully cooked Italian meatballs

1 can (28 ounces) diced tomatoes, undrained

3 cups beef broth

2 cups shredded cabbage

1 can (16 ounces) kidney beans, rinsed and drained

1 medium zucchini, sliced

1 cup fresh green beans, cut into 1-inch pieces

1 cup water

2 medium carrots, sliced

1 teaspoon dried basil

1/2 teaspoon minced garlic

1/4 teaspoon salt

1/8 teaspoon dried oregano

1/8 teaspoon pepper

1 cup uncooked elbow macaroni

1/4 cup minced fresh parsley

Grated Parmesan cheese, optional

1 In a 5-qt. slow cooker, combine the meatballs, tomatoes, broth, cabbage, kidney beans, zucchini, green beans, water, carrots and seasonings. Cover and cook on low for 5-1/2 to 6 hours or until vegetables are almost tender.

2 Stir in the macaroni and parsley; cook 30 minutes longer or until macaroni is tender. Serve with cheese if desired.

Yield: 6 servings (2-1/2 quarts).

Mulligatawny Soup

PREP: 20 MIN. ■ **COOK:** 6 HOURS

Mary Ann Marino
West Pittsburg, Pennsylvania
This is a delicious and satisfying soup, which I make with leftover chicken or turkey. My family enjoys this on crisp fall and winter days.

1 carton (32 ounces) chicken broth

1 can (14-1/2 ounces) diced tomatoes

2 cups cubed cooked chicken

1 large tart apple, peeled and chopped

1/4 cup finely chopped onion

1/4 cup chopped carrot

1/4 cup chopped green pepper

1 tablespoon minced fresh parsley

2 teaspoons lemon juice

1 teaspoon salt

1 teaspoon curry powder

1/2 teaspoon sugar

1/4 teaspoon pepper

2 whole cloves

1 In a 3- or 4-qt. slow cooker, combine all the ingredients. Cover and cook on low for 6-8 hours or until vegetables are tender. Discard cloves.

Yield: 8 servings (2 quarts).

Add some garnish. Mulligatawny Soup originated in Southern India as a spicy broth flavored with curry and other spices. When you serve up steaming bowls of this variation, add a traditional touch like shredded coconut or cooked rice.

Creamy Ham Chowder

PREP: 30 MIN. ■ **COOK:** 3-1/2 HOURS

Lee Bremson
Kansas City, Missouri
You'll dig into satisfaction when this thick and creamy chowder is on the menu. Loaded with comforting flavor, it's sure to make friends and family think you labored for hours perfecting it.

4 cups cubed peeled potatoes

2 tablespoons chopped onion

1/2 cup butter

3/4 cup all-purpose flour

1/4 teaspoon salt

1/4 teaspoon pepper

Pinch ground nutmeg

4 cups chicken broth

4 cups half-and-half cream

2 cups (8 ounces) shredded cheddar cheese

3 cups cubed fully cooked ham

1 package (16 ounces) frozen broccoli cuts, thawed and drained

1 Place potatoes in a large saucepan and cover with water. Bring to a boil. Reduce heat; cover and cook for 10-15 minutes or until tender.

2 Meanwhile, in a large saucepan, cook onion in butter over medium heat for 2 minutes. Stir in the flour, salt, pepper and nutmeg until blended. Gradually add broth. Bring to a boil; cook and stir for 2 minutes or until thickened. Stir in cream and cheese.

3 Transfer to a 5-qt. slow cooker. Drain potatoes; add to slow cooker. Stir in ham. Cover and cook on low for 3 hours.

4 Stir in broccoli. Cover and cook 30 minutes longer or until heated through and vegetables are tender.

Yield: 12 servings (about 3-1/2 quarts).

Black Bean 'n' Pumpkin Chili

(pictured above)

PREP: 20 MIN. ■ **COOK:** 4 HOURS

Deborah Vliet
Holland, Michigan
Our family loves this slow-cooked recipe. It's a wonderful variation on standard chili that freezes well and tastes even better as leftovers.

1 medium onion, chopped

1 medium sweet yellow pepper, chopped

2 tablespoons olive oil

3 garlic cloves, minced

3 cups chicken broth

2 cans (15 ounces each) black beans, rinsed and drained

2-1/2 cups cubed cooked turkey

1 can (15 ounces) solid-pack pumpkin

1 can (14-1/2 ounces) diced tomatoes, undrained

2 teaspoons dried parsley flakes

2 teaspoons chili powder

1-1/2 teaspoons dried oregano

1-1/2 teaspoons ground cumin

1/2 teaspoon salt

1 In a large skillet, saute onion, yellow pepper in oil until tender. Add garlic; cook 1 minute longer. Transfer to a 5-qt. slow cooker.

2 Stir in all the remaining ingredients. Cover and cook on low for 4-5 hours or until heated through.

Yield: 10 servings (2-1/2 quarts).

Colorful Minestrone

PREP: 40 MIN. ■ COOK: 7-1/2 HOURS

Tiffany Anderson-Taylor
Gulfport, Florida
Butternut squash, a leek and fresh kale make my minestrone different from most others. Not only do ingredients like these help keep the fat grams down, but they create a lovely blend of flavors.

1 medium leek (white portion only), thinly sliced

1 small onion, chopped

1 tablespoon olive oil

3 slices deli ham, chopped

2 garlic cloves, minced

2 quarts water

1 can (28 ounces) diced tomatoes, undrained

1 medium butternut squash, peeled, seeded and cubed

2 medium carrots, coarsely chopped

2 celery ribs, chopped

2 cups fresh baby spinach, cut into thin strips

1 cup fresh kale, trimmed and cut into thin strips

1 medium potato, peeled and cubed

1 tablespoon minced fresh rosemary

1 teaspoon salt

Pepper to taste

1 can (15 ounces) white kidney or cannellini beans, rinsed and drained

1 In a small skillet, saute leek and onion in oil for 2 minutes or until vegetables are tender. Add ham and garlic; cook 1 minute longer. Transfer ham mixture to a 5-qt. slow cooker.

2 Stir in water, vegetables, rosemary, salt and pepper. Cover and cook on low for 7-8 hours or until vegetables are tender.

3 Stir in the beans; cover and cook for 30 minutes.

Yield: 10 servings (3-1/2 quarts).

Healthy Tomato Soup

(pictured above)

PREP: 5 MIN. ■ COOK: 5 HOURS

Heather Campbell
Lawrence, Kansas
This soup is especially good with sandwiches and for dipping bread. To trim the sodium, I like to season it with spices and herbs rather than salt.

1 can (46 ounces) tomato juice

1 can (8 ounces) tomato sauce

1/2 cup water

1/2 cup chopped onion

1 celery rib with leaves, chopped

2 tablespoons sugar

1/2 teaspoon dried basil

3 to 5 whole cloves

1 bay leaf

1 In a 3-qt. slow cooker, combine all of the ingredients. Cover and cook on low for 5-6 hours or until heated through. Discard cloves and bay leaf.

Yield: 6 servings.

Roundup Chili

PREP: 35 MIN. ■ **COOK:** 6 HOURS

Linda Stemen
Monroeville, Indiana

Two types of meat make this not-too-spicy chili a hearty meal. It's a great choice for casual gatherings.

2 pounds lean ground beef (90% lean)

1 beef flank steak (1-1/2 pounds), cubed

1 medium onion, chopped

1 celery rib, chopped

1 can (29 ounces) tomato sauce

2 cans (14-1/2 ounces each) diced tomatoes, undrained

1 can (16 ounces) kidney beans, rinsed and drained

1 can (15 ounces) pinto beans, rinsed and drained

1 can (4 ounces) chopped green chilies

2 to 3 tablespoons chili powder

3 teaspoons ground cumin

2 teaspoons salt

2 teaspoons pepper

1/2 teaspoon ground mustard

1/2 teaspoon paprika

1/2 teaspoon cayenne pepper

1/4 teaspoon garlic powder

Hot pepper sauce, shredded cheddar cheese and additional chopped onion, optional

1 In a large skillet, cook the ground beef, flank steak, onion and celery over medium heat until meat is no longer pink; drain. Transfer to a 6-qt. slow cooker.

2 Stir in the tomato sauce, tomatoes, beans, chilies and seasonings. Cover and cook on low for 6-8 hours. Serve with hot pepper sauce, cheese and onion if desired.

Yield: 12 servings (3 quarts).

sides

Corn and Broccoli In Cheese Sauce

(pictured at left)

PREP: 10 MIN. ■ COOK: 3 HOURS

Joyce Johnson
Uniontown, Ohio

This dish is a standby. My daughter likes to add leftover ham to it for a simple one-dish supper.

- 1 package (16 ounces) frozen corn, thawed
- 1 package (16 ounces) frozen broccoli florets, thawed
- 4 ounces reduced-fat process cheese (Velveeta), cubed
- 1/2 cup shredded cheddar cheese
- 1 can (10-1/4 ounces) reduced-fat reduced-sodium condensed cream of chicken soup, undiluted
- 1/4 cup fat-free milk

1 In a 4-qt. slow cooker, combine the corn, broccoli and cheeses. In a small bowl, combine soup and milk; pour over vegetable mixture. Cover and cook on low for 3-4 hours or until heated through. Stir before serving.

Yield: 8 servings.

Old-Fashioned Dressing

PREP: 35 MIN. ■ COOK: 3 HOURS

Sherry Vink
Lacombe, Alberta, Canada

Remember Grandma's delicious turkey dressing? Taste it again combined with flavorful herbs and crisp veggies in this family favorite.

- 2 celery ribs, chopped
- 1 medium onion, chopped
- 1 cup sliced fresh mushrooms
- 1/2 cup butter, cubed
- 1/2 cup minced fresh parsley
- 2 teaspoons rubbed sage
- 2 teaspoons dried marjoram
- 1 teaspoon dried thyme
- 1 teaspoon poultry seasoning
- 1/2 teaspoon pepper
- 1/4 teaspoon salt
- 6 cups cubed day-old white bread
- 6 cups cubed day-old whole wheat bread
- 1 can (14-1/2 ounces) chicken broth

1 In a large skillet, saute the celery, onion and mushrooms in butter until tender. Stir in the seasonings. Place bread cubes in a large bowl. Add vegetable mixture and toss to coat. Stir in broth.

2 Transfer to a 3-qt. slow cooker coated with cooking spray. Cover and cook on low for 3-4 hours or until heated through.

Yield: 8 servings.

Slow-Cooked Bean Medley

(pictured above)

PREP: 25 MIN. ■ **COOK:** 5 HOURS

Peggy Gwillim
Strasbourg, Saskatchewan

I often change the variety of beans in this classic recipe, using whatever I have on hand to total five 15- to 16-ounce cans. The sauce makes any combination delicious! It's a side dish that's popular with everyone.

1-1/2 cups ketchup

2 celery ribs, chopped

1 medium onion, chopped

1 medium green pepper, chopped

1 medium sweet red pepper, chopped

1/2 cup packed brown sugar

1/2 cup water

1/2 cup Italian salad dressing

2 bay leaves

1 tablespoon cider vinegar

1 teaspoon ground mustard

1/8 teaspoon pepper

1 can (16 ounces) kidney beans, rinsed and drained

1 can (15-1/2 ounces) black-eyed peas, rinsed and drained

1 can (15-1/2 ounces) great northern beans, rinsed and drained

1 can (15-1/4 ounces) whole kernel corn, drained

1 can (15-1/4 ounces) lima beans, rinsed and drained

1 can (15 ounces) black beans, rinsed and drained

1 In a 5-qt. slow cooker, combine the ketchup, vegetables, brown sugar, water, Italian dressing, bay leaves, vinegar, mustard and pepper. Stir in the remaining ingredients. Cover and cook on low for 5-7 hours or until onion and peppers are tender. Discard the bay leaves.

Yield: 12 servings.

German Potato Salad With Sausage

PREP: 30 MIN. ■ **COOK:** 6 HOURS

Teresa McGill
Trotwood, Ohio

Hearty and saucy, this potato salad is an old family recipe that was updated using cream of potato soup to ease preparation. The sausage and sauerkraut give it a special zip.

8 bacon strips, diced

1 large onion, chopped

1 pound smoked kielbasa or Polish sausage, halved and cut into 1/2-inch slices

2 pounds medium red potatoes, cut into chunks

1 can (10-3/4 ounces) condensed cream of potato soup, undiluted

1 cup sauerkraut, rinsed and well drained

1/2 cup water

1/4 cup cider vinegar

1 tablespoon sugar

1/2 teaspoon salt

1/2 teaspoon coarsely ground pepper

1 In a large skillet, cook bacon over medium heat until crisp. Using a slotted spoon, remove to paper towels to drain. Saute onion in drippings for 1 minute. Add sausage; cook until lightly browned. Add potatoes; cook 2 minutes longer. Drain. Transfer sausage mixture to a 3-qt. slow cooker.

2 In a small bowl, combine the soup, sauerkraut, water, vinegar, sugar, salt and pepper. Pour over sausage mixture. Sprinkle with the bacon. Cover and cook on low for 6-7 hours or until the potatoes are tender.

Yield: 8 servings.

Creamy Macaroni and Cheese

PREP: 25 MIN. ■ **COOK:** 2 HOURS

Jennifer Babcock
Chicopee, Massachusetts
This is a great way to make America's most popular comfort food. The dish turns out cheesy, rich and creamy.

3 cups uncooked elbow macaroni

1 pound process cheese (Velveeta), cubed

2 cups (8 ounces) shredded Mexican cheese blend

2 cups (8 ounces) shredded white cheddar cheese

1-3/4 cups milk

1 can (12 ounces) evaporated milk

3/4 cup egg substitute

3/4 cup butter, melted

1 Cook the macaroni according to package directions; drain. Place in a greased 5-qt. slow cooker. Stir in the remaining ingredients. Cover and cook on low for 2-3 hours or until a thermometer reads 160°, stirring once.

Yield: 16 servings (3/4 cup each).

> **The classic look.** Elbow macaroni creates the classic look for mac and cheese. By switching out the macaroni with another small pasta, you can go for a different look. Try small shell pasta, rotini or even bow ties for a change of pace.

Italian Spaghetti Squash

PREP: 15 MIN. ■ **COOK:** 6-1/4 HOURS

Melissa Brooks
Sparta, Wisconsin

This is a unique and easy way to cook spaghetti squash. Be sure the squash is on the small or medium side so that it fits into the slow cooker after being cut in half.

---

1 medium spaghetti squash

1 cup sliced fresh mushrooms

1 can (14-1/2 ounces) diced tomatoes, undrained

1 teaspoon dried oregano

1 teaspoon salt

1/4 teaspoon pepper

3/4 cup shredded part-skim mozzarella cheese

1 Cut squash in half lengthwise; discard seeds. Place squash, cut side up, in a 6- or 7-qt. slow cooker. Layer with mushrooms, tomatoes, oregano, salt and pepper. Cover and cook on low for 6-8 hours or until squash is tender.

2 Sprinkle with cheese. Cover and cook for 15 minutes or until cheese is melted. When the squash is cool enough to handle, use a fork to separate the spaghetti squash strands.

Yield: 4 servings.

About spaghetti squash. Spaghetti squash can range in size from 4 to 8 pounds. For the Italian Spaghetti Squash recipe, look for one that is 4 to 5 pounds. When choosing a squash, look for one that feels heavy for its size and has hard rind that is free of blemishes. Unwashed spaghetti squash can be stored at room temperature for up to 3 weeks.

Nacho Hash Brown Casserole

(pictured above)

PREP: 15 MIN. ■ **COOK:** 3-1/4 HOURS

Pat Habiger
Spearville, Kansas

This tasty slow cooker recipe will free up your oven and produce the best hash browns ever. Soft and super cheesy, they make a comforting side dish for meat or poultry.

---

1 package (32 ounces) frozen cubed hash brown potatoes, thawed

1 can (10-3/4 ounces) condensed cream of celery soup, undiluted

1 can (10-3/4 ounces) condensed nacho cheese soup, undiluted

1 large onion, finely chopped

1/3 cup butter, melted

1 cup (8 ounces) reduced-fat sour cream

1 In a 3-qt. slow cooker coated with cooking spray, combine the potatoes, soups, onion and butter. Cover and cook on low for 3-4 hours or until potatoes are tender. Stir in sour cream. Cover and cook 15-30 minutes longer or until heated through.

Yield: 8 servings.

Slow-Cooked Creamy Rice

PREP: 25 MIN. ■ **COOK:** 2-1/2 HOURS

Laura Crane
Leetonia, Ohio
Serve this wonderful side with any stew. I use fresh herbs on hand along to add even more flavor.

3 cups cooked rice

2 eggs, lightly beaten

1 can (12 ounces) evaporated milk

1 cup (4 ounces) shredded Swiss cheese

1 cup (4 ounces) shredded cheddar cheese

1 medium onion, chopped

1/2 cup minced fresh parsley

6 tablespoons water

2 tablespoons canola oil

1 garlic clove, minced

1-1/2 teaspoons salt

1/4 teaspoon pepper

1 Combine all ingredients in a 3-qt. slow cooker. Cover and cook on low for 2-1/2 to 3 hours or until a thermometer reads 160°.

Yield: 8 servings.

Vegetable Medley

PREP: 5 MIN. ■ **COOK:** 5 HOURS

Terry Maly
Olathe, Kansas
This is a sensational side dish to make when garden vegetables are plentiful.

4 cups diced peeled potatoes

1-1/2 cups frozen whole kernel corn or 1 can (15-1/4 ounces) whole kernel corn, drained

4 medium tomatoes, seeded and diced

1 cup sliced carrots

1/2 cup chopped onion

3/4 teaspoon salt

1/2 teaspoon sugar

1/2 teaspoon dill weed

1/8 teaspoon pepper

1 In a 3-qt. slow cooker, combine all the ingredients. Cover and cook on low for 5-6 hours or until vegetables are tender.

Yield: 8 servings.

Coconut-Pecan Sweet Potatoes

(pictured above)

PREP: 20 MIN. ■ **COOK:** 5 HOURS

Rebecca Clark
Warrior, Alabama
It's great to be able to make a tempting sweet potato dish well ahead of dinnertime. This tasty recipe includes sweet coconut and crunchy pecans. It's yummy!

2 pounds sweet potatoes, peeled and cut into 3/4-inch cubes

1/4 cup packed brown sugar

2 tablespoons flaked coconut

2 tablespoons chopped pecans, toasted

1 teaspoon vanilla extract

1/2 teaspoon salt

1/4 teaspoon ground cinnamon

1 tablespoon butter, melted

1/2 cup miniature marshmallows

1 Place sweet potatoes in a 3-qt. slow cooker coated with cooking spray. In a small bowl, combine the brown sugar, coconut, pecans, vanilla, salt and cinnamon; sprinkle over sweet potatoes. Drizzle with butter.

2 Cover and cook on low for 5-6 hours or until potatoes are tender, sprinkling with marshmallows during last 5 minutes of cooking time.

Yield: 6 servings.

Ratatouille

PREP: 20 MIN. + STANDING ■ **COOK:** 3 HOURS

Jolene Walters
North Miami, Florida
Not only does this French-style recipe make a phenomenal side dish, but you can also serve it with sliced French bread for a warm but easy appetizer. Try it in the summer with your garden-fresh vegetables.

- 1 large eggplant, peeled and cut into 1-inch cubes
- 2 teaspoons salt, divided
- 3 medium tomatoes, chopped
- 3 medium zucchini, halved lengthwise and sliced
- 2 medium onions, chopped
- 1 large green pepper, chopped
- 1 large sweet yellow pepper, chopped
- 1 can (6 ounces) pitted ripe olives, drained and chopped
- 1 can (6 ounces) tomato paste
- 1/2 cup minced fresh basil
- 2 garlic cloves, minced
- 1/2 teaspoon pepper
- 2 tablespoons olive oil

1 Place eggplant in a colander over a plate; sprinkle with 1 teaspoon salt and toss. Let stand for 30 minutes. Rinse and drain well. Transfer to a 5-qt. slow cooker coated with cooking spray.

2 Stir in the tomatoes, zucchini, onions, green and yellow peppers, olives, tomato paste, basil, garlic, pepper and remaining salt. Drizzle with oil. Cover and cook on high for 3-4 hours or until vegetables are tender.

Yield: 10 servings.

Banana Applesauce

PREP: 20 MIN. ■ **COOK:** 3 HOURS

Judy Batson
Tampa, Florida
The recipe has evolved over the many years we have made it. This version has been a favorite at our Christmas dinners.

- 8 medium apples, peeled and cubed
- 1 medium ripe banana, thinly sliced
- 1 cup raisins
- 3/4 cup orange juice
- 1/2 cup packed brown sugar
- 1/4 cup honey
- 1/4 cup butter, melted
- 2 teaspoons pumpkin pie spice
- 1 small lemon
- 1 envelope instant apples and cinnamon oatmeal
- 1/2 cup boiling water

1 Place the apples, banana and raisins in a 3-qt. slow cooker coated with cooking spray. In a small bowl, combine the orange juice, brown sugar, honey, butter and pie spice; pour over apple mixture. Cut ends off lemon. Cut into six wedges and remove seeds. Transfer to slow cooker. Cover and cook on high for 3-4 hours or until apples are soft.

2 Discard lemon. Mash apple mixture. In a small bowl, combine oatmeal and water. Let stand for 1 minute. Stir into the applesauce.

Yield: 5-1/2 cups.

Change of fruit. *If you're a fan of pears, mix up a batch of Banana Pear Sauce. Use 8 peeled, cored and cubed pears for the apples. Try the sauce with Anjou, Bartlett, Bosc or Seckel pears.*

Squash Stuffing Casserole

(pictured above)

PREP: 15 MIN. ■ **COOK:** 4 HOURS

Pamela Thorson
Hot Springs, Arkansas
My friends just rave about this creamy dish. It's a snap to jazz up summer squash, zucchini and carrots with canned soup and stuffing mix.

- 1/4 cup all-purpose flour
- 1 can (10-3/4 ounces) condensed cream of chicken soup, undiluted
- 1 cup (8 ounces) sour cream
- 2 medium yellow summer squash, cut into 1/2-inch slices
- 1 small onion, chopped
- 1 cup shredded carrots
- 1 package (8 ounces) stuffing mix
- 1/2 cup butter, melted

1 In a large bowl, combine the flour, soup and sour cream until blended. Add the vegetables and gently stir to coat. Combine the stuffing mix and butter; sprinkle half into a 5-qt. slow cooker. Top with vegetable mixture and remaining stuffing mixture. Cover and cook on low for 4-5 hours or until vegetables are tender.

Yield: 8 servings.

"Everything" Stuffing

(pictured above)

PREP: 30 MIN. ■ **COOK:** 3 HOURS

Bette Votral
Bethlehem, Pennsylvania
My husband and father go crazy for this stuffing! It also freezes well so we can enjoy it even after Thanksgiving.

1/2 pound bulk Italian sausage	1/8 teaspoon pepper
4 cups seasoned stuffing cubes	1-3/4 cups sliced baby portobello mushrooms
1-1/2 cups crushed corn bread stuffing	1 package (5 ounces) sliced fresh shiitake mushrooms
1/2 cup chopped toasted chestnuts or pecans	1 large onion, chopped
1/2 cup minced fresh parsley	1 medium apple, peeled and chopped
1 tablespoon minced fresh sage or 1 teaspoon rubbed sage	1 celery rib, chopped
	3 tablespoons butter
1/8 teaspoon salt	1 can (14-1/2 ounces) chicken broth

1 In a large skillet, cook the sausage over medium heat until no longer pink; drain. Place in a bowl. Stir in stuffing cubes, corn bread stuffing, chestnuts, parsley, sage, salt and pepper.

2 In the same skillet, saute the mushrooms, onion, apple and celery in butter until tender. Stir into stuffing mixture. Add enough broth to reach desired moistness.

3 Transfer to a 5-qt. slow cooker. Cover and cook on low for 3 hours, stirring once.

Yield: 9 servings.

Hearty Wild Rice

PREP: 15 MIN. ■ **COOK:** 5 HOURS

Mrs. Garnet Pettigrew
Columbia City, Indiana
I switched this recipe from the oven to the slow cooker so I wouldn't need to keep an eye on it.

- 1 pound ground beef
- 1/2 pound bulk pork sausage
- 6 celery ribs, diced
- 2 cans (10-1/2 ounces each) condensed beef broth, undiluted
- 1-1/4 cups water
- 1 medium onion, chopped
- 1 cup uncooked wild rice
- 1 can (4 ounces) mushroom stems and pieces, drained
- 1/4 cup soy sauce

1 In a large skillet, cook beef and sausage over medium heat until no longer pink; drain. Transfer to a 5-qt. slow cooker.

2 Stir in the celery, broth, water, onion, rice, mushrooms and soy sauce. Cover and cook on high for 1 hour. Reduce heat to low; cover and cook for 4 hours or until the rice is tender.

Yield: 10-12 servings.

Editor's Note: Hearty Wild Rice is filling enough to be served as a main course with fresh whole wheat bread and a salad. Or use it as a side dish for any meaty entree.

Cranberry Relish

PREP: 5 MIN. + CHILLING
COOK: 6 HOURS

June Formanek
Belle Plaine, Iowa
This no-fuss, ruby-red condiment simmers away while I do other holiday preparations. It's especially well when served alongside turkey.

- 2 cups sugar
- 1 cup orange juice
- 1 teaspoon grated orange peel
- 4 cups fresh or frozen cranberries

1 In a 1-1/2-qt. slow cooker, combine sugar, orange juice and peel; stir until sugar is dissolved. Add the cranberries. Cover and cook on low for 6 hours. Mash the mixture. Chill several hours or overnight.

Yield: 10-12 servings (3 cups).

Winter Fruit Compote

PREP: 10 MIN.
COOK: 1-1/4 HOURS + COOLING

Esther Chesney
Carthage, Missouri
You can make this colorful and easy fruit relish up to a week in advance and refrigerate it. The compote makes a great accompaniment to turkey, chicken or pork.

- 1 package (12 ounces) fresh or frozen cranberries, thawed
- 2/3 cup packed brown sugar
- 1/4 cup orange juice concentrate
- 2 tablespoons raspberry vinegar
- 1/2 cup chopped dried apricots
- 1/2 cup golden raisins
- 1/2 cup chopped walnuts, toasted

1 In a 1-1/2-qt. slow cooker, combine the cranberries, brown sugar, orange juice concentrate and vinegar. Cover and cook on low for 1-1/4 to 1-3/4 hours or until cranberries pop and mixture is thickened.

2 Turn off the heat; stir in the apricots, raisins and walnuts. Cool to room temperature. Serve or refrigerate.

Yield: 2-1/2 cups.

Peachy Sweet Potatoes

PREP: 20 MIN. ■ **COOK:** 5 HOURS

Taste of Home Test Kitchen
It only takes six ingredients to create this sweet potato side dish. The recipe is on the sweet side, and the granola adds extra crunch.

- 2-1/4 pounds cubed peeled sweet potatoes
- 3/4 teaspoon salt
- 1/8 teaspoon pepper
- 1 cup peach pie filling
- 2 tablespoons butter, melted
- 1/4 teaspoon ground cinnamon
- 1/2 cup granola without raisins, optional

1 Place potatoes in a 3-qt. slow cooker coated with cooking spray. Toss with salt and pepper. Top with pie filling and drizzle with butter. Sprinkle with cinnamon. Cover and cook on low for 5-7 hours or until potatoes are tender. Sprinkle with granola if desired.

Yield: 6 servings.

Hot Fruit Salad

(pictured above)
PREP: 10 MIN. ■ **COOK:** 2 HOURS

Debbie Kimbrough
Lexington, Mississippi
This comforting side dish is convenient to make, and is delicious with poultry and beef. The warm medley also can be served over sliced buttery pound cake for dessert.

- 3/4 cup sugar
- 1/2 cup butter, melted
- 1/4 teaspoon ground cinnamon
- 1/4 teaspoon ground nutmeg
- 1/8 teaspoon salt
- 2 cans (15-1/4 ounces each) sliced peaches, drained
- 2 cans (15-1/4 ounces each) sliced pears, undrained
- 1 jar (23 ounces) chunky applesauce
- 1/2 cup dried apricots, chopped
- 1/4 cup dried cranberries

1 In a 3-qt. slow cooker, combine the sugar, butter, cinnamon, nutmeg and salt. Stir in all the remaining ingredients. Cover and cook on high for 2 hours or until heated through.

Yield: 10 servings.

Creamy Hash Brown Potatoes

(pictured above)

PREP: 5 MIN. ■ **COOK:** 3-1/2 HOURS

Julianne Brown
Springfield, Illinois

I like to fix a batch of these saucy potatoes for potlucks and big group gatherings. Convenient frozen hash browns, canned soup and flavored cream cheese make this side dish so quick to put together.

1 package (32 ounces) frozen cubed hash brown potatoes

1 can (10-3/4 ounces) condensed cream of potato soup, undiluted

2 cups (8 ounces) shredded Colby-Monterey Jack cheese

1 cup (8 ounces) sour cream

1/4 teaspoon pepper

1/8 teaspoon salt

1 carton (8 ounces) spreadable chive and onion cream cheese

1 Place potatoes in a lightly greased 3-qt. slow cooker. In a small bowl, combine the soup, cheese, sour cream, pepper and salt. Pour over potatoes and mix well. Cover and cook on low for 3-1/2 to 4 hours or until the potatoes are tender. Stir in the cream cheese.

Yield: 12-14 servings.

Slow Cooker Mashed Potatoes

PREP: 5 MIN. ■ **COOK:** 2 HOURS

Trudy Vincent
Valles Mines, Missouri

Sour cream and cream cheese add richness to these smooth, make-ahead potatoes. They're wonderful when time is tight because they don't require any last-minute mashing.

1 package (3 ounces) cream cheese, softened

1/2 cup sour cream

1/4 cup butter, softened

1 envelope ranch salad dressing mix

1 teaspoon dried parsley flakes

6 cups warm mashed potatoes (without added milk and butter)

1 In a large bowl, combine the cream cheese, sour cream, butter, salad dressing mix and parsley; stir in potatoes. Transfer to a 3-qt. slow cooker. Cover and cook on low for 2-4 hours.

Yield: 8-10 servings.

Editor's Note: This recipe was tested with fresh potatoes (not instant) in a slow cooker with heating elements surrounding the unit, not only in the base.

Slow-Cooked Applesauce

PREP: 20 MIN. ■ **COOK:** 6 HOURS

Susanne Wasson
Montgomery, New York

This chunky sweet applesauce is perfect alongside main entrees.

6 pounds medium apples (about 18 medium), peeled and sliced

1 cup sugar

1 cup water

1 teaspoon salt

1 teaspoon ground cinnamon

1/4 cup butter, cubed

2 teaspoons vanilla extract

1 In a 5-qt. slow cooker, combine the apples, sugar, water, salt and cinnamon. Cover and cook on low for 6-8 hours or until tender. Turn off heat; stir in butter and vanilla. Mash if desired. Serve warm or cold.

Yield: 12 cups.

Corn Spoon Bread

PREP: 15 MIN. ■ **COOK:** 3 HOURS

Tamara Ellefson
Frederic, Wisconsin
I make this comforting side dish with all of our holiday meals. It's moister than corn pudding made in the oven. It goes great with Thanksgiving turkey or Christmas ham.

1 package (8 ounces) cream cheese, softened
1/3 cup sugar
1 cup 2% milk
1/2 cup egg substitute
2 tablespoons butter, melted
1 teaspoon salt
1/4 teaspoon ground nutmeg
Dash pepper
2-1/3 cups frozen corn, thawed
1 can (14-3/4 ounces) cream-style corn
1 package (8-1/2 ounces) corn bread/muffin mix

1 In a large bowl, beat cream cheese and sugar until smooth. Gradually beat in milk. Beat in the egg substitute, butter, salt, nutmeg and pepper until blended. Stir in corn and cream-style corn. Stir in corn bread mix just until moistened.

2 Pour into a greased 3-qt. slow cooker. Cover and cook on high for 3-4 hours or until center is almost set.

Yield: 8 servings.

Care of leftovers. *After food has been cooked in a slow cooker, it can stay at room temperature for up to 2 hours. After that time, leftovers should be promptly packed up in airtight containers and refrigerated.*

Cheddar Spirals

(pictured above)

PREP: 20 MIN. ■ **COOK:** 2-1/2 HOURS

Heidi Ferkovich
Park Falls, Wisconsin
Our kids just love this and will sample a spoonful right from the slow cooker when they walk by. Sometimes I add cocktail sausages, sliced Polish sausage or cubed ham to the cheesy pasta for a hearty all-in-one dinner.

1 package (16 ounces) spiral pasta
2 cups half-and-half cream
1 can (10-3/4 ounces) condensed cheddar cheese soup, undiluted
1/2 cup butter, melted
4 cups (16 ounces) shredded cheddar cheese

1 Cook pasta according to package directions; drain. In a 5-qt. slow cooker, combine the cream, soup and butter until smooth; stir in the cheese and pasta. Cover and cook on low for 2-1/2 hours or until cheese is melted.

Yield: 12-15 servings.

Creamed Corn

(pictured above)

PREP: 10 MIN. ■ **COOK:** 3 HOURS

Barbara Brizendine
Harrisonville, Missouri
Five ingredients are all you'll need for my popular dinner accompaniment. It's wonderful no matter what the occasion is.

> 2 packages (one 16 ounces, one 10 ounces) frozen corn
>
> 1 package (8 ounces) cream cheese, softened and cubed
>
> 1/4 cup butter, cubed
>
> 1 tablespoon sugar
>
> 1/2 teaspoon salt

1 In a 3-qt. slow cooker coated with cooking spray, combine all the ingredients. Cover and cook on low for 3 to 3-1/2 hours or until the cheese is melted and the corn is tender. Stir just before serving.

Yield: 5 servings.

Creamy Red Potatoes

PREP: 10 MIN. ■ **COOK:** 5 HOURS

Elaine Ryan
Holley, New York
This side dish features cubed red potatoes that are cooked in a creamy coating until tender. Be sure to stir the mixture before serving to help the sauce thicken.

> 7 cups cubed uncooked red potatoes
>
> 1 cup (8 ounces) 4% cottage cheese
>
> 1/2 cup sour cream
>
> 1/2 cup cubed process cheese (Velveeta)
>
> 1 tablespoon dried minced onion
>
> 2 garlic cloves, minced
>
> 1/2 teaspoon salt
>
> Paprika and minced chives, optional

1 Place the potatoes in a 3-qt. slow cooker. In a blender or food processor, puree cottage cheese and sour cream until smooth. Transfer to a bowl; stir in the process cheese, onion, garlic and salt. Pour over potatoes and mix well.

2 Cover and cook on low for 5-6 hours or until potatoes are tender. Stir well before serving. Garnish with paprika and chives if desired.

Yield: 8 servings.

Rich Spinach Casserole

PREP: 10 MIN. ■ **COOK:** 2-1/2 HOURS

Vioda Geyer
Uhrichsville, Ohio
I found this recipe in an old slow cooker cookbook. When I took the side dish to our church sewing circle, it was a big hit.

> 2 packages (10 ounces each) frozen chopped spinach, thawed and well drained
>
> 2 cups (16 ounces) 4% cottage cheese
>
> 1 cup cubed process cheese (Velveeta)
>
> 3/4 cup egg substitute
>
> 2 tablespoons butter, cubed
>
> 1/4 cup all-purpose flour
>
> 1/2 teaspoon salt

1 In a 3-qt. slow cooker, combine all the ingredients. Cover and cook on low for 2-1/2 hours or until the cheese is melted.

Yield: 8 servings.

Slow-Cooked Bacon & Beans

PREP: 25 MIN. ■ **COOK:** 6 HOURS

Sue Livermore
Detroit Lakes, Minnestoa

Bacon adds subtle smokiness to this hearty side that's loaded with flavor. Serve it over rice for a tasty main dish.

1 package (1 pound) sliced bacon, chopped

1 cup chopped onion

2 cans (15 ounces each) pork and beans, undrained

1 can (16 ounces) kidney beans, rinsed and drained

1 can (16 ounces) butter beans, rinsed and drained

1 can (15-1/4 ounces) lima beans, rinsed and drained

1 can (15 ounces) black beans, rinsed and drained

1 cup packed brown sugar

1/2 cup cider vinegar

1 tablespoon molasses

2 teaspoons garlic powder

1/2 teaspoon ground mustard

1 In a large skillet, cook bacon and onion over medium heat until bacon is crisp. Using a slotted spoon, remove to paper towels to drain.

2 In a 4-qt. slow cooker, combine all the remaining ingredients; stir in bacon mixture. Cover and cook on low for 6-7 hours or until heated through.

Yield: 12 servings.

snacks & beverages

Slow Cooker Berry Cobbler

(pictured at left)

PREP: 15 MIN. ■ **COOK:** 2 HOURS

Karen Jarocki
Yuma, Arizona

I took my mom's oven-baked cobbler recipe and experimented with it until I came up with this version for slow cooking. With the hot summers here in Arizona, we can still enjoy this comforting dessert, and I don't have to turn on the oven.

1-1/4 cups all-purpose flour, divided

2 tablespoons plus 1 cup sugar, divided

1 teaspoon baking powder

1/4 teaspoon ground cinnamon

1 egg, lightly beaten

1/4 cup fat-free milk

2 tablespoons canola oil

1/8 teaspoon salt

2 cups unsweetened raspberries

2 cups unsweetened blueberries

2 cups low-fat vanilla frozen yogurt, optional

1 In a large bowl, combine 1 cup flour, 2 tablespoons sugar, baking powder and cinnamon. In a small bowl, combine the egg, milk and oil; stir into dry ingredients just until moistened (batter will be thick). Spread batter evenly onto the bottom of a 5-qt. slow cooker coated with cooking spray.

2 In a large bowl, combine the salt and remaining flour and sugar; add berries and toss to coat. Spread over batter. Cover and cook on high for 2 to 2-1/2 hours or until a toothpick inserted into cobbler comes out without crumbs. Top each serving with 1/4 cup frozen yogurt if desired.

Yield: 8 servings.

Warm Pomegranate Punch

(pictured at right)

PREP: 10 MIN. ■ **COOK:** 2 HOURS

Taste of Home Test Kitchen

If you're looking for something special to serve on a chilly evening, try this warming punch. It has a subtle tea flavor, and the juices create just the right balance of sweet and tart.

4 cups pomegranate juice

4 cups unsweetened apple juice

1/3 cup lemon juice

2 cups brewed tea

1/2 cup sugar

3 cinnamon sticks (3 inches)

12 whole cloves

1 In a 4- or 5-qt. slow cooker, combine the juices, tea and sugar. Place cinnamon sticks and cloves on a double thickness of cheesecloth; bring up corners of cloth and tie with string to form a bag. Add to slow cooker. Cover and cook on low for 2-4 hours or until heated through. Discard spice bag. Serve warm.

Yield: 2-1/2 quarts.

Butterscotch Apple Crisp

PREP: 10 MIN. ■ **COOK:** 2-1/2 HOURS

Jolanthe Erb
Harrisonburg, Virginia
This dessert classic gets a rich twist from butterscotch pudding.

> 3 cups thinly sliced peeled tart apples
> (about 3 medium)
> 1/3 cup packed brown sugar
> 1/4 cup all-purpose flour
> 1/4 cup quick-cooking oats
> 1/3 cup cook-and-serve butterscotch
> pudding mix
> 1/2 teaspoon ground cinnamon
> 1/4 cup cold butter
> Vanilla ice cream, optional

1 Place apples in a 1-1/2-qt. slow cooker. In a bowl, combine brown sugar, flour, oats, pudding mix and cinnamon. Cut in butter until mixture resembles coarse crumbs. Sprinkle over apples.

2 Cover and cook on low for 2-1/2 to 3-1/2 hours or until apples are tender. Serve with ice cream if desired.

Yield: 3 servings.

Party Sausages

PREP: 15 MIN. ■ **COOK:** 1 HOUR

Jo Ann Renner
Xenia, Ohio
Whenever I've served these, I have never had even one left over.

> 2 pounds fully cooked smoked sausage links
> 1 bottle (8 ounces) Catalina salad dressing
> 1 bottle (8 ounces) Russian salad dressing
> 1/2 cup packed brown sugar
> 1/2 cup pineapple juice

1 Cut sausages diagonally into 1/2-in. slices; cook in a skillet over medium heat until lightly browned. Transfer to a 3-qt. slow cooker; discard drippings. Add the dressings, sugar and juice to skillet; cook and stir over medium-low heat until sugar is dissolved. Pour over sausages. Heat on low for 1-2 hours or until heated through.

Yield: 16 servings.

Glazed Kielbasa

(pictured above)

PREP: 5 MIN. ■ **COOK:** 4 HOURS

Jody Sands Taylor
Richmond, Virginia
You'll need only three ingredients to prepare this pleasantly sweet treatment for sausage. Serve it as a main dish...or with toothpicks for a hearty appetizer.

> 3 pounds smoked kielbasa or
> Polish sausage, cut into 1-inch
> chunks

> 1/2 cup packed brown sugar
> 1-1/2 cups ginger ale

1 Place sausage in a 3-qt. slow cooker; sprinkle with brown sugar. Pour ginger ale over the top. Cover and cook on low for 4-5 hours or until heated through. Serve with a slotted spoon.

Yield: 12-16 servings.

Wassail Bowl Punch

PREP: 10 MIN. ■ **COOK:** 1 HOUR

Margaret Harms
Jenkins, Kentucky

All ages will enjoy this warming punch. The blend of spice, fruit and citrus flavors is scrumptious. You can assemble it before heading out for a winter activity and sip away the chill when you return.

4 cups hot brewed tea

4 cups cranberry juice

4 cups unsweetened apple juice

2 cups orange juice

3/4 cup lemon juice

1 cup sugar

3 cinnamon sticks (3 inches)

12 whole cloves

1 In a 5-qt. slow cooker, combine the tea, juices and sugar. Place the cinnamon sticks and cloves on a double thickness of cheesecloth; bring up corners of cloth and tie with string to form a bag. Add to slow cooker. Cover and cook on high for 1 hour or until punch begins to boil. Discard spice bag. Serve warm.

Yield: 3-1/2 quarts.

Keeping punch warm. *Let your guests serve themselves warm punch throughout the night. Place the punch in a slow cooker and set it to the low or warm setting. Keep a ladle on a saucer by the slow cooker so your guests can easily refill their cups.*

Chocolate Peanut Clusters

PREP: 10 MIN.
COOK: 2 HOURS + STANDING

Pam Posey
Waterloo, South Carolina
I turn to my slow cooker to prepare these convenient chocolate treats. Making candies couldn't be any easier!

---

1 jar (16 ounces) salted dry roasted peanuts
1 jar (16 ounces) unsalted dry roasted peanuts
1 package (11-1/2 ounces) milk chocolate chips
1 package (10 ounces) peanut butter chips
3 packages (10 to 12 ounces each) white baking chips
2 packages (11-1/2 ounces each) 60% cacao bittersweet chocolate baking chips

1 In a 5-qt. slow cooker, combine peanuts. Layer with the remaining ingredients in order given (do not stir). Cover and cook on low for 2 to 2-1/2 hours or until chips are melted.

2 Stir to combine. Drop by tablespoonfuls onto waxed paper. Let stand until set. Store in an airtight container at room temperature.

Yield: 4 pounds.

Luscious chocolate coating. Make your own chocolate clusters. Try replacing part or all of the peanuts with your favorite nut. Replace half the peanuts with raisins or create a special combination of pretzels, raisins, nuts and dry cereal.

Rice Pudding
(pictured above)

PREP: 15 MIN. ■ **COOK:** 3 HOURS + CHILLING

Jennifer Bennett
Salem, Indiana
For an old-fashioned sweet treat just like Grandma made, try this creamy pudding. It has a rich cinnamon flavor and is made wonderfully silky after whipped cream is stirred into it at the end.

1-1/4 cups 2% milk
1/2 cup sugar
1/2 cup uncooked converted rice
1/2 cup raisins
2 eggs, lightly beaten
1 teaspoon ground cinnamon
1 teaspoon butter, melted
1 teaspoon vanilla extract
3/4 teaspoon lemon extract
1 cup heavy whipping cream, whipped
Whipped cream and ground nutmeg, optional

1 In a 1-1/2-qt. slow cooker, combine the milk, sugar, rice, raisins, eggs, cinnamon, butter, vanilla and lemon extract. Cover and cook on low for 2 hours; stir.

2 Cover and cook 1-2 hours longer or until rice is tender. Transfer to a small bowl.

3 Cover and refrigerate for at least 1 hour. Just before serving, fold in whipped cream. If desired, garnish with additional whipped cream and nutmeg.

Yield: 4 servings.

Nacho Salsa Dip

PREP: 15 MIN. ■ **COOK:** 3 HOURS

Sally Hull
Homestead, Florida
This zesty dip is ideal for any get-together and allows me to spend more time with my guests. I always have requests to bring it when my husband and I attend get-togethers.

> 1 pound ground beef
>
> 1/3 cup chopped onion
>
> 2 pounds process cheese (Velveeta), cubed
>
> 1 jar (16 ounces) chunky salsa
>
> 1/4 teaspoon garlic powder
>
> Tortilla chips or cubed French bread

1 In a large skillet, cook beef and onion over medium heat until meat is no longer pink; drain well. Transfer to a greased 3-qt. slow cooker.

2 Stir in the cheese, salsa and garlic powder. Cover and cook on low for 3 hours. Stir; serve with tortilla chips or cubed bread.

Yield: 7 cups.

Party Meatballs

PREP: 10 MIN. ■ **COOK:** 3 HOURS

Debbie Paulsen
Apollo Beach, Florida
Meatballs are always great for parties. This is an easy twist on the usual recipe, and it's very fast to make.

> 1 package (32 ounces) frozen fully cooked homestyle meatballs, thawed
>
> 1 bottle (14 ounces) ketchup
>
> 1/4 cup A.1. steak sauce
>
> 1 tablespoon minced garlic
>
> 1 teaspoon Dijon mustard

1 Place meatballs in a 3-qt. slow cooker. In a small bowl, combine the ketchup, steak sauce, garlic and mustard. Pour over the meatballs. Cover and cook on low for 3-4 hours or until the meatballs are heated through.

Yield: about 6 dozen.

Mulled Pomegranate Sipper

(pictured above)

PREP: 10 MIN. ■ **COOK:** 1 HOUR

Lisa Renshaw
Kansas City, Missouri
This warm, comforting cider fills the entire house with an incredible aroma.

> 1 bottle (64 ounces) cranberry-apple juice
>
> 2 cups unsweetened apple juice
>
> 1 cup pomegranate juice
>
> 1/2 cup orange juice
>
> 2/3 cup honey
>
> 3 cinnamon sticks (3 inches)
>
> 10 whole cloves
>
> 2 tablespoons grated orange peel

1 In a 5-qt. slow cooker, combine the juices and honey. Place the cinnamon sticks and cloves on a double thickness of cheesecloth; bring up corners of cloth and tie with string to form a bag. Add to slow cooker. Cover and cook on low for 1-2 hours. Discard spice bag.

Yield: 16 servings (about 3 quarts).

Sweet 'n' Tangy Chicken Wings

PREP: 20 MIN. ■ **COOK:** 3-1/4 HOURS

Ida Tuey
Kokomo, Indiana
This saucy recipe is perfect for potlucks. Put the wings in before you prepare for the party, and in a few hours, you'll have wonderful appetizers!

3 pounds chicken wingettes and drumettes

1/2 teaspoon salt, divided

Dash pepper

1-1/2 cups ketchup

1/4 cup packed brown sugar

1/4 cup red wine vinegar

2 tablespoons Worcestershire sauce

1 tablespoon Dijon mustard

1 teaspoon minced garlic

1 teaspoon Liquid Smoke, optional

Sesame seeds, optional

1 Sprinkle chicken wings with a dash of salt and pepper. Broil 4-6 in. from the heat for 5-10 minutes on each side or until golden brown. Transfer to a greased 5-qt. slow cooker.

2 Combine the ketchup, brown sugar, vinegar, Worcestershire sauce, mustard, garlic, Liquid Smoke if desired and remaining salt; pour over wings. Toss to coat. Cover and cook on low for 3-1/4 to 3-3/4 hours or until chicken juices run clear. Sprinkle with sesame seeds if desired.

Yield: about 2-1/2 dozen.

Hot Fudge Cake

PREP: 20 MIN. ■ **COOK:** 4 HOURS

Marleen Adkins
Placentia, California
A cake baked in a slow cooker may seem unusual. But chocolaty smiles around the table prove how tasty it is. Sometimes, for a change of pace, I substitute butterscotch chips for chocolate.

1-3/4 cups packed brown sugar, divided

1 cup all-purpose flour

6 tablespoons baking cocoa, divided

2 teaspoons baking powder

1/2 teaspoon salt

1/2 cup 2% milk

2 tablespoons butter, melted

1/2 teaspoon vanilla extract

1-1/2 cups semisweet chocolate chips

1-3/4 cups boiling water

Vanilla ice cream

1 In a small bowl, combine 1 cup brown sugar, flour, 3 tablespoons cocoa, baking powder and salt. In another bowl, combine the milk, butter and vanilla; stir into dry ingredients just until combined. Spread evenly into a 3-qt. slow cooker coated with cooking spray. Sprinkle with chocolate chips.

2 In another small bowl, combine the remaining brown sugar and cocoa; stir in boiling water. Pour over batter (do not stir). Cover and cook on high for 4 to 4-1/2 hours or until a toothpick inserted near the center of the cake comes out clean. Serve warm with ice cream.

Yield: 6-8 servings.

Editor's Note: This recipe does not use eggs.

Mulled Dr. Pepper

(pictured above)

PREP: 10 MIN. ■ **COOK:** 2 HOURS

Bernice Morris
Marshfield, Missouri
When neighbors or friends visit us on a chilly evening, I'll serve this warm beverage with ham sandwiches and deviled eggs.

8 cups Dr. Pepper	1/2 teaspoon whole cloves
1/4 cup packed brown sugar	1/4 teaspoon salt
1/4 cup lemon juice	1/4 teaspoon ground nutmeg
1/2 teaspoon ground allspice	3 cinnamon sticks (3 inches)

1 In a 3-qt. slow cooker, combine all the ingredients. Cover and cook on low for 2 hours or until desired temperature is reached. Discard cloves and cinnamon sticks before serving.

Yield: 8-10 servings.

Hot Chili Cheese Dip

PREP: 20 MIN. ■ COOK: 4 HOURS

Jeanie Carrigan
Madera, California
I simplify party preparation by using my slow cooker to create this thick, cheesy dip. Your guests won't believe how good it is.

---

1 medium onion, finely chopped

2 teaspoons canola oil

2 garlic cloves, minced

2 cans (15 ounces each) chili without beans

2 cups salsa

2 packages (3 ounces each) cream cheese, cubed

2 cans (2-1/4 ounces each) sliced ripe olives, drained

Tortilla chips

1 In a small skillet, saute onion in oil until tender. Add garlic; cook 1 minute longer. Transfer to a 3-qt. slow cooker.

2 Stir in chili, salsa, cream cheese and olives. Cover and cook on low for 4 hours or until heated through, stirring occasionally. Stir before serving with the tortilla chips.

Yield: 6 cups.

Strawberry Rhubarb Sauce

(pictured above)

PREP: 15 MIN. ■ COOK: 4-1/4 HOURS

Nancy Cowlishaw
Boise, Idaho
The perfect addition to vanilla ice cream, my colorful fruit sauce features a delightful combination of rhubarb, apple and strawberry flavors. I also like to serve this delicious sauce over pancakes.

---

6 cups sliced fresh or frozen rhubarb, thawed

1 cup sugar

1/2 cup unsweetened apple juice

3 cinnamon sticks (3 inches)

1/2 teaspoon grated orange peel

1/4 teaspoon ground ginger

1 pint fresh strawberries, halved

Vanilla ice cream

1 Place the rhubarb, sugar, juice, cinnamon sticks, orange peel and ginger in a 3-qt. slow cooker. Cover and cook on low for 4-5 hours or until rhubarb is tender.

2 Stir in strawberries; cover and cook 15 minutes longer or until heated through. Discard cinnamon sticks. Serve with ice cream.

Yield: 4-1/2 cups.

Hot Spiced Cherry Cider

PREP: 5 MIN. ■ COOK: 4 HOURS

Marlene Wiczek
Little Falls, Minnesota
This cider is great to have waiting for you after being out in the cold.

---

1 gallon apple cider or juice

2 cinnamon sticks (3 inches)

2 packages (3 ounces each) cherry gelatin

1 Place cider in a 6-qt. slow cooker; add cinnamon sticks. Cover and cook on high for 3 hours. Stir in the gelatin; cook 1 hour longer. Discard cinnamon sticks before serving the cider.

Yield: 4 quarts.

Southwestern Nachos

PREP: 40 MIN. ■ **COOK:** 7-1/4 HOURS

Kelly Byler
Goshen, Indiana
Guests will go crazy when you serve two heaping pans of this creamy nacho casserole, with tender chunks of pork. You don't need to worry about filling the chip bowl...the tortilla chips are conveniently baked right in the dish!

2 boneless whole pork loin roasts (3-1/2 pounds each)

1 cup unsweetened apple juice

6 garlic cloves, minced

1 teaspoon salt

1 teaspoon Liquid Smoke, optional

2-1/2 cups barbecue sauce, divided

1/3 cup packed brown sugar

2 tablespoons honey

1 package (10 ounces) tortilla chip scoops

1-1/2 cups frozen corn

1 can (15 ounces) black beans, rinsed and drained

1 medium tomato, seeded and chopped

1 medium red onion, chopped

1/3 cup minced fresh cilantro

1 jalapeno pepper, seeded and chopped

2 teaspoons lime juice

1 package (16 ounces) process cheese (Velveeta), cubed

2 tablespoons milk

1 Cut each roast in half; place in two 5-qt. slow cookers. Combine the apple juice, garlic, salt and Liquid Smoke if desired; pour over meat. Cover and cook on low for 7-8 hours or until a meat thermometer reads 160°.

2 Remove pork from slow cooker; cool slightly. Shred with two forks and place in a very large bowl. Stir in 2 cups barbecue sauce, brown sugar and honey. Divide tortilla chips between two greased 13-in. x 9-in. baking dishes; top with pork mixture. Combine the corn, beans, tomato, onion, cilantro, jalapeno and lime juice; spoon over pork mixture.

3 Bake, uncovered, at 375° for 15-20 minutes or until heated through. Meanwhile, in a small saucepan, melt cheese with milk. Drizzle cheese sauce and remaining barbecue sauce over nachos.

Yield: 30 servings.

Editor's Note: When cutting hot peppers, disposable gloves are recommended. Avoid touching your face.

Gingered Pears

PREP: 35 MIN. ■ **COOK:** 4 HOURS

Catherine Mueller
St. Paul, Minnesota
My slow cooker allows me to serve a heartwarming dessert without much effort. Topped with caramel sauce, these tender pears feature a surprise filling of nuts and brown sugar.

> 1/2 cup finely chopped crystallized ginger
>
> 1/4 cup packed brown sugar
>
> 1/4 cup chopped pecans
>
> 1-1/2 teaspoons grated lemon peel
>
> 6 medium Bartlett or Anjou pears
>
> 2 tablespoons butter, cubed
>
> Vanilla ice cream and caramel ice cream topping, optional

1 In a small bowl, combine the ginger, brown sugar, pecans and lemon peel. Using a melon baller or long-handled spoon, core pears to within 1/4 in. of bottom. Spoon ginger mixture into the center of each.

2 Place pears upright in a 5-qt. slow cooker. Top each with butter. Cover and cook on low for 4-5 hours or until pears are tender. Serve with ice cream and caramel topping if desired.

Yield: 6 servings.

Mexican Fondue

(pictured above)
PREP: 15 MIN. ■ **COOK:** 1-1/2 HOURS

Nella Parker
Hersey, Michigan
A handful of items and a few moments of prep work are all you'll need for this festive fondue. It takes advantage of canned goods and other convenience items.

> 1 can (14-3/4 ounces) cream-style corn
>
> 1 can (14-1/2 ounces) diced tomatoes, drained
>
> 3 tablespoons chopped green chilies
>
> 1 teaspoon chili powder
>
> 1 package (16 ounces) process cheese (Velveeta), cubed
>
> French bread cubes

1 In a small bowl, combine the corn, tomatoes, green chilies and chili powder. Transfer to a 1-1/2-qt. slow cooker coated with cooking spray. Stir in cheese. Cover and cook on high for 1-1/2 hours, stirring every 30 minutes or until cheese is melted. Serve with bread cubes.

Yield: 4-1/2 cups.

Minister's Delight

PREP: 5 MIN. ■ **COOK:** 2 HOURS

Mary Ann Potter
Blue Springs, Missouri
A friend gave me the recipe several years ago, saying that a minister's wife fixed it every Sunday so she named it accordingly.

> 1 can (21 ounces) cherry or apple pie filling
>
> 1 package (18-1/4 ounces) yellow cake mix
>
> 1/2 cup butter, melted
>
> 1/3 cup chopped walnuts, optional

1 Place pie filling in a 1-1/2-qt. slow cooker. Combine cake mix and butter (mixture will be crumbly); sprinkle over filling. Sprinkle with walnuts if desired. Cover and cook on low for 2-3 hours. Serve in bowls.

Yield: 10-12 servings.

Saucy Cocktail Meatballs

PREP: 10 MIN. ■ **COOK:** 3 HOURS

Susie Snyder
Bowling Green, Ohio
My Grandmother served this every year at
Christmastime while I was growing up.

1 package (32 ounces) frozen fully cooked
homestyle meatballs, thawed

1 can (10-3/4 ounces) condensed tomato
soup, undiluted

1/3 cup chopped onion

1/3 cup chopped green pepper

2 tablespoons brown sugar

4 teaspoons Worcestershire sauce

1 tablespoon white vinegar

1 tablespoon prepared mustard

1 Place meatballs in a 3-qt. slow cooker. In
a small bowl, combine all the remaining
ingredients. Pour over meatballs. Cover
and cook on low for 3-4 hours or until
heated through.

Yield: about 6 dozen.

Tropical Tea

PREP: 15 MIN. ■ **COOK:** 2 HOURS

Irene Helen Zundel
Carmichaels, Pennsylvania
Brew a batch of this fragrant, flavorful tea
for your next family gathering. Your family
will love it.

6 cups boiling water

6 individual tea bags

1-1/2 cups orange juice

1-1/2 cups unsweetened pineapple juice

1/3 cup sugar

1 medium navel orange, sliced and halved

2 tablespoons honey

1 In a 5-qt. slow cooker, combine boiling
water and tea bags. Cover and let stand
for 5 minutes. Discard tea bags. Stir in
the remaining ingredients. Cover and
cook on low for 2-4 hours or until
heated through. Serve warm.

Yield: about 2-1/2 quarts.

Caramel Pear Pudding

(pictured above)

PREP: 20 MIN. ■ **COOK:** 3 HOURS

Diane Halferty
Corpus Christi, Texas
This is a lovely treat that uses pears that are seasonally available. It's easy
to fix and a comforting finale to any meal. I enjoy snacking on it in front
of the fireplace.

1 cup all-purpose flour

1/2 cup sugar

1-1/2 teaspoons baking
powder

1/2 teaspoon ground
cinnamon

1/4 teaspoon salt

1/8 teaspoon ground cloves

1/2 cup 2% milk

4 medium pears, peeled and
cubed

1/2 cup chopped pecans

3/4 cup packed brown sugar

1/4 cup butter, softened

1/2 cup boiling water

Vanilla ice cream, optional

1 In a large bowl, combine the flour, sugar, baking powder,
cinnamon, salt and cloves. Stir in milk until smooth. Add pears
and pecans. Spread evenly into a 3-qt. slow cooker coated with
cooking spray.

2 In a small bowl, combine brown sugar and butter; stir in boiling
water. Pour over batter (do not stir). Cover and cook on low for
3-4 hours or until pears are tender. Serve warm with ice cream
if desired.

Yield: 10 servings.

Slow-Cooked Salsa

PREP: 15 MIN.
COOK: 2-1/2 HOURS + COOLING

Toni Menard
Lompoc, California
I love the fresh taste of homemade salsa, but as a working mother, I don't have much time to make it. So I came up with this slow-cooked version that practically makes itself!

> 10 plum tomatoes
> 2 garlic cloves
> 1 small onion, cut into wedges
> 2 jalapeno peppers
> 1/4 cup cilantro leaves
> 1/2 teaspoon salt, optional

1 Core tomatoes. Cut a small slit in two tomatoes; insert a garlic clove into each slit. Place tomatoes and onion in a 3-qt. slow cooker.

2 Cut stem off jalapenos; remove seeds if a milder salsa is desired. Place the jalapenos in the slow cooker. Cover and cook on high for 2-1/2 to 3 hours or until the vegetables are softened (some may brown slightly); cool.

3 In a blender, combine the tomato mixture, cilantro and salt if desired; cover and process until blended. Store in the refrigerator.

Yield: about 2 cups.

Editor's Note: When cutting hot peppers, disposable gloves are recommended. Avoid touching your face.

Mulled Merlot

(pictured above)
PREP: 10 MIN. ■ **COOK:** 1 HOUR

Taste of Home Test Kitchen
This nicely spiced wine is sure to warm up your holiday guests!

> 4 cinnamon sticks (3 inches)
> 4 whole cloves
> 2 bottles (750 milliliters each) merlot
> 1/2 cup sugar
> 1/2 cup orange juice
> 1/2 cup brandy
> 1 medium orange, thinly sliced

1 Place cinnamon sticks and cloves on a double thickness of cheesecloth; bring up corners of cloth and tie with string to form a bag.

2 In a 3-qt. slow cooker, combine the wine, sugar, orange juice, brandy and orange slices. Add spice bag. Cover and cook on high for 1 hour or until heated through. Discard spice bag and orange slices. Serve warm in mugs.

Yield: 9 servings.

> *Blending hot ingredients.* Care should be taken when blending hot ingredients to avoid burns and splatters. That is why it is recommended to allow the ingredients to cool slightly before blending. If you blend hot ingredients, pressure builds up in the covered blender and may cause the blender top to pop off. If that occurs while you are processing the ingredients, they will splatter all over and you may get burned.

Reuben Spread

(pictured above)

PREP: 5 MIN. ■ **COOK:** 3 HOURS

Pam Rohr
Troy, Ohio
You'll need only five ingredients to stir up this hearty dip that tastes like a Reuben sandwich. It's requested at all the gatherings we attend.

2-1/2 cups cubed cooked corned beef
1 jar (16 ounces) sauerkraut, rinsed and well drained
2 cups (8 ounces) shredded Swiss cheese
2 cups (8 ounces) shredded cheddar cheese
1 cup mayonnaise
Snack rye bread

1 In a 3-qt. slow cooker, combine the corned beef, sauerkraut, cheeses and mayonnaise. Cover and cook on low for 3 hours, stirring occasionally. Serve warm with rye bread.

Yield: about 5 cups.

Editor's Note: Reduced-fat cheese and mayonnaise are not recommended for this recipe.

Chipotle Ham 'n' Cheese Dip

PREP: 15 MIN. ■ **COOK:** 1 HOUR

Lisa Renshaw
Kansas City, Missouri
During the busy holiday season, you just can't beat
convenient recipes like this one that let you visit with
guests instead of working away in the kitchen.

2 packages (8 ounces each) cream cheese, cubed

1 can (12 ounces) evaporated milk

8 ounces Gouda cheese, shredded

1 cup (4 ounces) shredded cheddar cheese

2 tablespoons chopped chipotle pepper in adobo sauce

1 teaspoon ground cumin

2 cups diced fully cooked ham

Fresh vegetables or tortilla chips

1 In a 3-qt. slow cooker, combine the cream cheese,
milk, cheeses, chipotle pepper and cumin. Cover
and cook on low for 40 minutes.

2 Stir in the ham; cook 20 minutes longer or until
heated through. Serve warm with vegetables or
tortilla chips.

Yield: 7 cups.

Slow Cooker Party Mix

PREP: 10 MIN. ■ **COOK:** 1 HOUR

Dana Hughes
Gresham, Oregon
Our parties usually include this mildly seasoned snack mix. Served warm from a slow cooker, the munchable mixture is very satisfying.

- 4 cups Wheat Chex
- 4 cups Cheerios
- 3 cups pretzel sticks
- 1 can (12 ounces) salted peanuts
- 1/4 cup butter, melted
- 2 to 3 tablespoons grated Parmesan cheese
- 1 teaspoon celery salt
- 1/2 to 3/4 teaspoon seasoned salt

1 In a 5-qt. slow cooker, combine cereals, pretzels and peanuts. Combine the butter, cheese, celery salt and seasoned salt; drizzle over cereal mixture and mix well. Cover and cook on low for 1 to 1-1/2 hours, stirring every 20 minutes. Serve warm or at room temperature.

Yield: about 3 quarts.

Hot Crab Dip

PREP: 10 MIN. ■ **COOK:** 2 HOURS

Terri Perrier
Simonton, Texas
Bits of sweet onion give this creamy dip a little unexpected crunch.

- 1 package (8 ounces) cream cheese, softened
- 1/2 cup finely chopped sweet onion
- 1/4 cup grated Parmesan cheese
- 1/4 cup mayonnaise
- 2 garlic cloves, minced
- 2 teaspoons sugar
- 1 can (6 ounces) crabmeat, drained, flaked and cartilage removed
- Assorted crackers

1 In a 1-1/2-qt. slow cooker, combine the cream cheese, onion, Parmesan, mayonnaise, garlic and sugar; stir in crab. Cover and cook on low for 2-3 hours or until heated through. Serve with crackers.

Yield: 2 cups.

Apple Cranberry Cider

(pictured above)

PREP: 5 MIN. ■ **COOK:** 2 HOURS

Kathy Wells
Brodhead, Wisconsin
Buffets are my favorite way to feed a crowd. This fruity cider can be made ahead, then kept warm in a slow cooker so people can serve themselves.

- 3 cinnamon sticks (3 inches), broken
- 1 teaspoon whole cloves
- 2 quarts apple cider or juice
- 3 cups cranberry juice
- 2 tablespoons brown sugar

1 Place cinnamon sticks and cloves on a double thickness of cheesecloth; bring up corners of cloth and tie with string to form a bag. In a 5-qt. slow cooker, combine the cider, cranberry juice and brown sugar; add spice bag. Cover and cook on high for 2 hours or until cider reaches desired temperature. Discard spice bag.

Yield: 11 cups.

Pepperoni Pizza Dip

PREP: 20 MIN. ■ COOK: 2-1/2 HOURS

Lisa Francis
Elba, Alabama
This tasty dip will be gone in a flash. It's a great appetizer for any party.

> 4 cups (16 ounces) shredded cheddar cheese
> 4 cups (16 ounces) shredded part-skim mozzarella cheese
> 1 cup mayonnaise
> 1 jar (6 ounces) sliced mushrooms, drained
> 2 cans (2-1/4 ounces each) sliced ripe olives, drained
> 1 package (3-1/2 ounces) slices pepperoni, quartered
> 1 tablespoon dried minced onion
> Assorted crackers

1 In a 3-qt. slow cooker, combine the cheeses, mayonnaise, mushrooms, olives, pepperoni and onion. Cover and cook on low for 1-1/2 hours; stir. Cover and cook for 1 hour or until heated through. Serve with crackers.

Yield: 5 cups.

Viennese Coffee

PREP: 10 MIN. ■ COOK: 3 HOURS

Sharon Delaney-Chronis
South Milwaukee, Wisconsin
This isn't your regular cup of Jo...it's a drink to savor.

> 3 cups strong brewed coffee
> 3 tablespoons chocolate syrup
> 1 teaspoon sugar
> 1/3 cup heavy whipping cream
> 1/4 cup creme de cacao or Irish cream liqueur
> Whipped cream and chocolate curls, optional

1 In a 1-1/2-qt. slow cooker, combine the coffee, chocolate syrup and sugar. Cover and cook on low for 2-1/2 hours. Stir in heavy cream and creme de cacao. Cover and cook 30 minutes longer or until heated through. Ladle coffee into mugs. Garnish with whipped cream and chocolate curls if desired.

Yield: 4 servings.

Marmalade Meatballs

(pictured above)

PREP: 10 MIN. ■ COOK: 4 HOURS

Jeanne Kiss
Greensburg, Pennsylvania
We had a pregame potluck at work, so I started cooking these meatballs in the morning. By lunchtime they were ready. They were a big hit!

> 1 bottle (16 ounces) Catalina salad dressing
> 1 cup orange marmalade
> 3 tablespoons Worcestershire sauce
> 1/2 teaspoon crushed red pepper flakes
> 1 package (32 ounces) frozen fully cooked homestyle meatballs, thawed

1 In a 3-qt. slow cooker, combine the salad dressing, marmalade, Worcestershire sauce and pepper flakes. Stir in meatballs. Cover and cook on low for 4-5 hours or until heated through.

Yield: about 5 dozen.

Gingerbread Pudding Cake

(pictured above)

PREP: 20 MIN. ■ **COOK:** 2 HOURS + STANDING

Barbara Cook
Yuma, Arizona

A handful of spices and a half cup of molasses give this delightful dessert a yummy, old-fashioned flavor. It's pretty, too, with a dollop of whipped cream and a mint sprig on top.

1/4 cup butter, softened

1/4 cup sugar

1 egg white

1 teaspoon vanilla extract

1/2 cup molasses

1 cup water

1-1/4 cups all-purpose flour

3/4 teaspoon baking soda

1/2 teaspoon ground cinnamon

1/2 teaspoon ground ginger

1/4 teaspoon salt

1/4 teaspoon ground allspice

1/8 teaspoon ground nutmeg

1/2 cup chopped pecans

TOPPING:

6 tablespoons brown sugar

3/4 cup hot water

2/3 cup butter, melted

1 In a large bowl, cream butter and sugar until light and fluffy. Beat in egg white and vanilla.

2 Combine molasses and water until blended. Combine the flour, baking soda, cinnamon, ginger, salt, allspice and nutmeg; add to creamed mixture alternately with molasses mixture, beating well after each addition. Fold in pecans.

3 Pour into a greased 3-qt. slow cooker. Sprinkle with brown sugar. Combine hot water and butter; pour over batter (do not stir). Cover and cook on high for 2 to 2-1/2 hours or until a toothpick inserted near the center of cake comes out clean. Turn off heat. Let stand for 15 minutes. Serve warm.

Yield: 6-8 servings.

Cherry Cola Chocolate Cake

(pictured at left)

PREP: 30 MIN. + STANDING
COOK: 2 HOURS + STANDING

Elaine Sweet
Dallas, Texas

For a truly different chocolate cake, try this almost effortless dessert...it's warm, moist and fudgy.

- 1/2 cup cola
- 1/2 cup dried tart cherries
- 1-1/2 cups all-purpose flour
- 1/2 cup sugar
- 2 ounces semisweet chocolate, chopped
- 2-1/2 teaspoons baking powder
- 1/2 teaspoon salt
- 1 cup chocolate milk
- 1/2 cup butter, melted
- 2 teaspoons vanilla extract

TOPPING:

- 1-1/4 cups cola
- 1/2 cup sugar
- 1/2 cup packed brown sugar
- 2 ounces semisweet chocolate, chopped
- 1/4 cup dark rum
- Vanilla ice cream and maraschino cherries, optional

1 In a saucepan, bring cola and dried cherries to a boil. Remove from heat; let stand for 30 minutes. In a bowl, combine flour, sugar, chocolate, baking powder and salt. Combine milk, butter and vanilla; stir into dry ingredients just until moistened. Fold in cherry mixture. Pour into a 3-qt. slow cooker coated with cooking spray.

2 For topping, in a saucepan, combine cola and sugars. Cook and stir until sugar is dissolved. Remove from heat; stir in chocolate and rum. Pour over cherry mixture; do not stir.

3 Cover and cook on high for 2 to 2-1/2 hours or until set. Turn off heat; let stand, covered, for 30 minutes. Serve warm with ice cream and maraschino cherries if desired.

Yield: 8 servings.

Barbecue Chicken Wings

PREP: 45 MIN. ■ **COOK:** 1 HOUR 35 MIN.

Jean Ann Herritt
Canton, Ohio

I got this spicy recipe from a friend but altered the ingredient amounts to adjust the hotness of the sauce. Make sure everyone has extra napkins... these wings are messy to eat but oh, so good!

- 3 pounds whole chicken wings
- 2 cups ketchup
- 1/2 cup honey
- 2 tablespoons lemon juice
- 2 tablespoons canola oil
- 2 tablespoons soy sauce
- 2 tablespoons Worcestershire sauce
- 1 tablespoon paprika
- 4 garlic cloves, minced
- 1-1/2 teaspoons curry powder
- 1/2 teaspoon pepper
- 1/8 teaspoon hot pepper sauce

1 Cut chicken wings into three sections; discard wing tips. Place wings in a greased 15-in. x 10-in. x 1-in. baking pan. Bake at 350° for 35-40 minutes or until chicken juices run clear.

2 In a large bowl, combine all the remaining ingredients. Pour 1/2 cup into a 3-qt. slow cooker. Drain chicken wings; add to slow cooker. Drizzle with remaining sauce. Cover and cook on low for 1 hour, basting occasionally.

Yield: 10 servings.

Editor's Note: Uncooked chicken wing sections (wingettes) may be substituted for whole chicken wings.

Slow Cooker Mexican Dip

PREP: 15 MIN. ■ **COOK:** 1-1/2 HOURS

Heather Courtney
Ames, Iowa
My husband, Jamie, and I love to entertain, and this hearty, seven-ingredient dip is always a hit. It couldn't be much easier to put together.

- 1-1/2 pounds ground beef
- 1 pound bulk hot Italian sausage
- 1 cup chopped onion
- 1 package (8.8 ounces) ready-to-serve Spanish rice
- 1 can (16 ounces) refried beans
- 1 can (10 ounces) enchilada sauce
- 1 pound process cheese (Velveeta), cubed
- 1 package tortilla chip scoops

1 In a Dutch oven, cook beef, sausage and onion over medium heat until meat is no longer pink; drain. Heat rice according to package directions. In a 3-qt. slow cooker, combine meat mixture, rice, beans, sauce and cheese. Cover and cook on low for 1-1/2 to 2 hours or until cheese is melted. Serve with tortilla scoops.

Yield: 8 cups.

Granola Apple Crisp

PREP: 20 MIN. ■ **COOK:** 5 HOURS

Barbara Schindler
Napoleon, Ohio
Tender apple slices are tucked beneath a sweet crunchy topping in this comforting crisp.

- 8 medium tart apples, peeled and sliced
- 1/4 cup lemon juice
- 1-1/2 teaspoons grated lemon peel
- 2-1/2 cups granola with fruit and nuts
- 1 cup sugar
- 1 teaspoon ground cinnamon
- 1/2 cup butter, melted

1 In a bowl, toss apples, lemon juice and peel. Transfer to a greased 3-qt. slow cooker. Combine cereal, sugar and cinnamon; sprinkle over apples. Drizzle with butter. Cover and cook on low for 5-6 hours or until the apples are tender.

Yield: 6-8 servings.

Mini Hot Dogs 'n' Meatballs

(pictured above)

PREP: 10 MIN. ■ **COOK:** 3 HOURS

Andrea Chamberlain
Macedon, New York
Hot appetizers don't come much simpler than this recipe. It always vanishes in minutes whenever I serve it. In fact, it's so popular I usually double the recipe if I have a larger slow cooker.

- 1 package (12 ounces) frozen fully cooked Italian meatballs
- 1 package (16 ounces) miniature hot dogs or smoked sausages
- 1 package (3-1/2 ounces) sliced pepperoni
- 1 jar (26 ounces) meatless spaghetti sauce
- 1 bottle (18 ounces) barbecue sauce
- 1 bottle (12 ounces) chili sauce

1 In a 5-qt. slow cooker, combine all the ingredients. Cover and cook on low for 3 hours or until heated through.

Yield: 8 cups.

Tangy Barbecue Wings

PREP: 1-1/2 HOURS ■ **COOK:** 3 HOURS

Sherry Pitzer
Troy, Missouri
When I took these savory appetizers to work, they were gone before I even got a bite! Spicy ketchup, vinegar, molasses and honey blend together in a tangy sauce that makes the wings lip-smacking good.

25 whole chicken wings (about 5 pounds)
2-1/2 cups hot and spicy ketchup
2/3 cup white vinegar
1/2 cup plus 2 tablespoons honey
1/2 cup molasses
1 teaspoon salt
1 teaspoon Worcestershire sauce
1/2 teaspoon onion powder
1/2 teaspoon chili powder
1/2 to 1 teaspoon Liquid Smoke, optional

1 Cut chicken wings into three sections; discard wing tip sections. Place chicken wings in two greased 15-in. x 10-in. x 1-in. baking pans. Bake, uncovered, at 375° for 30 minutes; drain. Turn wings; bake 20-25 minutes longer or until juices run clear.

2 Meanwhile, in a large saucepan, combine the ketchup, vinegar, honey, molasses, salt, Worcestershire sauce, onion powder and chili powder. Add Liquid Smoke if desired. Bring to a boil. Reduce heat; simmer, uncovered, for 25-30 minutes. Drain wings; place a third of them in a 5-qt. slow cooker. Top with about 1 cup sauce. Repeat layers twice.

3 Cover and cook on low for 3-4 hours. Stir before serving.

Yield: about 4 dozen.

Editor's Note: Uncooked chicken wing sections (wingettes) may be substituted for whole chicken wings.

Creamy Artichoke Dip

(pictured above)

PREP: 20 MIN. ■ **COOK:** 1 HOUR

Mary Spencer
Waukesha, Wisconsin
This rich dip is a family favorite. My sister, Teresa, got this recipe from a friend and she passed it along. It's loaded with cheese, artichokes and just the right amount of spice for a crowd-pleasing flavor.

2 cans (14 ounces each) water-packed artichoke hearts, rinsed, drained and coarsely chopped
2 cups (8 ounces) shredded part-skim mozzarella cheese
1 package (8 ounces) cream cheese, cubed
1 cup shredded Parmesan cheese
1/2 cup shredded Swiss cheese
1/2 cup mayonnaise
2 tablespoons lemon juice
2 tablespoons plain yogurt
1 tablespoon seasoned salt
1 tablespoon chopped seeded jalapeno pepper
1 teaspoon garlic powder
Tortilla chips

1 In a 3-qt. slow cooker, combine the artichokes, cheeses, mayonnaise, lemon juice, yogurt, salt, jalapeno and garlic powder. Cover and cook on low for 1 hour or until heated through. Serve with tortilla chips.

Yield: 5 cups.

Editor's Note: When cutting hot peppers, disposable gloves are recommended. Avoid touching your face.

Spice Coffee

PREP: 10 MIN. ■ **COOK:** 2 HOURS

Joanne Holt
Bowling Green, Ohio
Even those who usually don't drink coffee will find this special blend with a hint of chocolate appealing.

8 cups brewed coffee

1/3 cup sugar

1/4 cup chocolate syrup

1/2 teaspoon anise extract

4 cinnamon sticks (3 inches)

1-1/2 teaspoons whole cloves

Additional cinnamon sticks, optional

1 In a 3-qt. slow cooker, combine the coffee, sugar, chocolate syrup and anise extract. Place cinnamon sticks and cloves in a double thickness of cheesecloth; bring up corners of cloth and tie with string to form a bag. Add to slow cooker. Cover and cook on low for 2-3 hours.

2 Discard spice bag. Ladle coffee into mugs; garnish each with a cinnamon stick if desired.

Yield: 8 cups.

Cranberry Sauerkraut Meatballs

PREP: 15 MIN. ■ **COOK:** 4 HOURS

Lisa Castelli
Pleasant Prairie, Wisconsin
I tried these meatballs at a birthday party, and now I make them all the time.

1 can (14 ounces) whole-berry cranberry sauce

1 can (14 ounces) sauerkraut, rinsed and well drained

1 bottle (12 ounces) chili sauce

3/4 cup packed brown sugar

1 package (32 ounces) frozen fully cooked homestyle meatballs, thawed

1 In a 4-qt. slow cooker, combine the cranberry sauce, sauerkraut, chili sauce and brown sugar. Stir in meatballs. Cover and cook on low for 4-5 hours or until heated through.

Yield: 5-1/2 dozen.

Fruit Salsa

(pictured above)

PREP: 10 MIN. ■ **COOK:** 2 HOURS

Florence Buchkowsky
Prince Albert, Saskatchewan
Serve this fruity salsa anywhere you'd use ordinary salsa. My son and I experimented with different ingredients to find the combination we liked best.

3 tablespoons cornstarch

4 teaspoons white vinegar

1 can (11 ounces) mandarin oranges, undrained

1 can (8-1/2 ounces) sliced peaches, undrained

3/4 cup pineapple tidbits

1 medium onion, chopped

1/2 each medium green, sweet red and yellow pepper, chopped

3 garlic cloves, minced

Tortilla chips

1 In a 3-qt. slow cooker, combine the cornstarch and vinegar until smooth. Stir in the fruit, onion, peppers and garlic. Cover and cook on high for 2 hours or until thickened and heated through, stirring occasionally. Serve with tortilla chips.

Yield: 4 cups.

Chili Cheese Dip

(pictured above)

PREP: 20 MIN. ■ **COOK:** 4-1/2 HOURS

Sandra Fick
Lincoln, Nebraska

After trying to create a Mexican soup, I ended up with this outstanding dip that eats like a meal. My husband and two young children love it! Now it's popular for football games or family gatherings.

1 pound lean ground beef (90% lean)

1 cup chopped onion

1 can (16 ounces) kidney beans, rinsed and drained

1 can (15 ounces) black beans, rinsed and drained

1 can (14-1/2 ounces) diced tomatoes in sauce

1 cup frozen corn

3/4 cup water

1 can (2-1/4 ounces) sliced ripe olives, drained

3 teaspoons chili powder

1/2 teaspoon dried oregano

1/2 teaspoon chipotle hot pepper sauce

1/4 teaspoon garlic powder

1/4 teaspoon ground cumin

1 package (16 ounces) reduced-fat process cheese (Velveeta), cubed

Corn chips

1 In a large skillet, cook beef and onion over medium heat until meat is no longer pink; drain. Transfer to a 5-qt. slow cooker.

2 Stir in the beans, tomatoes, corn, water, olives, chili powder, oregano, pepper sauce, garlic powder and cumin. Cover and cook on low for 4-5 hours or until heated through; stir in cheese.

3 Cover and cook for 30 minutes or until cheese is melted. Serve with corn chips.

Yield: 8 cups.

Caramel Hot Chocolate

PREP: 10 MIN. ■ **COOK:** 4-1/4 HOURS

Maureen Mitchell
Calgary, Alberta
Perfect on a chilly day, this hot chocolate is so luscious thanks to a caramel candy bar.

4 cups nonfat dry milk powder

3/4 cup baking cocoa

1/2 cup sugar

8 cups water

1 Caramello candy bar (2.7 ounces), chopped

Whipped cream and grated chocolate, optional

1 In a 3-qt. slow cooker, combine the milk powder, cocoa and sugar; gradually whisk in water. Cover and cook on low for 4 hours or until hot. Add candy bar; stir until melted. Garnish with whipped cream and grated chocolate if desired.

Yield: about 2 quarts.

Hot Holiday Cider

PREP: 10 MIN. ■ **COOK:** 3 HOURS

Cindy Tobin
West Bend, Wisconsin
This warm, slightly tart cider is perfect for a holiday open house.

2 quarts apple cider or juice

1 quart cranberry juice

2 cups orange juice

1/2 cup sugar

3 cinnamon sticks (3 inches)

1 teaspoon whole allspice

1 teaspoon whole cloves

1 In a 5- or 6-qt. slow cooker, combine the cider, juices and sugar. Place the cinnamon sticks, allspice and cloves on a double thickness of cheesecloth; bring up corners of cloth and tie with string to form a bag. Place in slow cooker. Cover and cook on low for 3-4 hours. Discard spice bag. Serve warm in mugs.

Yield: 14 servings (3-1/2 quarts).

Cranberry-Stuffed Apples

(pictured above)

PREP: 10 MIN. ■ **COOK:** 4 HOURS

Graciela Sandvigen
Rochester, New York
Cinnamon, nutmeg and walnuts add a homey autumn flavor to these eye-appealing stuffed apples.

5 medium apples

1/3 cup fresh or frozen cranberries, thawed and chopped

1/4 cup packed brown sugar

2 tablespoons chopped walnuts

1/4 teaspoon ground cinnamon

1/8 teaspoon ground nutmeg

Whipped cream or vanilla ice cream, optional

1 Core apples, leaving bottoms intact. Peel top third of each apple; place in a 5-qt. slow cooker. Combine the cranberries, brown sugar, walnuts, cinnamon and nutmeg; spoon into apples. Cover and cook on low for 4-5 hours or until apples are tender. Serve with whipped cream or ice cream if desired.

Yield: 5 servings.

Sweet Kahlua Coffee

PREP: 10 MIN. ■ **COOK:** 4 HOURS

Ruth Gruchow
Yorba Linda, California
I have this beverage brewing in my slow cooker at my annual Christmas open house.

>   2 quarts hot water
>   1/2 cup Kahlua
>   1/4 cup creme de cacao
>   3 tablespoons instant coffee granules
>   2 cups heavy whipping cream
>   1/4 cup sugar
>   1 teaspoon vanilla extract
>   2 tablespoons grated chocolate

1   In a 4-qt. slow cooker, combine first four ingredients. Cover and cook on low for 3-4 hours. In a large bowl, beat cream until it begins to thicken. Add sugar and vanilla; beat until stiff peaks form. Ladle coffee into mugs. Garnish with whipped cream and grated chocolate.

Yield: 9 servings (2-1/4 quarts).

Ginger Tea Drink

(pictured above)

PREP: 15 MIN. ■ **COOK:** 2 HOURS

Alexandra Marcotty
Cleveland Heights, Ohio
Looking for something new and unique to serve to guests? Let this soothing green tea simmer while you concentrate on preparing other dishes for your gathering. Everyone is sure to ask for this heartwarming recipe.

>   4 cups boiling water
>   15 individual green tea bags
>   4 cups white grape juice
>   1 to 2 tablespoons honey
>   1 tablespoon minced fresh gingerroot
>   Crystallized ginger, optional

1   In a 3-qt. slow cooker, combine boiling water and tea bags. Cover and let stand for 10 minutes. Discard tea bags. Stir in the remaining ingredients. Cover and cook on low for 2-3 hours or until heated through.

2   Strain if desired before serving warm. Garnish with candied ginger if desired.

Yield: 2 quarts.

Crunchy Candy Clusters

PREP: 15 MIN. ■ **COOK:** 1 HOUR

Faye O'Bryan
Owensboro, Kentucky
Before I retired, I took these yummy peanut butter bites to work for special occasions.

>   2 pounds white candy coating, coarsely chopped
>   1-1/2 cups peanut butter
>   1/2 teaspoon almond extract, optional
>   4 cups Cap'n Crunch cereal
>   4 cups crisp rice cereal
>   4 cups miniature marshmallows

1   Place candy coating in a 5-qt. slow cooker. Cover and cook on high for 1 hour. Add peanut butter. Stir in extract if desired. In a large bowl, combine the cereals and marshmallows. Stir in the peanut butter mixture until well coated. Drop by tablespoonfuls onto waxed paper. Let stand until set. Store at room temperature.

Yield: 6-1/2 dozen.

Hot Wing Dip

(pictured above)

PREP: 10 MIN. ■ **COOK:** 1 HOUR

Coleen Corner
Grove City, Pennsylvania
Since I usually have all the ingredients on hand, this is a
great go-to recipe when unexpected guests show up.

2 cups shredded cooked chicken

1 package (8 ounces) cream cheese, cubed

2 cups (8 ounces) shredded cheddar cheese

1 cup ranch salad dressing

1/2 cup Louisiana-style hot sauce

Tortilla chips and/or celery sticks

Minced fresh parsley, optional

1 In a 3-qt. slow cooker, combine the chicken, cream
cheese, cheddar, salad dressing and hot sauce.
Cover and cook on low for 1 hour or until cheese
is melted. Serve with chips and/or celery. Sprinkle
with parsley if desired.

Yield: 4-1/2 cups.

> **Hot beef dip.** Use the basic wing dip recipe and
> modify it for a savory beef dip. Omit the chicken
> and chop 1 or 2 packages of thinly sliced dried
> beef, then substitute Monterey Jack cheese for
> the cheddar.

indexes

GENERAL RECIPE INDEX

This index lists the recipes by food category and major ingredient, so you can easily locate recipes that suit your needs.

Beef and Lamb Stew, 55
Beef and Three-Bean Chili, 194
Beef Barley Soup, 178
Beef Roast Dinner, 20
Brisket 'n' Bean Burritos, 43
Brisket with Cranberry Gravy, 52
Burgundy Beef, 35
Butternut Beef Stew, 58
Cajun-Style Pot Roast, 50
Chipotle Beef Sandwiches, 22
Coffee-Flavored Beef Roast, 47
Colony Mountain Chili, 191
Corned Beef Supper, 29
Double-Onion Beef Brisket, 33
Flank Steak Roll-Up, 19
Flavorful Beef Stew, 13
Forgotten Minestrone, 186
Garlic Beef Stroganoff, 49
German-Style Short Ribs, 20
Glazed Corned Beef Dinner, 31
Green Chili Beef Burritos, 23
Hearty Beef Vegetable Stew, 16
Hearty French Dip Sandwiches, 50
Hearty Short Ribs, 14
Hungarian Goulash, 36
Hungarian Stew, 23
Italian Beef on Rolls, 53
Italian Pot Roast, 34
Italian Roast with Alfredo Potatoes, 52
Loaded Vegetable Beef Stew, 25
Mexican Beef Stew, 41
Mushroom 'n' Steak Stroganoff, 38
Mushroom Pepper Steak, 24
No-Fuss Swiss Steak, 17
Picante Beef Roast, 26
Polynesian Roast Beef, 42
Pot Roast with Gravy, 18
Pot Roast with Mushroom Gravy, 27
Reuben Spread, 233
Roast Beef and Gravy, 32
Roundup Chili, 205
Round Steak Italiano, 28
Seasoned Short Ribs, 27
Slow-Cooked Caribbean Pot Roast, 28
Slow-Cooked Coffee Beef Roast, 54
Slow-Cooked Pot Roast, 9
Slow-Cooked Short Ribs, 51
Slow-Cooked Steak Fajitas, 57
Slow Cooker Fajitas, 48
Slow Cooker Sauerbraten, 37
Smothered Round Steak, 58
Southwestern Beef Stew, 46
Southwestern Beef Tortillas, 39
Special Slow-Cooked Beef, 10
Steak Burritos, 15
Steak Strips with Dumplings, 44
Sweet-Sour Beef, 57
Swiss Steak Supper, 59
Tangy Pot Roast, 9
Tender Beef Brisket, 54

Tex-Mex Beef Sandwiches, 12
Texas Beef Barbecue, 36
Texas-Style Beef Brisket, 41
Traditional Beef Stew, 29
Vegetable Beef Stew, 38
Zippy Beef Fajitas, 16
Zippy Steak Chili, 199

BEVERAGES
Apple Cranberry Cider, 235
Caramel Hot Chocolate, 243
Ginger Tea Drink, 244
Hot Holiday Cider, 243
Hot Spiced Cherry Cider, 228
Mulled Dr. Pepper, 227
Mulled Merlot, 232
Mulled Pomegranate Sipper, 225
Spice Coffee, 241
Sweet Kahlua Coffee, 244
Tropical Tea, 231
Viennese Coffee, 236
Warm Pomegranate Punch, 221
Wassail Bowl Punch, 223

BROCCOLI
Broccoli Potato Soup, 187
Corn and Broccoli in Cheese Sauce, 207
Creamy Ham Chowder, 203
Slow-Cooked Ham 'n' Broccoli, 101

BURRITOS (also see Enchiladas, Fajitas, Tacos & Tortillas)
Brisket 'n' Bean Burritos, 43
Fiesta Chicken Burritos, 120
Green Chili Beef Burritos, 23
Pork Burritos, 67
Steak Burritos, 15

CABBAGE (also see Sauerkraut)
All-Day Soup, 181
Butternut Beef Stew, 58
Corned Beef Supper, 29
Creamy Cabbage-Pork Stew, 91
Forgotten Minestrone, 186
Loaded Vegetable Beef Stew, 25
Sweet 'n' Tender Cabbage Rolls, 40
Veggie Meatball Soup, 201

CARROTS
All-Day Soup, 181
Apple Chicken Stew, 131
Beef and Lamb Stew, 55
Beef Roast Dinner, 20
Chicken Stew over Biscuits, 152
Chunky Pasta Sauce, 159
Confetti Casserole, 32
Corned Beef Supper, 29
Creamy Cabbage-Pork Stew, 91
Flavorful Beef Stew, 13
Glazed Corned Beef Dinner, 31

Ground Beef Stew, 17
Hearty Beef Vegetable Stew, 16
Lemon Chicken Breast with Veggies, 111
Loaded Vegetable Beef Stew, 25
Meat Sauce for Spaghetti, 166
Meatball Stew, 39
Mexican Pork Roast, 93
No-Fuss Potato Soup, 177
No-Fuss Swiss Steak, 17
Pork and Pinto Beans, 81
Pork Chili Verde, 105
Pot Roast with Mushroom Gravy, 27
Sage Turkey Thighs, 151
Savory Winter Soup, 187
Slow-Cooked Pork Roast Dinner, 88
Smoky Bean Stew, 82
Southwestern Beef Stew, 46
Spicy Seafood Stew, 171
Sweet 'n' Sour Sausage, 84
Sweet Potato Lentil Stew, 162
Sweet Sausage 'n' Beans, 61
Sweet-Sour Beef, 57
Swiss Steak Supper, 59
Tangy Pot Roast, 9
Texas Stew, 18
Thai Shrimp and Rice, 162
Traditional Beef Stew, 29
Turkey Leg Pot Roast, 144
Turkey Thigh Supper, 143
Two-Bean Chili, 174
Zippy Bean Stew, 159

CAULIFLOWER
Beef and Lamb Stew, 55
Cream of Cauliflower Soup, 197

CHEESE
Cheddar Spirals, 217
Chili Cheese Dip, 242
Chipotle Ham 'n' Cheese Dip, 234
Corn and Broccoli in Cheese Sauce, 207
Creamy Macaroni and Cheese, 209
Hearty Cheese Tortellini, 161
Hot Chili Cheese Dip, 228
Mexican Fondue, 230
Nacho Hash Brown Casserole, 210
Parmesan Potato Soup, 178
Pepper Jack Chicken, 114
Veggie-Sausage Cheese Soup, 196

CHERRIES
Cherry Cola Chocolate Cake, 238
Easy and Elegant Ham, 92
Hot Spiced Cherry Cider, 228
Minister's Delight, 230
"Secret's in the Sauce" BBQ Ribs, 96
Sweet Onion & Cherry Pork Chops, 96

ALPHABETICAL RECIPE INDEX

This handy index lists every recipe in alphabetical order, so you can easily find your favorite recipe.